—————————— MUSLIM WOMEN IN WAR AND CRISIS ——————————

MUSLIM WOMEN IN WAR AND CRISIS

Representation and Reality

EDITED BY FAEGHEH SHIRAZI

UNIVERSITY OF TEXAS PRESS
Austin

A University Cooperative Society Subvention Grant was awarded by the
University of Texas at Austin for the publication of this manuscript.

∞ The paper used in this book meets the minimum requirements of
ANSI/NISO Z39.48-1992 (R1997) (Permanence of Paper).

Library of Congress Cataloging-in-Publication Data
Muslim women in war and crisis : representation and reality /
edited by Faegheh Shirazi.
p. cm.
Includes bibliographical references and index.
ISBN 978-0-292-72884-4
1. Muslim women—Press coverage. 2. Muslim women—Social conditions.
I. Shirazi, Faegheh, 1952–
HQ1170.M8475 2010
305.48'69709045—dc22
2009053616

*This book is dedicated to
the memory of my parents,
Dr. Mahmood Shirazi and Aghdas Simafar,
to my children, Ramin and Geeti,
and to all women whose lives
have been impacted by war*

CONTENTS

NOTE FROM THE EDITOR

Transliteration and Key Terms

The transliteration of Arabic, Persian, Urdu, Bengali, and Bosniak has been preserved exactly as submitted by the contributors to this collection. Variations on the same word—for example, *hejab* and *hijab*—appear in these essays, kept in the original to acknowledge various differences in pronunciation, spelling, and regional preferences throughout the Muslim world.

In searching for an appropriate title for this collection, a title that would do justice to the content, I decided on *Muslim Women in War and Crisis: Representation and Reality.* I use the term "representation" in the title to denote any form of textual expression or visual image that either advances religious, political, or marketing agendas or reflects personal responses to experiences of violence and war. This collection speaks to various forms of representation, such as fine art, memoir, news and media reports, poetry, and graphic art interweaving text and image (specifically designed for public spaces).

The terms "war" and "crisis" refer to any form of military combat force between nations, invasion of a nation, colonization of a country, internal civil war, revolution, ethnic cleansing, act of terrorism, or any form of hostility causing loss of lives or property and/or leading to the creation of refugees and displaced persons.

INTRODUCTION

FAEGHEH SHIRAZI

This volume reflects a deep interest in the politics of "image" and the ways in which images dominate and seduce by investing power in particular signifiers, tropes, and descriptions. The multivoiced text, written by scholars and journalists from across the world, revolves around dual themes: the reality and the representation of women caught in war and crises. What ties the chapters together is a collective concern for women who are subjected to violence in various manifestations. Whether physical or psychological, direct or indirect, whether promulgated by external and internal forces or by religious majorities intent on genocide, the issue of direct or threatened violence against women informs each essay.

Many of the contributors have lived through the times they discuss. For some, including the editor of this volume, their personal lives have been affected firsthand by war. Indeed, this project taps into the traumatic effects of war on my own family, friends, and community. As an eighteen-year-old, I left Abadan, Iran—unaware that I would never be able to return. My family home, my father's business, all beloved childhood memories and spaces were entirely obliterated by Iraqi bombs. Across the decades, colleagues and acquaintances, most of them women, have shared their personal stories concerning war and national struggle. The more I spoke with them, the more I realized the universality of our experiences, despite differences in culture, language, and religious background.

One objective of this project was to document and disseminate stories like my own. In the process, I began to notice significant disparities between firsthand accounts and analyses of the events on which those accounts were based. This subject-object tension, with the attendant dichotomy of women cast either as victims or as political agents, piqued my interest and informed my decision to juxtapose the two separate themes of reality and representation in a single volume.

GENDER AND WAR: THE REALITY

Women and children make up 80 percent of refugees worldwide. As soldiers, as refugees, and as survivors of war-related incidents and sexual violence, women are often affected by war in markedly different ways from men. According to the United Nations Office for the Coordination of Humanitarian Affairs, the protection of women in armed conflict—and their centrality to conflict prevention, peacekeeping, and peace building—is a matter of increasing concern to the international community. The UN Security Council passed a resolution in October 2000 to "expand the role of women in UN field-based operations, especially among military observers, civilian police, human rights workers, and humanitarian personnel."[1] Yet the deliberate killing, rape, mutilation, forced displacement, abduction, trafficking, and torture of women and girls continue unabated.

In times of civil war or strife when male family members are drafted into the military, arrested by government or occupying forces, or killed in combat, women assume primary responsibility for their households and carry the burden of ensuring the immediate survival of family members. At these critical times, women and girls face continued threats to their safety and security, not only during the conflict, but also in the postconflict phase. The aftermath of any war is frequently marked by significant social and political upheaval. Women who have been subjected to gender-specific control within their communities during peacetime will be especially at risk. If these women become victims of rape, forced prostitution, or other sexual violations at the hands of the "enemy," the impact is staggering. Women caught in political repression or social upheavals are often manipulated, exploited, and used as scapegoats.

For example, it is not unusual for young women, often against their will, to be assigned suicide missions. In September 2008 a fifteen-year-old Iraqi girl, who had apparently been drugged, turned herself in to village police—explaining that female family members had fitted her with a vest of explosives and directed her to a schoolyard where she was to await further instructions. In 2007 eight female suicide bombers were documented in Iraq. In 2009 authorities arrested Samira Ahmed Jasmin, known as Umm al-Mumineen (Mother of Believers), who was suspected of recruiting more than eighty female suicide bombers, and on February 13, 2009, forty people were reported killed in one bombing incident.[2] Generally, women draw less suspicion than men, and security checks tend to be less comprehensive for women due to the social protocol of honoring a woman's modesty. For these reasons, militant organizations increasingly recruit women. Although there are instances in which women voluntarily join with men in armed struggle, more often they are responding to pressure exerted by family, community, and religious leaders. One sees this, for example, in the exhortations of Sheikh Ahmed Ismail Yassin, cofounder and spiritual leader of Hamas, who issued a *fatwa* (religious ruling) "that gave permission to women to participate in suicide attacks as well as listing the rewards in 'Paradise' that these female martyrs would receive upon their deaths."[3] Perhaps the most chilling aspect of this female jihad-martyrdom can be best expressed in the phrase "dying to kill." Literally, young women who are facing honor killing themselves as a result of having "sullied" their family's purity are given the choice: either be killed by family members or die as martyrs.[4]

The motivations of female suicide attackers vary according to circumstance. Although it is difficult to profile the typical female suicide bomber, one can observe certain patterns:

> Like male suicide bombers, women who do attack tend to be younger and more educated than their peers. Some reports indicate that certain women are motivated by revenge for male relatives or spouses killed in the continuing violence, while other anecdotal evidence suggests that others are unwittingly used to transport explosives that are remotely detonated.
>
> Nor are female suicide attackers unique to Iraq. There is a long history of such attacks by Sri Lankan, Chechnyan, Palestinian, and Turkish terrorists. The Tamil Tigers in Sri Lanka have used women most frequently, conducting some 200 suicide attacks of which 30 to 40 percent involved women.[5]

The impact of any crisis on a nation, initiated by internal or external forces, always exerts a significant toll on the general populace, most often women and children. Images of women during any crisis can be reshaped to project various identities. Especially in the post-9/11 era, images of Muslim women have been used to further radical policies, as a means of regulating society. Religious and political authorities view women as integral to societal regulation; they must be controlled, tamed, and dominated. Under the guise of glorifying the value and status of women, societal norms are adopted and women's images targeted. In such contexts, for a more orthodox reinterpretation of Islamic values, women's bodies have become the testing ground for new political policies. These values are then intertwined with regional traditions and fed to the populace as the way to salvation. In Sharia-based nations—primarily throughout the Middle East but in other Muslim communities as well—Islamic authorities continue to embrace extremist poli-

cies.[6] In Iran, for example, "the Islamic state has adopted an increasingly conservative religious interpretation of the role of women, and excluded them
from the social and political mainstream."[7] Roksana Bahramitash refers to
this process of rigidly interpreting the Qur'an to promote political agendas
as "Islamic fundamentalism."

DEFINING FUNDAMENTALISM

Some scholars suggest that the terms "fundamentalism" and "fundamentalist"
are neither static nor uniform. While I concur with this assessment entirely,
collective agreement on terminology is key to any thoughtful discussion regarding Islamic resurgence. Terms take shape and assume different meanings
depending on the perspectives and disciplines of the scholars engaged in the
debate. According to Mahmood Mamdani,[8] one should eschew the term
"fundamentalism" — which he describes as a *cultural* phenomenon — in favor
of the term "political Islam" to describe an Islam that has embraced violence
as central to political action. Olivier Roy supports this distinction by suggesting that "fundamentalism" and "cultural worldview" are synonymous.[9]

Dilip Hiro claims that fundamentalism is "the effort to define the fun-
damentals of a religious system and adhere to them."[10] According to Minoo
Moallem, fundamentalism exists within every religion and "is not peculiar
to an Islamic context."[11] Moallem situates "fundamentalism as a modern
discursive formation . . . with a genealogy and history of representation."[12]
She further states that although application of the term "fundamentalism"
may seem problematic, running the risk of demonizing Islam, employing it
is useful for "an understanding of both religion and secularism."[13]

"Fundamentalism" can refer to a wide spectrum of movements or attitudes, from religious revivalism to extremist political movements. I view it
as a political ideology rooted historically in a religious community's specific
social and cultural environments. In this collection of essays, the various authors treat the concept of fundamentalism in relation to their own academic
training, experience, and observation.

THE LEGACY OF ORIENTALISM

Over the past two decades — in particular, since September 11, 2001 — violence
has engulfed Islamic societies; the brutal and bloody face of war has become
commonplace. Bombarded by media coverage of these horrific images, indi-

viduals living in the West have formed overt and subtle impressions of what Islam stands for. When major television networks persist in substituting the word "fundamentalist" for "terrorist" and prestigious print venues such as the *New York Times* or the *Wall Street Journal* invariably juxtapose the terms "fundamentalism" and "terrorism," how can Western audiences be expected to sift through the confusion? An analysis of reports from the *New York Times* between September 2001 and September 2003 revealed that "the dominant representations of Muslim men [were as] violent and dangerous[,] and Muslim women [were presented] as victims of oppression. The dominant images of both Muslim men and women served the same purpose: They established the need [for the West] to intervene to rescue the men and control the men."[14]

How can the West know what it means to be Muslim and, perhaps especially, what it means to be a Muslim woman? How to explain the stubborn survival of traditions and practices in Islamic societies without reinforcing stereotypes? How to avoid portraying Muslim women as inferior to women of other religious faiths without resorting to apologetic and self-glorifying accounts of Islam today and throughout history?

Historic accounts of Muslim women reflect what Edward Said describes as Orientalism: "a style of thought based upon an ontological and epistemological distinction made between the Orient and . . . the Occident in which Western culture and societies are essentially and inherently superior to Eastern ones."[15] Muslim women, in early accounts left by European travelers, are acknowledged as "little more than black shadows in the corner of the Bedouin tent."[16] Travel accounts of the Orient as early as the seventeenth century depict Middle Eastern women as symbols of a backward, idle culture. For example, in 1665 Jean Thévenot wrote in his *Voyage du Levant*, "This great idleness causes the women to be depraved, and they apply all of their mind to the search for means of distraction."[17] Among nineteenth-century European writers who visited Algeria, Egypt, and Palestine were Théophile Gautier and Gustave Flaubert. Flaubert's description of the Oriental woman is especially telling:

[She is] . . . no more than a machine; she makes no distinction between one man and another man. Smoking, going to the baths, painting her eyelids and drinking coffee—such is the circle of occupation to which her existence is confined.[18]

Interestingly, European travelers rarely attempted to converse with Muslim women; one might say they preferred representation to reality. According to Judy Mabro, "Few travellers to the Middle East or North Africa ever found themselves in a position where they could really communicate with women living there, and even fewer had any interest in learning how *their* society was perceived by the people they were observing."[19] The Middle Eastern man, as counterpart, is also portrayed in the travel literature as something lesser, not quite a real man. In Western representations of Islamic masculinity, men are perceived as despots or victims, either domineering patriarchs or oppressed by colonial power. Images, whether visual or textual, put forth by a narcissistic West, tend to encapsulate men and women of the Orient in a colonization of the spirit.[20]

Victorian travelers such as C. M. Doughty, the Burtons, and the Blunts did much to further the colonial perception of the feminized Middle East, that is, as territory meant to be penetrated. The Orient itself, Europe's cultural and spiritual opposition, was often conceived of as female. A century later, in his novel *The Stranger,* Albert Camus called attention to this same tension when the Arab protagonist refuses to offer his sister to French colonialists. The introduction to Malek Alloula's *The Colonial Harem* states, "Possession of Arab women came to serve as a surrogate for and means to the political and military conquest of the Arab World."[21] In short, Orientalism, the product of a four-thousand-year relationship between Europe and Asia, resulted in a historicization of the Muslim woman as either sexually idealized or oppressed. In his book *Covering Islam,* Said insists that Orientalism is still very much alive today, pointing to the media's projection of negative images of Muslims.[22]

MEDIA REPRESENTATIONS

Most of the authors included in this volume agree on one point: the Western media's representations of Muslim women, whether veiled or exposed, passive or wielding weapons, have fit quite neatly into "dominant geopolitical discourses" and have served as the "main repositories of the West's sense of fear, fascination, and superiority vis-à-vis the Muslim world."[23] Elizabeth Poole speaks to this critical role of the media and their success in having superseded all other institutions in the cultural production of knowledge.[24]

The manner in which Western media interpret and present the roles of Muslim women is the focus of several chapters. Post-9/11 media representations in the West of Muslim women, for example, focused almost entirely on Afghanistan. Afghanistan became the first prism through which Americans would consider Muslim women. As a result, Western images of Muslim women have disproportionately reflected images of individuals who are oppressed and helpless.

Two chapters in this volume focus exclusively on women's experience in Afghanistan, a nation that has endured more than twenty-five years of armed struggle. Carol Mann's essay, "From Refugee Camp to Kabul: The Influence of Fundamentalism on Afghanistan's Politics and Women," underscores the defeat of positive reform in Afghanistan. According to Mann, this failure to reform has produced a unique phenomenon—one of reactionary modernity rather than a return to the archaic past. Owing to a weak central government in Afghanistan and strong rural tribal influence, she states, "the configuration that is affecting women today was produced by the unique political evolution in Pakistani refugee camps which then percolated towards Kabul." Mann investigates what it means to be a Muslim woman caught in the violence, patriarchy, and insecurity of post-Taliban Afghanistan. Valentine Moghadam, too, has perceived the dilemma of Afghan women as linked directly to the consequences of "a tribal social structure, warlordism, and state compromises."[25]

Lina Abirafeh, in "Gendered Aid Interventions and Afghan Women: Images versus Realities," suggests that a particular discourse on Afghan women was created to justify intervention—a discourse that was not contextualized and that largely denied Afghan women's agency. Media images of downtrodden women beneath the *burqa* helped to fuel the rhetoric of "liberation" and "empowerment" characterizing aid interventions. However, women in Afghanistan might say that they have been neither liberated nor empowered, despite the rhetoric. Abirafeh's study is the result of perceptions and experiences accrued during almost four years of fieldwork in Afghanistan. Her research, based on interviewing numerous Afghan women involved with or participating in aid programs, leads to crucial questions: Are Afghan women passive victims or active social participants? Are they in need of liberation by the West or is their *burqa*-clad image one more opportunity to further political agendas?

The news media's part in shaping women's images is also explored by Sara Struckman in her essay, "'Black Widows' in the *New York Times*: Images of Chechen Women Rebels." Struckman is interested in the media's treatment of Chechen women involved in suicide bombings and other violent acts. "Black widow" was a term coined by the press to explain women's violent involvement in the Chechen independence struggle from the Russian Federation. Struckman examines how the *New York Times* questioned this explanation, yet felt compelled to offer other culturally acceptable and gender-appropriate reasons to account for what motivated the Chechen women rebels. In doing so, the *Times* simultaneously broke away from and remained faithful to the media's role as a "circuit of culture."

Fauzia Ahmad explores media representations of Muslims—specifically, British Muslim women—following the London bombings of July 7, 2005, and attempted bombings in London and Glasgow during June 2007. Ahmad questions whether those projected images reflect lived realities or merely a victim-based pathology of Muslim women selectively maintained by the mainstream media. According to Ahmad, after the terrorist attack on London's public transport system, Muslim women in Britain—especially those highly visible in their *hijab, jilbab,* or *niqab*—experienced particular vilification on the streets, in the media, and from some politicians. Some women were spat on or verbally abused. Others were refused entry on public transport or had their *hijabs* pulled off and, in more serious cases, became targets of physical violence.

Ángeles Ramírez focuses on the *hijab* issue in Spain, an understudied country. In her chapter, "Muslim Women in the Spanish Press: A Subaltern Image," Ramírez sheds light on the phenomenon of Maurophobia (Spain's postcolonial relationship with Morocco) and suggests that the press successfully transformed Maurophobia into Islamophobia after the train attack in Madrid by terrorists. Since the 2004 attack, Spanish newspapers have presented Muslim women in one of two ways: either they wear the headscarf, or they do not. The absence of a headscarf signals adaptation, modernity, and culture. Its presence threatens Spain's democratic values. Ramírez cites Antonio Elorza, a political scientist who writes prolifically for the newspaper *El País.* Elorza states that obstacles hindering Muslims in the West are "the spirit of violence," which is connected to the ideology of *jihad* and the inferiority of women in Islam. Sexist constructions of the headscarf, although targeting a particular group (Moroccan Muslim women immigrating to Spain), represent a critique of all Muslim society. This racist style of thought and expression, deeply rooted in the Oriental discourse, exemplifies a form of ongoing psychological abuse against Muslims in general and against Muslim women in particular.

Omar Sacirbey, in his essay "Images of Muslim Women in Post-9/11 America," points to the quandary in which American Muslim women find themselves: they face hostility and violence from non-Muslim Americans for wearing the *hijab* and spiteful disapproval from fellow Muslims for *not* wearing the *hijab.* Sacirbey alludes to an American fifteen-year-old high school student who, curious about discrimination against Muslim women in the United States, decided to wear a *burqa* for a day (in 2007) and record her experience. She was subjected to abusive remarks—"Hey, we rape your women!"—underscoring, in Sacirbey's words, "a persistent animosity toward American Muslims that is driven largely by the terrorist attacks of 9/11 and the wars in Afghanistan and Iraq."[26] Given that Muslim American women have begun to take proactive steps to shape their images in the media, Sacirbey continues to question whether impartial news coverage can undo bigotry or significantly affect the seemingly reflexive response of distrust and hostility engendered by the sight of a woman in a *hijab*.

The Lebanese author Nada S. Fuleihan also delves into the significance of the *hijab* in her chapter, "In Search of Identity: *Hijab* Recollections from West Beirut." The 1982 Israeli invasion of Lebanon and the subsequent siege of West Beirut brought devastation and humiliation on Muslims. As a result, a resurgence of Islamic fundamentalism and fervor took hold in southern Lebanon and West Beirut. Many young Muslim women—university students and professionals who had not previously followed Islamic proscriptions for modest apparel—decided to adopt the *hijab*. This provoked widely diverse community responses, from total rejection to respectful admiration. Even Fuleihan, raised in the Christian tradition, admitted that this act gave voice to her "own suppressed feelings of anger and loss." Fuleihan demonstrates how the *hijab* became a dramatic symbol for Lebanese women. For some, it was a declaration of faith, a form of resistance to Israeli actions; for others, it meant submission to coercion from family and community. Indeed, the *hijab* itself came to represent a dichotomy between women as activists and women as passive victims.

VICTIMIZATION VERSUS POLITICAL AGENCY

In the feminist narratives of liberation, debate continues over the concept of women's agency in the contexts of war and social crises. One must not assume that all women are passive (i.e., victims) and all men are active (i.e., oppressors). Doing so denies women what Katherine Gibson and Julie Graham have described as "resistant agency."[27] In this respect, the term "agency" refers to a woman's refusal to be a victim and to fight back instead. In other words, violence against women is not an "inevitable truth" but rather a "language script" to be rewritten. The script that women make use of may take multiple forms. Eloquence does not necessarily come from words inscribed on the page; rather, it may occur in the most unexpected ways.

For example, in 2005 women artists—all masters of textile traditions—documented their lived realities of war in Michigan State University's exhibition *Weaving of War, Fabrics of Memory*. From Afghanistan to Laos, from

Lebanon to South Africa, these women captured and expressed their personal experiences of the reality of war by weaving, embroidering, and quilting textiles. Many of them eschewed the traditions of nonfigurative design to embrace literal, pictorial imagery: assault rifles, pistols, hand grenades, helicopters, tanks. This extraordinary folk art demonstrates the way in which women use "self-presentation" to "survive, reflect, and remember aggression." The exhibition catalogue continues:

> Whether the works are narrative tapestries that depict scenes of executions, refugees fleeing war-torn lands, or ethnic cleansing, or whether the works are simply garments and household objects with motifs of helicopters and machineguns, these objects defy simple interpretation.[28]

Thus, even women—both Muslim and non-Muslim—who are allowed no voice, power, or control in their immediate social environments manage to preserve the individual and collective realities of war.

Another example of resistant agency is Shirin Neshat's photography and, more recently, her video installations. According to Iftikhar Dadi, "Neshat has arguably come to occupy the position of the most significant visual interpreter of the status of Muslim women universally."[29] Neshat, an Iranian American, is referred to as "a visual theorist of the body." Her images, adorned with calligraphy, may be understood and appreciated aesthetically even by Western art audiences unfamiliar with Persian culture or language. The meaning deepens significantly for audiences who can easily read and understand the text. In general, Neshat's photographic work focuses primarily on the Iranian postrevolutionary woman and her place in the public sphere; specifically, her figure as representation.[30]

Nada Shabout's chapter, "Images and Status: Visualizing Iraqi Women," recounts the many changes Iraqi women have experienced since the 1968 revolution created the Arab Socialist Baʿath Party. It provides a comparative examination of posters, public monuments, and paintings produced by extremist Iraqi women of the time. Shabout also discusses the status of Iraqi women artists and their role in transforming contemporary visual representations.

Although Iraqi women have suffered endlessly, whether at the mercy of the Baʿathist regime, under economic sanctions imposed by the West, or, more recently, during the extended U.S. occupation, like their Iranian counterparts, as Miriam Cooke eloquently points out, these women no longer embrace "their expected role of Mater Dolorosa. [No longer] do [they] quietly lament and submit to a fate that might be cruel, pointless violence."[31] Instead they are finding gender-specific ways to resist aggression. As writers and artists, as mothers and lawyers, they are accessing public spaces and refusing to remain invisible victims.

Rita Stephan offers a good example of this by examining in her essay the nonviolent active struggle by Lebanese women who took to the streets, joining their male counterparts, during the Beirut protests of March 8 and March 14, 2005. Once accused of being indifferent to political processes and outcomes, Lebanese women became liberators and resisters, participating alongside men in the Cedar Revolution to oust Syria from Lebanese soil. As women assumed leadership roles in the Lebanese freedom movement, they created a more tolerant, less violent, and more feminized style of protest. The Cedar Revolution left an indelible image of women as active and equal citizens in their society. Against a backdrop of three decades of war—and threatened by the likelihood of Hezbollah's violent exchanges with Israel—stands a new breed of Lebanese woman, such as Sirine Ahmad, age forty-seven, who claims indignantly that "Hezbollah does not have the right to decide to take [Lebanon] back into war."[32] It is this emerging activism that Rita Stephan highlights—women who represent a new form of patriotism in Lebanon, insisting on a normal life after so many years of war, death, and misery. Stephan is also concerned with how the media captured and projected images of Muslim women during the anti-Syrian protests in Lebanon, given that these images ultimately had an impact on the perceptions and decisions of regional policy makers.

Sya'afatun Almirzanah focuses on Muslim women's daily realities in conflict and postconflict situations in the Aceh region of Sumatra and in Ambon (Maluku), Indonesia. Her essay, "The Peace Brokers: Women of Aceh and Ambon," chronicles the peacemaking roles of Indonesian Muslim women. In the late 1990s the struggle between Indonesian security forces and the Free Aceh Movement, an armed insurgency, exploded in brutal warfare in which each side violated human rights with impunity. The Ambon conflict represents the most deadly violence in Indonesian history since the 1960s—resulting in the death and displacement of a large portion of the population. Almirzanah discusses the specific effects on Muslim women of conflict and crisis, stressing the importance of their political agency vis-à-vis postwar rebuilding efforts, as well as their contributions to the August 2005 peace agreement signed in Helsinki between insurgents and the Indonesian government.

MASTERS OF MANIPULATION AND EXPLOITATION

Because family values and the role of women as wives and mothers are core elements in the development of any society, women especially are viewed as fortresses against the infiltration of foreign values and practices. Defending chastity and maintaining national and family honor become paramount. In a patriarchal society, value systems such as honor and shame align neatly with proscribed religious doctrine. Thus when patriarchal value systems are at risk, women's behavior must be controlled and closely monitored, even to the extent of instructing women in proper forms of clothing and public behavior. In the extreme, women are silenced in the name of religion and cultural tradition. As Nafis Sadiq, former executive director of the UN Population Fund, counters, "Tradition must not be used to oppress, but to empower."[33]

Zilka Spahić-Šiljak, in "Images of Women in Bosnia, Herzegovina, and Neighboring Countries, 1992–1995," begins by tracing the status and roles of Balkan women in public life starting in 1946. She then analyzes the images of women projected during the 1992–1995 Balkan war, images that reflected ethno-national politics and ideologies prevalent at that time. As Kesic Vesna has written, "Nationalistic political discourse defined women as mothers of the nation, responsible for the continuation of national identity and maintaining tradition."[34] The chapter addresses gender-based violence during the war, in particular, rape and other forms of sexual abuse, which proved highly successful in transforming women's bodies into symbols of national territory to be conquered and defeated.[35] Current research on the Balkan tragedy— research that references mass killings and gang rapes—supports the assertion that women were primarily raped for reasons of national, religious, and ethnic identity rather than for reasons based on sexuality.[36]

Reducing women to sexualized bodies and silencing their agency through acts of violence is the story of other nationalist tragedies as well. The torture, rape, abduction, murder, and suicide committed by Hindu and Muslim men against Muslim and Hindu women, respectively, during the partition of colonial India provides historical context for Shamita Basu's contribution to this collection, "Nation and Selfhood: Memoirs of Bengali Muslim Women." Basu highlights two female Muslim writers at the time of partition (1947), describing their memoirs as much more than mere stories or historical recollections. Rather, these personal narratives represent multiple voices of protest, agony, and criticism requisite for breaking the linearity and certainty of tradition.

In both memoirs Gandhi stands as an iconic figure, encouraging women to participate in political resistance through the *charkha* and *khadi* movements. Muslim women viewed Gandhi's ideology of nonviolence as a way to offset existing patriarchal and fundamentalist paradigms. Gandhi's vision not only attempted to create a multireligious community but also offered a symbiotic relationship with feminism. The partition of the subcontinent, as reflected in the historical narratives of these Muslim women, was considered nothing less than a tragic betrayal of nonviolence.

Another example of Muslim women having been used and abused to construct religious-national identity is reflected in Faegheh Shirazi's chapter, "The Islamic Republic of Iran and Women's Images: Masters of Exploitation." The Islamic Revolution ushered in a new era of violence against women in the name of religious morality. For instance, the Islamic regime created and supported a female commando network called the Sisters of Zaynab (Khaharan e Zaynab); their duties included patrolling streets and targeting women dressed "immodestly." Punishments ranged from scolding and name calling to jail sentences and fines. More zealous members of the Zaynab commando units would wipe off women's lipstick with a razor blade hidden in a handkerchief. In 1983 an amendment was added to the Iranian constitution stating that women who violated codes of public chastity by appearing without religiously sanctioned veiling in streets and in public view would be subject to receiving up to seventy-four lashes.[37]

Shirazi recalls the Islamic government's massive orchestration of traditional myths and collective symbols to control public sentiment during Iran's revolution and during the 1980s. She cites religious-political messages behind posters, banners, and stamps created in the 1980s and analyzes the purposeful semantic fusion of *hejab* (veiling) and *jihad* (holy war), especially in the context of martyrdom. As suggested by Peter Chelkowski and Hamid Dabashi, the persuasive effects of public myths and collective symbols significantly contributed to the achievement of the Islamic Republic's wartime objectives.[38] Although Iranian women were not physically present on the battlefield, they were expected to be martyrs by proxy. That is, they were expected to perform their patriotic duty with enthusiasm by willingly sacrificing sons, brothers, husbands, fathers, and friends to war.

During the same Iran-Iraq war, on the other side of the border in Baghdad, lived the poet Hassan al-Nassar. Abbas Kadhim, in his essay in this volume, explores Al-Nassar's poetry to underscore the phenomenon of sacrifice and its violent psychological impact on the lives of Iraqi women. Al-Nassar lived through two devastating wars and a ruinous era of sanctions under Saddam Hussein's government. Unlike other poets of his stature, he passionately devoted his time to writing about those whom he perceived as silent victims of war—Iraqi women. As Kadhim points out, Al-Nassar's poetry celebrates forgotten Iraqi widows who, through no choice of their own, shouldered all the sorrows of war and none of its glory.

Just as the Ba'ath Party exploited Iraq's population, both male and female, to serve Saddam's totalitarian objectives, so it is that authoritarian regimes today throughout the Maghreb continue to subvert basic rights in their own countries. Nadia Marzouki's essay examines women's rights in Tunisia, Morocco, and Algeria. Marzouki points out that any attempt to help North African women is doomed to fail as long as the Maghreb's authoritarian regimes remain unchallenged. She also questions the presupposition that the main solution to Maghrebi women's problems must be either purely Islamic or purely secular, and she makes a compelling case by arguing that supporting these women's nongovernmental organizations (NGOs) translates into supporting the very authoritarian states responsible for deplorable conditions against which women are struggling.[39] In reading Marzouki's essay, one begins to understand the reason for the sense of futility and frustration experienced by women working to advance basic rights in this region. In short, not only have Maghrebi rulers held women's issues hostage "either to avoid or to simulate political openness[,] . . . [but] the opposition (secular and Islamist) has also been adept at using the issues of women to support their own interests."[40]

HOMELAND INSECURITY

After September 11, 2001, U.S. citizens began to grasp the daily trials of individuals living in war-torn regions throughout the world. While many Americans called for tolerance and understanding, others engaged in relentless harassment of Muslim citizens, including anyone who appeared to be Muslim or of Middle Eastern descent. The result was to forever damage American Muslims' sense of belonging. The adoption by the U.S. government of new security measures served to exacerbate their feelings of exclusion. Louise Cainkar points out:

> These measures . . . included mass arrests, secret and indefinite detentions, prolonged detention of "material witnesses," closed hearings and use of secret evidence, government eavesdropping on attorney-client conversations, FBI home and work visits, wiretapping, seizures of property, removals of aliens with technical visa violations, and mandatory special registration. At least 100,000 Arabs and Muslims living in the United States . . . personally experienced one of these measures.[41]

In addition, in the post-9/11 climate, negative public sentiment toward Arabs and Muslims has been fomented by "sensationalized media portrayals of Muslims and strong anti-Muslim/anti-Islamic rhetoric from the political right."[42] Muslim communities have reported increased incidences of workplace discrimination, interrogations, and property seizures.

As the "war against terrorism" unfolds and Islam continues to be perceived with suspicion and hostility, the veil is no longer associated simply with Muslim women; rather, it has become a symbol of Islam. According to Bailey and Tawadros, "In the aftermath of 11 September, the veil has become synonymous with cultural and religious differences that have been presented to us repeatedly as unbridgeable, alien, and terrifying."[43] Muslim women, easily identified in *hijab*, are especially vulnerable to hate crimes. For example, "On October 5, 2003, a Muslim woman wearing *hijab* was attacked from behind in a K-Mart parking lot in Springfield, Virginia. The white male teenager attacker allegedly shouted, 'You terrorist pig!' before running away. The woman was treated for a 2–3 inch deep wound on her lower back at a local hospital and released."[44]

My intention in compiling this book is in part to counter the Islamophobia that pervades contemporary literature, media, and government policy—not only in the United States but also in Europe. Particularly in the wake of the Madrid (2004) and London (2005) terrorist bombings, "the parameters of . . . institutionalized xeno-racism—anti-foreignness—have been expanded to include minority ethnic communities that have been settled in Europe for decades—simply because they are Muslim."[45] At the same time, this study is also meant to illuminate the flaws of the Islamic world—its absence of political freedom, open debate, and pluralism, all of which create a breeding ground for Islamic fundamentalism. Muslims must not eschew constructive criticism or deny the need for self-criticism.

This volume, whose contributors draw on primary sources such as poetry, prose, diaries, news reports, and visual media, begins with Central and South Asia and moves east to west, ending with a Muslim perspective from the United States. The essays represent cultural viewpoints as diverse as the regions in which they originate. Whether in Kandahar or New York City, the Muslim woman continues to be an enigmatic symbol and an ongoing source of Western fascination. More to the point, it is the Muslim woman who bears the terrible burdens of international, covert political operations. For example, during the USSR-Afghan conflict, U.S. aid was funneled into the hands of extremist Afghan Islamic groups (i.e., the Taliban). It is well documented that "one of the most favored of these groups was headed by Gulbuddin Hekmatyar, a man known for throwing acid in the faces of women who refused to wear the veil, and whose group received as much as 50% of US aid."[46] Beneath "the rubble left behind by the game of super power politics played on Afghan [and Iraqi] bodies and communities" are countless displaced women and their families.[47] Some will bear the scars permanently; some will remain refugees indefinitely.

Multiple factors influence women's alternatives in times of war, especially in patriarchal societies where men enjoy privileges linked to education, employment, property rights, and family status. Perhaps this disparity is most dramatic at the level of basic resources, that of food. The following testimony of a sixty-eight-year-old female Kurdish refugee demonstrates this point:

> When we fled to Turkey it was very difficult to get food. All the younger men ran fast and got all the food the Americans were handing out. We only had my husband with us and he can't run. So we ended up as a family without food. This happened to all the women who fled without their men. We were just left out as if we weren't there. Three of my grandchildren died in those mountains.[48]

The United Nations High Commission on Refugees (UNHCR) reports that even when food supplies are adequate in refugee camps, malnourished (and, on occasion, starving) women and children appear alongside healthy-looking, well-fed men. In camp environments patriarchal traditions are rigidly observed; men and boys are fed first, resulting in a higher mortality rate for the female refugee population.[49]

This book attempts to provide a realistic picture of countless Muslim women caught in the snares of war and militarization. Along with the other contributing writers, my goal is to foster meaningful dialogue concerning the plight of these women and, in doing so, quicken the cessation of their exploitation and abuse. It is my hope that readers in policy studies and those working with NGOs, as well as students in the fields of Middle Eastern studies, Islamic studies, gender studies, and anthropology, will find this publication useful.

NOTES

1. Swanee Hunt and Cristina Posa, "Women Waging Peace," *Foreign Policy*, no. 124 (May–June 2001), 38–47.

2. "Leader of Iraqi Female Suicide Bomber Network Arrested," Associated Press, February 4, 2009; Robert H. Reid, "Iraqi Female Suicide Bomber Kills at Least 40 Shiite Pilgrims," Associated Press, February 13, 2009.

3. http://en.wikipedia.org/wiki/Female_suicide_bomber. Accessed September 5, 2008.

4. http://jihadwatch.org/archives/019780.php. Accessed September 5, 2008.

5. www.usnews.com/articles/news/iraq/2008/07/28/the-rising-number-of-female-suicide-bombers-in-iraq.html. It is interesting to note that, according to *Marie Claire* magazine (www.marieclaire.com/world/articles/female-suicide-bomber), the Hindu-based Tamil suicide commando squad known as the Black Tigers (LTTE) contains the largest number of female suicide bombers in the world. Accessed September 5, 2008.

6. Sharia is Islamic law.

7. Roksana Bahramitash, "Islamic Fundamentalism and Women's Economic Role: The Case of Iran," *International Journal of Politics, Culture, and Society* 16, no. 4 (Summer 2003): 558.

8. www.asiasource.org/news/special_reports/mamdani.cfm. Mahmood Mamdani, interviewed May 5, 2004, by Nermeen Shaikh of AsiaSource. Accessed August 21, 2008.

9. www.foreignaffairs.org/20050101fareviewessay84113b/mahmood-mamdani/whither-political-islam.html/Mahmood Mamdani. "Whither Political Islam?" [review of Olivier Roy, *Globalized Islam: The Search for a New Ummah*], *Foreign Affairs,* January–February 2005. Accessed August 21, 2008.

10. Dilip Hiro, *Holy Wars: The Rise of Islamic Fundamentalism* (New York: Routledge, 1989), 1–2.

11. Minoo Moallem, *Between Warrior Brother and Veiled Sister: Islamic Fundamentalism and the Politics of Patriarchy in Iran* (Berkeley: University of California Press, 2005), 9.

12. Ibid., 10.

13. Ibid.

14. Smeeta Mishra, "'Saving' Muslim Women and Fighting Muslim Men: Analysis of Representations in the *New York Times*," *Global Media Journal* 6, no. 11 (Fall 2007). http://lass.calumet.purdue.edu/cca/gmj/fa07/gmj-fa07-mishra.htm. Accessed August 27, 2008.

15. Edward Said, *Orientalism* (New York: Vantage Books, 1979), 2; cited in Elizabeth Poole's *Reporting Islam: Media Representations of British Muslims* (London: I. B. Tauris, 2002), 28.

16. Jean Thévenot, *Voyage du Levant;* quoted in Malek Alloula, *The Colonial Harem* (Minneapolis: University of Minnesota Press, 1986).

17. Quoted in Alloula, *The Colonial Harem*, 95.

18. Sarah Graham-Brown, *Images of Women: the Portrayal of Women in Photography of the Middle East, 1860–1950* (New York: Columbia University Press, 1988), 9.

19. Judy Mabro, *Veiled Half-Truths: Western Travelers' Perceptions of Middle Eastern Women* (London: I. B. Taurus, 1991), 23. Emphasis added.

20. Amal Treacher, "Reading the Other: Women, Feminism, and Islam," *Studies in Gender and Sexuality* 4, no. 1 (2003): 59–71.

21. Alloula, *The Colonial Harem*.

22. Edward W. Said, *Covering Islam: How the Media and the Experts Determine How We See the Rest of the World* (New York: Pantheon Books, 1981).

23. Ghazi-Walid Falah, "The Visual Representation of Muslim/Arab Women in Daily Newspapers in the United States," in *Geographies of Muslim Women: Gender, Religion, and Space,* ed. Ghazi-Walid Falah and Caroline Nagel (New York: Guilford Press, 2005), 318.

24. Poole, *Reporting Islam.*

25. Valentine M. Moghadam, "Peace-Building and Reconstruction with Women: Reflections on Afghanistan, Iraq, and Palestine," in *Empowerment: From Patriarchy to Women's Participation, Movements, and Rights in the Middle East, North Africa, and South Asia,* ed. Valentine M. Moghadam (Syracuse: Syracuse University Press, 2007), 331.

26. Ibid.

27. J. K. Gibson-Graham, "Beyond Global vs. Local: Economic Politics outside the Binary Frame," in *Geographies of Power,* ed. Andrew Herod and Melissa W. Wright (Oxford: Blackwell, 2004).

28. Ariel Zeitlin Cooke and Marsha MacDowell, eds., *Weavings of War: Fabrics of Memory* [exhibition catalogue] (Lansing: Michigan State University Museum, 2005).

29. Iftikhar Dadi, "Shirin Nashat's Photographs as Postcolonial Allegory," *Signs: Journal of Women in Culture and Society* 34, no. 1 (2008): 130.

30. For examples of Neshat's work, see the following Web site with John Lekay's interview: www.heyokamagazine.com/HEYOKA.4.FOTOS.ShirinNeshat.htm.

31. Miriam Cooke, "Baghdad Burning: Women Write War in Iraq," *World Literature Today* 81, no. 6 (November 2007): 23–26. For more information, see Riverbend, *Baghdad Burning: Girl Blog from Iraq,* foreword Ahdaf Soueif, introd. James Ridgeway (New York: Feminist Press at CUNY, 2005).

32. Hassan M. Fattah, "Violence Opens Old Wounds from Lebanon's Past," July 14, 2006, www.nytimes.com/2006/07/14/world/middleeast/14lebanon.html. Accessed September 5, 2008.

33. K. Barnes, R. Chiarelli, C. Cohn, R. Johal, M. Kihunah, and M. Olsen, "UN Security Council 1325 on Women, Peace, and Security—Six Years On Report," October 2006, vii.

34. Kesic Vesna, "Gender and Ethnic Identities in Transition: The Former Yugoslavia-Croatia," in *From Gender to Nation,* ed. Rada Ivekovic and Julie Mostov (New Delhi: Feminist Publishing in India, 2004), 65.

35. For more information, see Jasmina Kuzmaovic's "Legacies of Invisibility: Past Silence, Present Violence against Women in the Former Yugoslavia," in *Women's Rights, Human Rights: International Feminist Perspectives,* ed. Julie Peters and Andrea Wolper (New York: Routledge, 1995), 57–61.

36. For more information on wartime rape as a collective security problem, see Lene Hansen, "Gender, Nation, Rape: Bosnia and the Construction of Security," *International Feminist Journal of Politics* 3, no. 1 (April 2001): 55–75.

37. I found these notes in a booklet titled *Simaye Hijab* [Face of the Veil] (Tehran: Ma'avenate Mobareze ba mafasede ijtima'iye naja [Ministry of Fight against Immorality] 1373 H.), 17.

38. Peter Chelkowski and Hamid Dabashi, *Staging a Revolution: The Art of Persuasion in the Islamic Republic of Iran* (New York: New York University Press, 1999).

39. For another perspective on this same issue, see Bruce Maddy-Weitzman, "Women, Islam, and the Moroccan State: The Struggle over the Personal Status Law," *Middle East Journal* 59, no. 3 (July 2005): 393–410.

40. Louis Dris-Aït-Hamadouche, "Women in the Maghreb: Civil Society's Actors or Political Instruments?" *Middle East Policy* 14, no. 4 (Winter 2007): 124, 126, 118.

41. Louise Cainkar, "The Impact of the September 11 Attacks and Their Aftermath on Arab and Muslim Communities in the United States," *GSC Quarterly* 13 (Summer–Fall 2004). http://programs.ssrc.org/gsc/publication/quarterly13/cainkar.pdf.

42. Ibid.

43. David Bailey and Gilane Tawadros, eds., *Veiling, Representation, and Contemporary Art* (Cambridge, MA: MIT Press, 2003), 18.

44. Ibid.

45. Liz Fekete, "Anti-Muslim Racism and the European Security State," *Race and Class* 46, no. 1 (2004): 4.

46. Charles Hirschkind and Saba Mahmood, "Feminism, the Taliban, and Politics of Counter-Insurgency," *Anthropological Quarterly* 75, no. 2 (Spring 2002): 343.

47. Ibid., 342.

48. Mary-Wynne Ashford and Yolanda Huet-Vaughn, "The Impact of War on Women," in *War and Public Health,* ed. Barry S. Levy and Victor W. Sidel (Oxford: Oxford University Press, 1997), 188.

49. Ibid.

PART ONE

CENTRAL AND SOUTH ASIA

I

THE PEACE BROKERS
Women of Aceh and Ambon

SYAʿAFATUN ALMIRZANAH

It is beyond dispute that a child, even before it begins to write the alphabet and gathers worldly knowledge, should know what the soul is, what truth is, what love is and what forces are hidden in the soul. It should be the essence of true education that every child learns this and in the struggle of life be able more readily to overcome hatred by love, falsehood by truth and violence by taking on suffering itself.

—MOHANDAS K. GANDHI

This chapter explores the role of women during the conflict and postcon-flict eras in Indonesia's Aceh province and in Ambon, the capital city of Maluku.[1] Moreover, it examines the peacemaking roles of Christian and Muslim women who have promoted harmony and worked to eliminate exist-ing prejudice in their communities. It also concentrates on the wide range of obstacles women have faced—socially, economically, and politically—over the thirty years of civil conflict and the survival strategies they have had to adopt.

MUSLIMS AND CHRISTIANS: A TRADITION OF *PELA*

Since the fall of President Suharto in May 1998, Indonesia has faced political, economic, and social crises. Racial and religious clashes, resulting in riots throughout the country, proved daily events. This was a horizontal rather than a vertical struggle, in that communities from widely different religious backgrounds were involved and the conflict was aggravated by constantly shifting demographics. It would seem that above all other factors religion played the most crucial role in the sectarian strife.

Richard Fox, observing the media treatment of the violence in Maluku, noted that early "sensational" reports on the role of religion in the violence were eventually replaced by more formal analyses of structural interests organizing against the order of the nation-state. This, in Fox's view, provides evidence of "an implicit theory of human action according to which people do not *really* act on the basis of 'religious' motivation."[2] Academic observers, too, have tended to downplay the role of religion in the conflict, insisting that what appears to be a religious war is on closer analysis actually a struggle motivated by socioeconomic, political, and territorial grievances.[3] For example, while most of the world's press depicts the conflict in Aceh as one of militant Islam against a largely secular government, the war is as much about political self-determination and control over the province's vast natural gas reserves as it is about religious ideology.

In many cases, what appears to be religious strife more often has its roots in ethnic conflict. For example, when migrants who are followers of one religion move to a region that is predominantly a different religion, tensions run high, especially when the migrant community acquires a strong position in the local economy or becomes sufficiently numerous to challenge the indigenous community's grip on local politics. This dynamic has featured prominently in both of Indonesia's "religious wars." In Maluku, the conflict between Muslim migrants and indigenous Christians was the relevant trigger, much more than any disagreement involving indigenous Muslims.[4] The common perception in the West that this conflict was the result of a Muslim campaign to eliminate Christians is incorrect. In fact, Christians were no less involved in killing Muslims than Muslims were in killing Christians.

In the Indonesian media, Maluku was portrayed as a region in which relations between Christians and Muslims had always been harmonious. This interfaith tranquility was largely the effect of a centuries-old alliance system called *pela.* According to *pela,* a village of one faith is matched with a sister village of another faith so that, for example, Christians helped build mosques and Muslims helped build churches.

On a recent visit to Ambon, I found this dynamic still present. For example, I attended a festival known as *panas pela* and *panas gandong*—between a Muslim community and a Christian community.[5] *Panas* is translated as "hot" and in this case refers to the "warming up" of relations between the two communities. *Pela* may be translated as "family relationship built between two villages for mutual support in the event of any attack." *Gandong* means "family relationship between Muslims and Christians based on blood oath." The celebration of *panas pela* or *panas gandong* is meant to reconnect, strengthen, and vivify the feelings of familial relations.

Indeed, the city of Ambon and the Maluku islands in general have long been home to both Muslims and Christians, and the occurrence of violent interfaith conflict has until recently been extremely rare and restricted in scope. Islam was propagated under the auspices of the Ternate Sultanate;[6] the influence of this sultanate extended through much of eastern Indonesia and, in the years prior to European contact, as far afield as the Philippine archipelago. The Portuguese imported Roman Catholicism to the Moluccas in the sixteenth century and established a network of forts and small settlements during the heyday of the spice trade. In the seventeenth century, the Dutch East India Company replaced the Portuguese as the sole purchaser of Moluccan spices, bringing Protestant missionaries in its wake. Throughout the centuries, it was the *pela* system of alliances between local settlements (*negeri*) that helped to sustain reciprocity and cooperation between Muslim and Christian villages and neighbors.[7]

Tragically, the most recent conflict has fatally damaged the Maluku community. Social relations have been disrupted. There has been a marked increase in social divisions according to religion (such as the segregation of Muslim and Christian housing),[8] and the long-established practice of pluralism, tolerance, and solidarity is withering away.

CIVIL WAR: IMPACT ON WOMEN'S LIVES

At the northernmost tip of Sumatra, the largest island in the Republic of Indonesia's vast archipelago, a civil war has simmered for over a quarter century. Aceh, popularly called Serambi Makkah (Veranda to Mecca) was the first part of the archipelago to be converted to Islam. Aceh is a center of Islamic scholarship and, since the seventeenth century, has produced some of the greatest Sufi saints and poets of the Malay world. It has been ruled for many centuries by sultanates portraying themselves as the center of moral, cultural, and political authority.[9]

Unlike Ambon, the conflict in Aceh can be termed a vertical conflict, pitting the central government of Indonesia against a grassroots insurgency, the Free Aceh Movement (GAM). The reasons for this Acehnese rebellion are complex and numerous, "among them economic inequality, class conflict, poverty and lack of the most basic infrastructure, access to schools and higher education."[10] Thus this conflict is about the reorganization of the nation-state and capital, about social justice for the victims, orphans, and widows of systematic, planned murders of state terror. The central government has been waging counterinsurgency operations in Aceh, the largest of which was conducted during the military emergency from May 2003 to May 2004. Like the conflict in Maluku and North Maluku, violence in Aceh has cost thousands of lives and has resulted in vast numbers of refugees.

Indeed, the crises and conflicts—political, religious, and ethnic—that have beset Indonesia, Ambon and Aceh in particular, have had a serious impact on women's lives. Women have been at the receiving end of increased pressures and violence in both the familial and social spheres. Furthermore, they have faced increased demands as caregivers and providers, while at the same time their freedom of movement and actions have been curtailed. Indeed, they have borne the brunt of the anger and frustration of male relatives who are humiliated because they cannot fulfill their traditional role as providers. Women have had to shoulder most of the burden of caring for tens of thousands of men and children injured during the many years of conflict.

In Ambon, when most of the men were still at war, women from opposing groups (Christian and Muslim) became the frontier peace guard—by engaging in and promoting economic activities at the market and by caring for each other. Women from Kei, in Southeast Maluku, for example, "served time" by camping out in the middle of a bridge for a month so that finally the two groups agreed to renegotiate.

A Muslim woman, living in Batu Merah in Ambon and making her living by selling souvenirs, told me that she was primarily concerned with helping the injured and supplying food to refugees and other victims of war.[11] Whenever she runs out of provisions, instead of losing hope, she begins again from nothing. She said that she never feels afraid. As evidence of her fearlessness, she explained that she was hiding Christians in her own house to prevent them from being killed by fellow Muslims. They would remain with her until it was safe for them to return to their homes.

PEACEMAKERS: THE CARING WOMEN'S MOVEMENT

To many people in Ambon, or in Maluku province, it would be unimaginable that there still exists a group of Muslim and Christian women in Ambon who have a keen sense of humanity and a desire for peace. In the heat of the conflict, a small group of Moluccan women from the Muslim and Christian communities have come together, realizing that violence will never solve existing problems. From their point of view, it is women who must develop alternate strategies to put an end to conflict.

The first meeting, mediated by the governor's wife at the request of Christian women, was neither pleasant nor promising.[12] Mistrust and anger were palpable, as accusatory fingers pointed back and forth. To their great credit, however, neither group of women gave up on the other. Instead, they continued to meet, sharing stories about their personal experiences of the conflict. The storytelling process helped them to realize their common plight as victims. That acknowledgment brought them closer together. They continued to meet, forming deep friendships and collectively planning courses of action—such as demanding an end to the violence, working with youth who were recruited to throw bombs, and empowering women to become agents of reconciliation and peace.[13]

This intercommunal network of women called itself the Gerakan Perempuan Peduli (GPP), or Caring Women's Movement. As a coalition of women, they officially declared their position on September 4, 1999. They voiced "the conscience of women" before the Maluku governor; the head of the Pattimura Military Regional Command, Brig. Gen. Max Tamaela; and the (at the time) chief of Maluku Provincial Police, Col. Bugis Saman.[14]

The GPP remains a nonprofit organization with no representative office. More than forty women activists from Protestant, Muslim, and Catholic communities are involved in the movement. Their objective is to provide aid to those women and children in Maluku who have lost nearly everything: their schools, their childhoods, their parents, husbands, and villages. The GPP organizes rallies against violence while supporting women and children who are victims of the war. In close cooperation, they have agreed and are determined to make the people of the Moluccas realize that violence is not the answer.

One of the more prominent Muslim GPP members is Ibu Tum, sister of Governor Latuconsina.[15] She has been part of a peacekeeping force helping war victims, either by providing necessary logistics or showing up at the battlefield. She also supports a key GPP peace-building program referred to as "Closing the Gap," which addresses prejudice, mistrust, and suspicion between Christians and Muslims in the Moluccas. Both men and women participate in the intensive program. For six days they live in the same house, eat and work together, share stories, and laugh and cry together. In short, Christian and Muslim men and women learn to live with one another again in spite of their religious and ethnic differences.

Ibu Tum conducts other peace-oriented activities as well, such as "Live-Ins," which bring women from diverse religious traditions together for a week. She pointed out that although touching "others" is *haram* (prohibited),[16] the activities she has developed allow participants to begin working together. They also engage in exercises geared toward "trauma healing."[17] Despite many challenges, the women's passionate spirit to cease all forms of violence and conflict has not been dampened.

Slowly but surely, the GPP in Maluku has made itself known to the wider community by visiting camps for displaced persons, organizing workshops on trauma counseling, and undertaking activities involving children in both Christian and Muslim communities. They have also approached Catholic and Protestant priests, Muslim teachers and clerics.[18]

Another organization, Arika Mahina, is a nongovernmental organization (NGO) involved in assisting victims of warfare by providing low-interest loans to help individuals, both women and men, start small businesses to support their families. One of the victims I met had been badly burned when she boarded a ship with a bomb hidden on board. When it exploded, she hesitated to jump because she could not swim. Eventually she was forced into the water and managed to survive, although her face and body were damaged irreparably. Afterwards she became an introvert, avoiding the company of others because of the way she looked. Eventually, with the help of Arika Mahina, an NGO working specifically to assist children and disabled victims of war, she was able to purchase a *warung* (small store) and has developed new confidence.[19]

During Sultan Iskandar Muda's reign in the seventeenth century, Aceh became the cosmopolitan center of Islamic learning. In the same century, Aceh was ruled by a succession of Acehnese queens. As heads of state, the four queens who successfully rose to the throne were Tajul Alam Safiatudin Shah (1641–1675), Nur Al-Alam Nakiyyat al-Din Shah (1675–1678), ʿInayat Shah Zakiyyat al-Din (1678–1688), and Kamalat Shah (1688–1699).[20] According to Mernissi, "They reigned despite the fact that their political enemies had imported from Mecca a fatwa that declared that 'it was forbidden by [religious] law for a woman to rule.'"[21]

In fact, the women of Aceh have left prodigious legacies over the centuries and have behaved heroically, especially during the anticolonial struggles against the Dutch. I refer to women such as Tjut Nyak Dhien (1848–1908), who assumed a position of leadership after her husband was killed while leading an anticolonial resistance movement. Other women served as guerrilla fighters alongside their husbands, resisting Dutch colonialism. One woman named Pocut Baren (1641–1700?) became commander of a warship battling the Portuguese, replacing her slain husband, the admiral Malahayati. The term "Inong Balee," in fact, refers to those widows who have continued their husbands' struggle for freedom. Given their courageous resistance to colonial forces, it is not surprising that many of these widows eventually assumed prominent and influential political roles.

Because of their proud history of female leaders, the Acehnese have remained a strongly matriarchal society—in spite of a deeply Islamic background. In every *gampong* (village) in Aceh, there has been a gathering space allocated for women to learn about Islam, to discuss and share information. This space, referred to as *balee ureung inong*,[22] has traditionally functioned as a center for women's activities and now serves to ensure that women's rights are guaranteed in the postconflict reconstruction process. It is in this place that the problems and rights specific to women are discussed and resolved. Unfortunately, as women have been increasingly relegated to the domestic sphere, both the influence of women in the public sphere and the availability of women's public spaces have diminished. In contrast, men engage in debates and discussion in public spaces such as *warung kopi* (coffee shops).[23]

INTERNATIONAL INFLUENCE IN ACEH

Discourse surrounding the role of Acehnese women has become increasingly important—especially since the 2004 tsunami tragedy—as many international aid organizations have transported staff, some of whom are Muslim, to Aceh. Most of these Muslim outsiders, with a Taliban mind-set, have been shocked and surprised to discover Indonesian women stepping into activities and start-up businesses usually undertaken by men. Research findings suggest that most aid organizations involved in postconflict or posttsunami disaster relief are women's organizations. These include Relawan Perempuan untuk Kemanusiaan (RpuK), or Women Volunteers for Humanity; Kelompok Kerja Transformasi Gender Aceh (KKTGA), or Aceh Gender Transformation Group; Solidaritas Perempuan (Women's Solidarity); 'Aisyiah Muhammadyah; and Perempuan Islam (Islamic Women). Indeed, most crisis centers are staffed by women—such as PCC (People's Crisis Center) and Yayasan Matahari (Matahari Foundation). Still other women's organizations work to promote livelihood opportunities for women in the postconflict period, such as LBH-APIK, Yayasan Hati Nurani, and Pengembangan Aktifitas Sosial Ekonomi Aceh (PASKA), the latter led by Faridah Hariani, recipient of the Yap Thian Him Award, established to honor those working for human rights.

Euro-American and First World feminists working within the international solidarity network tend to universally categorize Third World women as docile victims and inferior subordinates. They have difficulty conceiving of a matrifocal culture in Aceh (in terms of gender, a relatively egalitarian culture). Indeed, Western feminists tend to categorize Acehnese women as victimized and suffering.[24] According to the author Jacqueline Aquino Siapno, in matrifocal cultures such as Aceh and in most parts of Sumatra, not "all women are at risk."[25] As one Amnesty International report claims, not all of them are easily intimidated and certainly not all of them are powerless and subordinated.

Some of the women I interviewed refused to be labeled as victims. For example, a woman from Lhok Sukon recounted how several soldiers had shown up outside her house early one morning. Her husband, who was ill, knew the soldiers were there and warned his wife to stay indoors. Because she needed to take ablution for *fajar* prayer,[26] she disregarded his plea. As she was preparing to leave, two soldiers knocked at the door and forced her to a hillside area where other soldiers were waiting. There she was raped repeatedly. Afterwards, the soldiers brought her back home, warning her not to tell anyone about what had happened. However, her very bright son noted the name and official register number of one of the men. With this number in hand, she went to the military base and reported the incident. As a result of her refusal to be intimidated and labeled a victim, the soldiers were tried in court and imprisoned.[27]

Another woman I interviewed eschewed the role of "suffering wife." She told me that her husband, a GAM member, stayed in the mountains for days at a time, returning home only sporadically. On one of these occasions, he returned with another woman. What was most interesting, and revelatory, to me was the manner in which the woman told her story. She did not at all seem sad; in fact, she even laughed while she spoke. I asked her, "Why do you seem so happy about what happened? Don't you feel sad at all?" She replied, "There is no benefit in feeling sad! He is gone!" She is genuinely happier now since she no longer has to fear being the wife of a rebel.

This is almost the same sentiment that Siapno discovered when interviewing an Acehnese woman whose husband had been sentenced to three years in prison. The woman did not miss her husband for a moment. Instead, she claimed that his imprisonment was her freedom and his freedom, her imprisonment; he had been a domineering husband, never allowing her to go anywhere.[28]

The only effective mode for silencing women has been to deny them access to participation in the independence movement (Aceh Merdeka). Ironically, the movement claims to struggle on behalf of women. Also, elite urban feminists claim to represent these silenced women while frequently categorizing them as submissive and subordinate in the elitist discourse.

As Siapno writes:

Like other women in political movements for independence where women's participation is marginalized, Acehnese women tend to have profoundly cynical, if not contemptuous attitudes toward Aceh Merdeka male leaders who claimed to be struggling for democracy but who, in fact, did not practice democratic values in their own homes. [One of the men who was] interviewed . . . said, matter-of-factly, that he was her [his wife's] representative, and did not therefore need her opinion.[29]

Unfortunately, well-meaning scholars, human rights workers, solidarity groups, and women's NGOs are all guilty of generating narratives that tend to silence and subordinate poor women, even while ostensibly trying to help them. In her critique of the political-economic, representational, and ethical problems concealed in overzealous practices of human rights, donor-driven agendas, Gewald writes:

> Within every community that is able to voice its violation of rights, there are those groups and individuals who are unable to articulate it. . . . [W]ho is speaking for whom? What is the location of power that enables them to speak for others? What forms of violence do these representations perform? If it is not individuals but non-profit groups who are speaking, then we must engage critically with the nature of the "local" and "grassroots" claims that are being made by these groups.[30]

Women in the postconflict areas of Ambon and Aceh have voiced a strong desire for the creation of a women's organization working exclusively on the economic empowerment of widows and orphans, instead of an organization primarily seeking justice through "human rights" and the court system. It has frequently been the case that well-funded groups with a specific mandate can demonstrate solidarity only on *their* terms rather than on the terms of those women with whom they supposedly sympathize.[31]

In fact, the majority of women I interviewed in Ambon and Aceh agreed that their most pivotal need is economic empowerment. What they require from relief organizations is support to sustain their families, which includes feeding and providing for their children. Some are trying to operate small businesses, modest enterprises that encompass a wide range of skills—from laundering other people's clothes to opening a small *warung* (shop) to serving as makeup artists (especially for brides) to making foodstuffs for sale.

Many widowed women have been robbed of ownership rights to the land they cultivated with their husbands for years. Because income-generating options are so limited, some women have been forced to engage in prostitution in order to survive and to obtain food for their families. In the midst of the challenging and delicate task of piecing together a broken country, women (comprising more than half of the population) stand at the center of recuperation and development efforts. They are at once collective agents of change and individuals with specific and critical needs that must be addressed as efficiently as possible.

Unlike Ambonese women, who were often directly involved in warfare, actually fighting on the battlefield, Acehnese women have adopted subtler strategies. As Siapno points out, the Acehnese women's relative absence in this nationalist movement should not be viewed as a marker of female subordination and marginalization. Instead, "their agency and power are not explicitly articulated in modern, progressivist political movements or coalitions . . . but rather in more indigenous forms of local feminism and exercises of power that are not often examined in Euro-American analysis of gender agency."[32] Thus Acehnese women have indeed participated actively in (and have been deeply affected by) the struggle, although they have neither held highly visible public positions nor participated in overt forms of opposition.

Siapno cites an interview by Kerry Brogan with an Acehnese woman whose husband had been killed. The interview demonstrates how individual women who have experienced the critical impacts of violence are forced into an attitude of stoicism. Brogan recorded:

> Two years after [the husband's] death, some soldier approached . . . [the woman named] Maya and started sexually harassing her. They asked where her husband was, but she was too scared to reveal that he was dead, for fear that this would leave her vulnerable to further harassment from the military. . . . [In the interview] she [Maya] described what happened to her husband without displaying much emotion. But when we asked what life was like for her now, she immediately began to cry, perhaps because the day-to-day hardships are easier to grieve over than the inexplicable death of her husband.[33]

Indeed, in my interviews with GAM wives whose rebel husbands had died in the conflict, although it was difficult for them to accept their personal losses, the prospect of attempting to survive from day to day was even more difficult. One respondent became hysterical when contemplating her responsibility as sole breadwinner for her family.

CONCLUSION

In conditions of warfare, violence, and bloodshed it is challenging if not impossible for women to pursue a progressive agenda.[34] They lack access even to the most basic services that may eventually be provided in postconflict situations. Once the fighting has ceased, the "invisibility" of many female ex-combatants renders them unable to gain access to the services and benefits they are due. In fact, keeping their ex-combatant role secret, or invisible, may be key to their survival. As a result, women who have been active in armed struggle often find their return to civilian life extremely difficult. Communities tend to stigmatize them for contributing to the destruction inflicted on the community and for stepping out of traditional gender roles. Furthermore, female combatants who have been raped, forcibly impregnated, or infected with HIV/AIDS face heightened discrimination on their reintegration to home or receiving communities.

Few would argue that women's equal participation in political life—as voters, candidates, and members of electoral committees—is integral to their general advancement in any society or culture. And yet, across the globe, women remain underrepresented in political and decision-making positions, a phenomenon that results in the perpetuation of policies and practices that do not serve women's needs equally with those of men. This disparity is especially dangerous in postconflict settings, where the voices of women must be heard in order to ensure equitable and sustainable reconstruction.

In most countries, elections are scheduled a few years after the signing of a peace agreement to give citizens a chance to select leaders who will guide them into the subsequent phases of reconstruction. Such has been the case in Aceh. Postconflict elections can be an opportunity for women to vote for candidates who will have a favorable impact on their lives. On the other hand, this can also be a time in which progressive policies supporting women that had been introduced during or immediately after the conflict may be stripped away. If women are not allowed or encouraged to participate at every level of decision making and if women's perspectives are not integrated accordingly, then the goals of equality, development, and peace cannot be attained.

Women in both Ambon and Aceh face obstacles at the polls due to coercion, threats, and intimidation by male relatives. Compared to men, women have less access to information and fewer opportunities for education. In postconflict settings, when the foundations of a new society are being built, surmounting such barriers is of vital importance if new constitutions and new legislation are to reflect the experiences, insights, and needs of women.

In the postconflict areas of Aceh and Ambon, women have organized for peace and are continuing to do so—not only in their respective communities but at the regional and national levels as well. However, the reality is that they are rarely a part of the official peace process from the start. This marginalization of women denies half the population equal access to the political process and denies all people the benefits of an invaluable female perspective. Also, formal negotiations that exclude women have little hope of widespread popular support. It is not enough to include a few "token women," however capable, at the highest levels of decision making. Many more women need to be included—especially those with an understanding of social justice and gender equality issues.

Indeed, almost no Acehnese women have been included in decisions concerning postconflict issues, not even issues that immediately and vitally affect them. Not surprisingly, the reconstruction and reconciliation process has yet to provide any significant relief for or support to the women of Aceh. The same holds true in Ambon. During my visit to both islands in July 2006, I witnessed many women still living in barracks. These women typify the discrimination to which I refer.

In times of war and crisis, then, women should be acknowledged as invaluable resources—whether at the negotiation table, or during reconstruction, or when policy is being crafted. Especially women with firsthand experience of conflict, as well as those who have suffered untold misfortune, deserve pivotal, substantive roles in reshaping their communities. It is these women, in Indonesia and elsewhere, with the potential to construct sustainable frameworks for peace.

NOTES

1. Maluku is the Indonesian name for the Moluccas, a group of islands located between Sulawesi and New Guinea.

2. Richard Fox, Conflict@Ambon.Net. Excerpt from a paper titled "Media, Practice, Antagonism: Rethinking the Role of Mass Communication Research in Asia," presented at Nanyang Technological University, Singapore, June 11–12, 1999, 4. Available at the_ religious_subject@indonesia.net.

3. See Kirsten E. Schulze, "Laskar Jihad and Conflict in Ambon," *Brown Journal of World Affairs* 10, no. 1 (Spring 2002); Robert W. Hefner, ed., *The Politics of Multiculturalism and Citizenship in Malaysia, Singapore, and Indonesia* (Honolulu: University of Hawaiʻi Press, 2001).

4. Jacquest Bertrand, "Legacies of the Authoritarian Past: Religious Violence in Indonesia's Moluccan Islands," *Pacific Affairs* 75, no. 1 (Spring 2002): 57–85.

5. The festival I attended was held in Ambon on July 20, 2006.

6. Ternate is an island located in North Maluku, Eastern Indonesia. This island kingdom belonging to the Islamic Sultanate played a significant role in terms of commerce from the thirteenth to seventeenth centuries.

7. For more information on the *pela* system, see Dieter Bartels, "Guarding the Invisible Mountain: Intervillage Alliances, Religious Syncretism and Ethnic Identity among Ambonese Christians and Moslems in the Moluccas" (Ph.D. dissertation, Cornell University, 1977).

8. I witnessed this segregation firsthand during my visit to Ambon.

9. Jacqueline Aquino Siapno, *Gender, Islam, Nationalism and the State of Aceh: The Paradox of Power, Co-optation and Resistance* (New York: Routledge Curzon, 2002), 25.

10. Ibid., 30.

11. Interview in Ambon on July 20, 2006. This woman was approximately fifty years old.

12. This meeting was held immediately after the conflict occurred.

13. From interview with Kiki Shamal, Ambon, July 2006.

14. Oktavianus Pinontoan, "Christian, Muslim Women Promote Peace in Maluku," *Jakarta Post,* December 31, 2002.

15. Muhammad Saleh Latuconsina was governor in Ambon when the conflict occurred.

16. According to Islamic law.

17. Based on interview with Ibu Tum Latuconsina in her home, Ambon, July 24, 2006.

18. Oktavianus Pinontoan, "Christian, Muslim Women Promote Peace in Maluku," *Jakarta Post,* December 31, 2002.

19. Interview with Sara (pseudonym; real name withheld), the burn victim, and her mother in their home, July 25, 2006.

20. See Fatimah Mernisi, *The Forgotten Queens of Islam,* trans. Mary Jo Lakeland (Minneapolis: University of Minnesota Press, 1993).

21. Ibid., 110. Cited in Siapno, *Gender, Islam, Nationalism and the State of Aceh,* 51.

22. B*alee ureung inong* literally translates as "a place for young women to gather."

23. Siapno, *Gender, Islam, Nationalism and the State of Aceh,* 108.

24. Ibid., 181.

25. Ibid., 182.

26. *Fajar* refers to an Islamic prayer before sunrise.

27. Interview with this woman from Lhok Sukon (and her friends) in Lhokseumawe, July 2006.

28. Siapno, *Gender, Islam, Nationalism and the State of Aceh,* 22–23.

29. Telephone interview with Agam (pseudonym; real name withheld), July 12, 2006.

30. Inderpal Gewald, *Scattered Hegemonies: Postmodernity and Transnational Feminist Practices* (Minneapolis: University of Minnesota Press, 1994), 5–7. Quoted in Siapno, *Gender, Islam, Nationalism and the State of Aceh,* 180.

31. Siapno, *Gender, Islam, Nationalism and the State of Aceh,* 185.

32. Jacqueline Aquino Siapno, "Gender, Nationalism and the Ambiguity of Female Agency," in *Frontline Feminism, Women, War, and Resistance,* ed. Marguerite R. Waller and Jennifer Rycenga (New York: Garland, 2000), 27.

33. Kerry Brogan, "The Forgotten Costs of Counter-Insurgency in Aceh," *Inside Indonesia,* March 1997, 4, quoted in Siapno, *Gender, Islam, Nationalism and the State of Aceh,* 286.

34. Susan Blackburn, "Gender Violence and the Indonesian Political Transition," *Asian Studies Review* 23, no. 4 (1999): 6.

2

NATION AND SELFHOOD

Memoirs of Bengali Muslim Women

SHAMITA BASU

During periods of political and social upheaval, new and often unforeseen opportunities arise from the disruption of the status quo. This chapter focuses on the creation of Muslim women's political agency in India, beginning with the mid-nineteenth-century anticolonial struggle and culminating with the 1947 partition of India and Pakistan. It attempts to trace the development of Muslim feminist consciousness during this period and celebrates the memoirs of two Muslim Bengali women whose vision of liberation from patriarchal domination was significantly influenced by the violent transition from colonialism to national independence.

GENDERING OF A NATION: HINDU VERSUS MUSLIM

For centuries, Muslim women in the Bengal region of India have lived solitary lives of *abarodh,* or seclusion.[1] This prohibitive level of seclusion proved an ideal structure to uphold male domination and prevent the questioning of male authority. Only when political upheaval unsettled the still, predictable waters of this stagnant tradition was change possible—a disruption secretly welcomed by Muslim women caught in rigid patriarchal snares.

The success of India's twentieth-century nationalism was dependent on the mobilization of large masses of people, a grassroots activism that necessarily cut across gender and caste lines. This political phenomenon provided women with a new opportunity to escape from their narrow domestic spheres and join in the process of collective political action. Indeed, it was hoped that this newly emerging nationalism might very well translate into a new political agency for women.

As far as Hindu Bengali women were concerned, political participation — albeit in a limited form — acquired legitimacy and "respectability" as a sacred act of patriotism.[2] Within Hindu nationalist political discourse, attempts were made to "gender" the nation as a powerful feminine mother. These attempts had far-reaching implications in terms of generating widespread social approval for women participating in violent, extremist acts. *Bande Mataram*, "Hail the Mother," became the most popular patriotic slogan of Hindu nationalism. Powerful female figures in Hindu Bengali patriotic literature were celebrated, remarkable women who had contributed to the formation of social codes considered daring during their lifetimes.

This veneration of the nation as quintessentially feminine did not meet with the same approval in contemporary Muslim society. Neither the principle of energy embodied in female Hindu deities, such as Durga, nor figures of feminine modesty and tolerance as celebrated by Gandhi in Hindu epics (e.g., Sita, the ideal wife of Rama) were embraced with equal fervor by Muslims. A corresponding Muslim reconstruction did take place, however; that is, "the Aryan Goddesses were replaced by an ideal woman, a modern-day Ayesha or Fatima [female Muslim warriors of antiquity like Khaola were sometimes celebrated, but they never became household words]."[3] The all-important role of mother, or the feminine, in Hindu society never attained the same religious and political symbolism among Muslims. Given "the newly awakened and politicized sense of separate identity, a section of [the Islamic] community viewed the worship of mother earth and motherland with some misgivings, as a concept not in keeping with the monotheistic tenets of Islam."[4]

POLITICAL STRUGGLE AND THE MEMOIR

I would like to call attention to two memoirs, *Smriteer Paata* (1962) (Pages from Memory), by Sayeeda Manowara Khatun (1909–1981), and *Ekale Amader Kaal* (1988) (Our Past in the Present Time), by Sufia Kamal (1911–1999). A study of these Muslim women's memoirs reveals how they observed and maneuvered the path of political struggle and violence, often as witnesses from behind the *purdah*. The memoirs document the ways in which Muslim women began to perceive myriad possibilities for self-transformation as a result of the emergence of colonial modernity and nationalist struggle. Apart from offering an alternate trajectory of nationalist history, women's narratives such as these are especially significant in creating an entirely new register, documenting women's oppression and recounting how anticolonial nationalism allowed them to challenge patriarchal oppression while developing new personal identities.

These women witnessed mass uprisings that ripped through the subcontinent, imperialist violence that culminated in events such as the Jallian-walabagh massacre, the Khilafat struggle,[5] and finally the outbreak of riots during the partition. Against this backdrop of unspeakable violence in the public arena, these two memoirs serve as constant reminders of the domestic violence that women quietly endured in the privacy of their own homes and communities.

Khatun's *Smriteer Paata* and Kamal's *Ekale Amader Kaal* provide glimpses into history, revealing how Muslim Bengali women emerged onto the political stage. Within these short narratives, the voices of Muslim women are re-covered. The images they recall of an enslaved nation clearly reflect their own subjugation. The nationalist struggle translates into their personal struggle against seclusion and segregation, while the revolt of the colonized subjects becomes their fervent desire for liberation from patriarchal domination.

Two simultaneous narratives are interwoven throughout the memoirs. One describes events leading to the formation of new nation-states. The other recounts how these women were profoundly transformed as their collective fate became linked with the political destiny of the newly emerging nations. These memoirs are much more than mere stories or historical recollections. Rather, they represent multiple voices of protest, agony, and criticism requi-site for breaking the linearity and certainty of tradition.

Having become objectified and ossified symbols of community honor, Muslim women were confined within the walls of patriarchal households and their voices silenced. They were frequently spoken of but never allowed to speak about themselves. From this dark perspective, the sights and sounds of war and strife stirred these women's will and imagination, ultimately driving them into the public sphere. What the memoirs signify is a passionate desire to break from seclusion, a longing to belong to and participate in the politics of emancipation.

THE MARGINS OF MODERNITY: OPPORTUNITY AND SUPPRESSION

At the dawn of the twentieth century, both Manowara Khatun and Sufia Kamal were born into the old Muslim aristocracy. These Muslim elites, in particular the *sharif* classes,[6] were drawn to the British educational system and to British institutions that reinforced the glory of a cosmopolitan, enlight-ened, and classical Islam. However, this cosmopolitan worldview did not in any way address women's liberation. Women were merely onlookers to this transitional era of unprecedented changes in community and polity.[7] Muslim women never fully inhabited the domain of modernity as Hindu upper-class women did. Instead, theirs was an ambiguous social space just on the margins of modernity. What Khatun and Kamal convey is a passionate desire to go beyond the margins, to engage in and be part of the politics of emancipation. Studies of Bengali Muslim women have shown that the

> structures of the traditional family in the *andarmahal* [domain of domesticity within a household] had by the late nineteenth century given rise to distorted notions of seclusion designed to control women's sexuality. This, coupled with the fact that upper-class women had no economic and social role in the public domain, led to a total separation of the public and the private spheres in the *sharif* society. But no form of power and control is isolated from resistance, which generates in its turn an impetus to change.[8]

Both Khatun and Kamal poignantly describe a desire to become learned women and to revolt against seclusion. As modern politics intruded into shared community spaces, it also made its way into the dark recesses and corridors of secluded domesticity; this incursion of modernity gradually began to break the silences, introduce questions, and provoke resistance to traditional family structures.

The renaissance of reform and modernization that took place in colonial Bengal gave rise to "new" Muslim women. The role model for these elite Muslim women was the English-educated Brahmo-Hindu woman—the *bhadramahila*.[9] It is argued that "by the end of the [nineteenth] century, there was an articulate group of women able to make their voices heard through public institutional channels hitherto confined to men. This type of modern woman became known as the *bhadramahila*."[10] Literature was one of the powerful agencies of Bengal renaissance, which began in the mid-nineteenth century.

The Bengal renaissance also expressed itself through powerful political, religious, scientific, and artistic movements, especially among the growing middle-class intelligentsia. It was this indigenous group of individuals that responded to the Western colonial discourses on Enlightenment and modernity. Most of the "new" Muslim women wrote in Bengali, which emerged as a modern vernacular. In Bengal as elsewhere, Islam was continuously interpreted and reshaped as different social classes in different periods became its dominant carriers and representatives.[11] For Bengali Muslims,

> the *sharif* family [was] the central institution of the private sphere comprised in the main of those who were not supposed to be seen, let alone

participate in the world outside. . . . This was a natural consequence of the gender inequality inherent in a patriarchal scheme of things. The familial space was perhaps the only domain where women—rich and poor—derived any significance and meaning from their lives, and its structure was a key element in maintaining prescribed gender relations.[12]

An unintended consequence of nationalist modernity was that the newly educated middle-class and aristocratic women—mostly Hindu, but to a limited degree Muslim women as well—had to be accommodated within the public and political national spheres. Beginning in the late nineteenth century, those Bengali women longing for a public role became involved in social reform movements. With the introduction of formal education for women, upper-class urban Hindus and especially Brahmo women took advantage of the modernist reform movements and adopted the newly defined roles of what the Indian feminist historian Tanika Sarkar refers to as political "achievers." The term "achiever" not only connotes activism but also suggests that those women were socially acclaimed for their contributions to public life.

However, not all Bengal Muslim women enjoyed the same advantages. Addressing this social phenomenon, Kamal explains:

From 1910 or perhaps earlier the national independence struggle, [the] militant nationalist strategy, [the] movement against the first partition of Bengal, and the constitution of the Muslim League took place. Stories and news of mass agitation were also reaching women in the interior spaces of Muslim households. But it was not possible for Muslim women to actively participate in politics like the non-Muslims, except that my family was partly involved in the boycott movement.[13]

Though ripples of rebellion made their way into domestic spaces, very little actually changed for Muslim women in seclusion, especially in terms of everyday practices. Judith Butler, who theorized extensively on "gender performativity," has demonstrated that gender comes into being through performance of repetitive actions in the social sphere, actions that are codified or scripted by social conventions and hegemonic ideologies.

Khatun provides an example of such practices when alluding to her elder brother. Indeed, it was he who made all-important decisions for female family members—including denying Khatun the opportunity to pursue a formal education. Kamal too expresses indignation in the face of patriarchal injunctions. She is especially amazed and disappointed by the attitudes of her uncle, a man considered learned and cosmopolitan. In spite of possessing a reasonably liberal disposition, as well as one of the largest private libraries in their town, he prohibited Kamal from receiving a formal education.[14]

The making of Muslim women's agency in colonial Bengal cannot be understood when disassociated from the commonplace practices prescribed and normalized by a male hierarchy. Butler has shown how the role of performativity cannot be understood outside the context of iterability, that is, a regularized and constrained repetition of norms. This repetition is not performed *by* a subject; instead, it is what enables a subject and constitutes the temporal condition for the subject. This iterability implies that "performance" is not a singular "act" or event but a ritualized production, a ritual reiterated under and through constraint, under and through the force of prohibition and taboo, with the threat of ostracism and even death controlling and compelling the shape of the production. Again, the significance does not lie in the repetitive act being performed by a subject or individual; rather, what is significant is that the repetitive act enables, or empowers, an individual and constitutes the temporal conditions for him or her.[15]

CONFINEMENT, DESIRE, AND MIMESIS

During the partition movement that would divide India and Pakistan, women longed to transcend their stereotypical roles as passive, domestic caregivers. They dreamed of adopting behaviors associated with action and transformation, behaviors socially and normatively gendered as male. Hindu women had more opportunities to emulate these activist behaviors, such as picketing or taking part in armed rebellion. Because upper-class Bengali Hindu women were the early beneficiaries of formal Western education, they were more able than their Muslim counterparts to engage in public and literary activities. Beginning in the early twentieth century, Hindu women also became involved in direct terrorist activities and armed struggle. Muslim women had few opportunities in this regard. Only later, when more women from middle-class Hindu Bengali families joined the nationalist struggle, did Western-educated elite Muslim women become actively involved. In general, women wanted to redefine and expand their sphere of activities and their roles—and they wanted to do so by emulating qualities traditionally associated with men: fearlessness, willingness to take risks and provoke authority, courage in the face of certain danger.

Khatun's memoir reflects this desire to move with the wave of change, to be part of the new political mobility. She documents sights and sounds of agitation all around her, including songs by the Khilafatists. "We used to run around all over the household trying to catch a glimpse of them," she writes, "from the windows, the balconies, and the rooftop. I used to wish so badly to join them and work for the cause of the nation."[16] Recalling the era when men were recruited into World War II, Khatun makes it clear that, from her standpoint, a man's opportunity to fight a war was far more fortunate than a woman's domestic confinement. Feeling paralyzed, she laments that "as British subjects it was not possible for Indian Muslims to travel to Turkey and take part in the holy war; otherwise, it would have been far better to die there as martyrs."[17] How much more glorious to die as a martyr than live life without purpose! In fact, dying as a martyr seemed the ultimate solution to all life's problems.[18]

The memoirs reflect a steadfast admiration for the iconic male figure of a martyr, one who symbolizes courage and resistance in the face of brutal opposition. In a self-revealing moment, Khatun recalls that she secretly desired a young revolutionary named Basiruddin. She was stirred by this young man who attracted thousands of patriotic Indians, both Hindus and Muslims, many of whom followed him to the prison gates of Jessore, chanting the slogans *Bande Mataram* and *Allah o Akbar*.[19] She recalls thinking to herself:

> Lucky is the man who could sacrifice everything for the nation and even go to jail for the cause. Had he a wife, how proud would she have felt for him now. She would have been deeply honored for being the wife of such a noble man. One has to be immensely fortunate to be a wife of such a hero. People lecture that one has to respect one's husband, but how many women find a man worthy of honor and respect.[20]

Custom required women to respect their husbands, and therefore most women were coerced into being respectful. Men like Basiruddin presented an exception to this rule, men for whom women could abandon their hearts and whose nobility they could truly respect.[21] Patriots and martyrs emerged as surrogate agents of power that these women could admire, even desire, without actually possessing. For example, Khatun recalls:

> In the pages of *Moslem Bharat* I saw the picture of the revolutionary poet Kazi Nazrul Islam, dressed as a *havildar*[22] [and] standing upright in a heroic posture as if he is telling us through the words of his poem, "My head is always held high." Beside the picture was inscribed his memorable poem *Bidrohi* (The Rebel), and in the same book was the famous composition on Kemal Pasha's victory. What a stirring description of heroism, what thunderous rhythm of the poem![23]

She continues:

> Such was the valor of the great poet who was born during the time of
> the Non-Cooperation movement. It was through his thoughts, poems,
> and songs that a sleeping nation and Islam discovered its lost spirit. [So
> that] when the son of George V visited the country, the whole nation
> was paralyzed by strikes, [and] the British government conducted mass
> arrests, ruthlessly beating protesters. Yet the protesters continued singing
> the songs of freedom, declaring "You will never be able to suppress us by
> *lathis*;[24] the bloody struggles will only increase our strength even if you
> put us in jail."[25]

Without any narrative break, Khatun's memoir moves from images of courage and resistance to an overwhelming sadness about her powerlessness. The
nationalist struggle becomes a metonymy for her own need to struggle against
confinement. She laments:

> At home we too dedicated our body and soul to the nationalist cause,
> but we were handicapped by sorrow and misery. We were isolated and
> imprisoned within our domestic world, tired and oppressed by chains of
> *aborodh*. Our lives were gradually sinking in confinement, and one day it
> would collapse. In Turkey, during the reigns of Sultan Abdul Hamid and
> Sultan Abdul Majid Khan, *purdah* restrictions were strictly enforced. No
> women dared to educate themselves or violate the norms. But even in
> that oppressive society extraordinary women like Khaleda Khanam were
> born. Her father encouraged her to go to America to study. We don't have
> such opportunities in this country. That is why we are in this state of
> degradation.[26]

Because Khatun's narrative is unbroken, it is challenging to identify the
point where admiration for patriotic courage ends and regret for her own
state of subjugation begins. Constant desire, admiration, and longing for a
space in the public arena in which a courageous struggle for freedom could
be enacted permeates the text. The subjugated body of the colonized nation
and the oppressed soul of women seamlessly and symbolically merge.

For Muslim women suffering from a sense of confinement and exclusion, the sights and sounds of patriotic fervor provided release; that is, the
sense of national solidarity seemed to reach out and include them. Mass uprisings, protests, rallies, meetings, fasts, boycotts—all created internal solidarity across communities and provided a "second life for the people, who

for a time entered the utopian realm of community, freedom, equality, and abundance."[27]

THE GANDHIAN MOMENT

Khatun and Kamal, as witnesses to historic and often tumultuous events, longed to use changing political circumstances as leverage to push for new social roles for themselves. Nationalism held the seeds of emancipation and empowerment, and perhaps no one left a stronger mark on the emerging feminism than Gandhi. In both memoirs he stands as an iconic figure, encouraging women to participate in political resistance through the *charkha* and *khadi* movements,[28] symbolic yet productive acts that women could engage in from their domestic space. To a great extent the introduction of *charkha* and *khadi* was also an attempt on the part of the Mahatma to feminize the nationalist movement.

Both memoirs include anecdotes about Gandhi's attempt to bring Hindus and Muslims together. Khatun recalls his clarion call for unification. Her family, like millions of others in India, joined the Civil Disobedience movement in boycotting all British goods. Khatun recalls the experience of national unity:

> The caliph was ousted, and the Muslims kept a one-day *roza*,[29] and the family boycotted English goods; the chain of imperialism in this period culminated in the massacre at Jallianwalabag when the whole nation stood as one in its outrage against imperialist actions.

The narrative continues, "Our beautiful *sarees*, lovely coats, *achhkan*, and western shoes were burnt [by us]."[30] Although young women particularly prized their *sarees*, they derived great satisfaction from such acts of sacrifice. They were especially pleased to boycott British goods and to adopt nationalist practices such as weaving *sarees* on the *charkha*. From their secluded sphere of domesticity, women felt as if they were forging an imaginary communion with patriots in the public domain. Khatun passionately describes the patriotism of India's Muslims following the Jallianwalabagh massacre, citing how her family took to *charkha* and *khadi* and supported the role played by Shaokat Ali and Mohammed Ali's mother, known as B'Amma. The Ali brothers were radical anti-British Pan-Islamicists who led the Khilafat movement. As such, they served as iconic figures, inspiring an entire generation of Muslims in India. Shaokat Ali was jailed in 1919 for publishing (what the British charged were) seditious materials and organizing protests. He was also elected the first president of the Khilafat conference. He was rearrested and imprisoned from 1921 to 1923 for supporting Mahatma Gandhi and the Indian National Congress during the Non-Cooperation movement (1919–1922).[31]

Khatun writes, "We gave up wearing *bilayti* [English or Western clothes], and three or four different types of *charkha* . . . arrived at home. *Kamala Charkha, Bangalakshmi Charkkha, Ahmedabad Charkha.* We all used to weave on these spinning wheels."[32]

Numerous women began weaving on spinning wheels at home; others took to the streets in protest against police. In her memoir, Khatun finds inspiration in the story of Joan of Arc, a simple French peasant girl who defied all power and authority. Why couldn't she and other ordinary women do the same?[33] She recalls, "Women publicly went out picketing, joined meetings, rallies, and protests. Their lives were images of fulfillment being able to work for the cause of the nation."[34] At the same time, she laments her own predicament (seclusion at home), which leaves her feeling hopeless and useless for any mission or cause.

Gandhian teachings went straight to the heart of this feminine angst, especially stirring emotions against enforced confinement. Although he did not seek a permanent reversal of the traditional role of women, Gandhi succeeded in opening and extending the political sphere to women through his carefully crafted aesthetic of resistance.

NEW NATIONS, NEW WOMEN

Women's primary concern in the world of colonial Bengal, then, was twofold: emancipation and a desire to participate in public life. These became the leitmotiv of the *nari jagaran,* or women's awakening:

> In 1929 *Saogat* [a Muslim women's journal] published three articles which referred more directly to the phenomenon of *jagaran* (awakening). The first, Fazilatun Nessa's piece, was titled "Muslim Narir Mukti" [The Liberation of Muslim Women] and she gave her views on what the word [*mukti*] meant to her: "The word *mukti* implies emancipation of one's inner self. To render one's independent self to the world and to society and be regulated by the dictates of one's own reason—that is freedom of self."[35]

Earlier generations of Muslim women had found self-definition by serving as healers and caregivers for the young, sick, and poor. Khatun's narrative suggests a cynical withdrawal from this earlier paradigm of feminine value. She recalls that her mother taught a beggar girl to sing. A member of the older generation of Muslim women, her mother would have seen this small effort to uplift the disadvantaged as eminently more virtuous than engaging in public activities meant to bring about social transformation. Here the author and her mother represent diverging social values, one honoring a more private sphere of activities, the other lauding public endeavors. Indeed, the generation of women to which Khatun belonged was eager to trade the world of domesticity for the pursuit of literate, metropolitan cultural practices and beliefs. "Every day," she recalls, "we used to read at least two newspapers in detail." She records that Muslim women behind the *purdah* devoured poems by Tagore and Hemchandra. Their delight in reading and reciting poems brought the Hindu and Muslim poets together, if only in a virtual sense.

Sufia Kamal tried her hand at publishing short stories, which were appreciated by Hindus and Muslims alike. Although her husband supported her attempt to begin a literary career, the patriarchs of the family fiercely opposed it. This opposition marked Kamal's transition from domesticity to social activism. In the face of family disapproval, she became a social worker and joined Gandhi's Khadi movement. Her sense of personal empowerment is palpable as she vividly recollects the first *saree* woven by her own hands on the *charkha*.[36] She later became a peace activist and played an important role in the Bangladesh language movement. She proudly describes her successful literary career, especially the praise she received from the poets Nasirruddin, Tagore, and Kazi Nazrul Islam. Each of them greatly admired her poems and held her in the highest esteem. Tagore especially appreciated her poetry, and she was overwhelmed by this love and admiration.[37]

Like Kamal, Khatun ultimately achieved literary and professional success. Gifted with an entrepreneurial spirit, she began by teaching herself to embroider and knit and ultimately sent her products to the marketplace. At the same time she demonstrated an eagerness for education. A Christian teacher living with her family supported her desire to learn by offering lessons at home.[38] Eventually Khatun taught literacy skills to underprivileged girls, in addition to writing and publishing poems for children.

EXILE AND MELANCHOLY

For both Kamal and Khatun, partition meant separation from friends and relatives remaining on the other side of the border. This self-imposed exile resulted in a pervasive feeling of sadness that gripped the populace. Moving into the domain of a new nation did not necessarily translate into a sense of homecoming.

In writing about earlier years (1931–1938), Kamal observes, "Life meandered through myriad experiences of turbulence and nightmare. Love and loss, joy and consolation coexisted but what cannot be forgotten is the horror of famine, war and the perennial battle for freedom."[39] She recalls the wave of feminist consciousness released by the Pakistan nationalist movement and laments that the movement later degenerated into a deplorable, tyrannical Islamic theocratic state. Her narrative alludes to brutal efforts by the state to suppress the Bengali identity of the Muslim community in Bangladesh.

She suggests that for women exile may be a permanent state of being, whether exiled from one's homeland or exiled from one's right to self-expression and self-empowerment. Even the dramatic creation of new nation-states did not bring Bangladeshi women relief in any permanent sense but only led to their entrapment in a new series of unspeakable atrocities. Freedom in some ultimate sense constantly eluded them.

Kamal poignantly describes her arrival in Dhaka:

> When I came to Dhaka, the well-known Lila Nag, our very favorite *Liladi* [sister Lila] who had established the *Naree Shiskha Mandir* [temple of learning for women], had by then organized the joint Hindu–Muslim Peace Committee. I joined the peace movement. Many women came forward to organize peace committees far and wide, even outside the city limits and suburbs. At any point in time, no matter one's native country, it is only when women, putting aside their misery and poverty, come forward does one realize the special role that women and mothers have to play in ushering in peace. Day after day we were witnesses to inconsolable tears flowing from the eyes of the destitute women, homeless, torn asunder from friends and families. Sometimes there were desperate and violent outbursts, while others would narrate their stories, laughing and crying.[40]

Kamal's memoir ends with the agony of partition, the creation of East Pakistan, and the reprehensible attempts to replace Bengali with Urdu as the national language. The author declares that in her long sojourn through different periods of history what cannot be forgotten is the inevitable downfall of ignorant, greedy, and violent regimes—and the integral role of women fighting against oppression, torture, and brutality. Understandably, melancholy seeps into the narrative as Kamal contemplates the significance of what she is writing:

After all, how will it ever be possible for this history to be narrated? Those who knew nothing about Hindustan and Pakistan laid down their lives for the cause of freedom; women faced unspeakable brutalities[,] . . . [and in the end] the violence that I saw defies narration. I don't know who will write this history of Bangladesh, about floods, famines, and pestilence and the march of skeletons and pile of corpses. The cries of oppressed women haunt me, those who have fought against hunger [and] illiteracy and for peace. I was always at the forefront of this movement.[41]

Scholars of partition history have recently argued that "there is a remarkable complementary relation between the problems internal to history and the demands and desire of memory, so much so that they become the integral parts of a single operation, the historical operation."[42] As to the importance of these memoirs, Sayeeda Manowara Khatun and Sufia Kamal made a conscious political choice to remember history, not only to commemorate the past, but also to discard it. Memory became a powerful force behind political activism; it kept alive the sense of alienation, dissent, and discontent to be recovered as an instrument of power and critical analysis.

NOTES

Translations from the Bengali works *Smriteer Paata* by Sayeeda Manowara Khatun and *Ekale Amader Kaal* by Sufia Kamal are mine.

1. It may be useful to contrast *abarodh* with *purdah*. In some Muslim societies *purdah* is a system of screening women from strangers—particularly males—by means of a veil or curtain. In ancient times this was also practiced in some extremely conservative Hindu families as well. Hindu women were referred to as *paradanasheens,* or women behind the *purdahs.* The extreme form of *purdah* is *abarodh.* Women are strictly prohibited from moving away from their private areas; usually, this means they cannot leave their residence or domestic space. The practice of *abarodh* is intended to strictly segregate and prohibit women from entering the public sphere.

2. For a detailed discussion of Hindu women's political participation in Bengal in the 1920s and 1930s, see Tanika Sarkar, "Politics and Women in Bengal: The Conditions and Meaning of Participation," *Indian Economic and Social History Review* 21, no. 1 (1984).

3. Sonia Nishat Amin, *The World of Muslim Women in Colonial Bengal* (Leiden: Brill, 1996), 31.

4. Ibid., 92.

5. After the defeat of the Ottoman Empire, rumors circulated that a harsh peace treaty was going to be imposed on the sultanate. As a result, the Khilafat movement gained momentum in 1919–1920. Three major Khilafat demands were presented as part of

diplomatic efforts in Paris in March 1920. The first demand stated that the Turkish sultan Khalifa would retain control over spaces sacred to Islam. The second insisted that he be left sufficient territory over which he would rule and defend the Islamic faith. The third demand stated that the region known as Jazir-ul-Arab (Arabia, Syria, Iraq, and Palestine) had to remain under Muslim sovereignty.

6. *Sharif* refers to the aristocratic lineage within the Muslim community. These individuals comprise a wealthy upper-class, usually landowning gentry.

7. I refer to the transition from the Islamic culture of the Mughal rule to that of British colonialism. This transition had a special impact on the Muslim mind, as the supremacy of Islamic traditional culture and authority faded—to be replaced by a culture of modernity. This new culture included Western Enlightenment philosophy, the British educational system, and the British system of government.

8. Amin, *The World of Muslim Women in Colonial Bengal*, 270.

9. *Bhadramahila* alluded to a woman who received a formal Western education and who was trained in the ways of public life. The term offers a gender counterpart to *bhadralok*, the elite Western educated gentleman.

10. Meredith Borthwick, *The Changing Role of Women in Bengal, 1849–1905* (Princeton: Princeton University Press, 1984), xxi.

11. Richard M.Eaton, *Essays on Islam and Indian History* (New Delhi: Oxford University Press, 2000), 273.

12. Amin, *The World of Muslim Women in Colonial Bengal*, 37.

13. Sufia Kamal, *Ekale Amader Kaal* (Dacca: Jnan Prakashani, 1988), 31–32.

14. Ibid., 12.

15. Judith Butler, *Bodies That Matter: On the Discursive Limits of Sex* (New York: Routledge, 1993), 95.

16. Sayeeda Manowara Khatun, *Smriteer Paata* (Dacca, 1962), 45.

17. Ibid.

18. Ibid.

19. *Bande Mataram* was used by Hindu militant nationalists. Muslims raised the Arabic slogan *Allah o Akbar,* meaning "God (or Allah) is Great," as a battle cry.

20. Khatun, *Smriteer Paata*, 46.

21. Khatun, *Smriteer Paata*, 45–46.

22. Havildar was a rank equivalent to sergeant in the British Indian Army.

23. Khatun, *Smriteer Paata*, 46.

24. *Lathis* are long, heavy, iron-clad bamboo sticks traditionally used as weapons in armed combat and most commonly used by police in India.

25. Khatun, *Smriteer Paata*, 46.

26. Ibid., 47–48.

27. Colin Counsell and Laurie Wolf, eds., *Performative Analysis: An Introductory Coursebook* (London: Routledge, 2001), 217.

28. *Charkha* is a spinning wheel that was used in the home to weave clothes. *Khadi* is a coarse handwoven cloth. The *charkha* and *khadi* were part of the Gandhian Non-Cooperation movement. *Charkha* and *khadi* served in the alternate, indigenous cottage

industry that would buttress the program of economic noncooperation by boycotting British goods. On the one hand, it was expected to deal a blow to British industrial enterprise while fostering a village-based economy. On the other hand, it provided women with a sense of belonging in the nationalist movement without their publicly taking part in meetings or armed struggle.

29. *Roza* is the Arabic word for fasting, a practice observed during the Muslim celebration of Ramadan. Here *roza* served as an act of protest against the ousting of the caliph.

30. Khatun, *Smriteer Paata,* 45.

31. The Ali brothers eventually became disillusioned with the Indian National Congress and Gandhi's leadership. In 1928 Shaokat Ali demanded separate elections for Muslims.

32. Khatun, *Smriteer Paata,* 46.

33. Ibid., 46.

34. Ibid.

35. Amin, *The World of Muslim Women in Colonial Bengal,* 274.

36. Kamal, *Ekale Amader Kaal,* 35.

37. Ibid., 51.

38. Khatun, *Smriteer Paata,* 50.

39. Ibid., 52.

40. Ibid., 52–53.

41. Ibid., 55–56.

42. Ranabir Samaddar, "The Historiographical Operation: Memory and History," *Economic and Political Weekly,* June 3, 2006, 2238.

3

FROM REFUGEE CAMP TO KABUL

The Influence of Exile on Afghan Women

CAROL MANN

Between 1980 and 1990, some 6 million Afghan citizens fled their homeland, primarily in the direction of Iran and Pakistan. By 1990, there were
3,274,000 officially registered refugees living in Pakistan (another 500,000 to
one million were unaccounted for).[1] Seventy percent of refugees resided in
the North-West Frontier Province (NWFP).[2] Urban refugees systematically
fled to cities, settling into what became semi-suburban shantytowns, whereas
the rural population joined family or village members in camps, attempting
to re-create familiar social units.

Since March 2002, more than 4.7 million refugees have returned to Afghanistan. It was estimated that in 2008 approximately 2 million refugees
were still living in Pakistan. Because the situation in Afghanistan continues to
be unstable, camp life often represents a safe and desirable alternative. Even
when major camps close, many of the inhabitants simply move on to other
refugee settlements within the country, refusing the pitiful $100 handout
offered by the United Nations High Commission for Refugees (UNHCR)
for repatriation. Why return to a homeland where the prospect of peace remains as distant as it has for the past thirty years? An entire generation of
Afghan refugees has grown up in the camps. Sustained only by yearnings for
an imagined homeland, their identity and expectations are products of harsh
camp life.

The particular configuration that has linked the destinies of the border
populations of Pakistan and Afghanistan has resulted in long-term consequences, especially for Afghan women. Members of the Taliban have been
much demonized by the West, depicted as instigators of reactionary politics
against women. This delayed reaction from the West, precipitated by the
events in the United States of September 11, 2001, came six long years after
the Taliban swept into power. Many suggest that the Western response to
the Taliban has been nothing more than a propaganda tool to justify allied
intervention in Afghanistan.

In this chapter, I demonstrate how the previous generation of Western-supported *mujahedin*, initially fighting America's proxy war against the Soviet Union, were the precursors paving the way for Taliban excesses. I further argue that since the fall of the pro-Soviet government in Afghanistan, women especially have suffered from a combination of hard-line Islamist radicalization and the exacerbation of traditional patriarchal practices promoted in Pakistani refugee camps over the past twenty-eight years. The ideological mix emanating from the camps, unique in the Muslim world, has successfully eliminated Afghan alternative secular nationalist discourses. This includes the subversion of progressive Islamic trends, all of which were present in the late 1970s, before the 1978 pro-Communist coup. As Edward Said has argued, this represented a clash within a single civilization, rather than a clash between East and West, as suggested by Samuel Huntington.[3] These progressive alternatives were swept away by massive Western support of the *mujahedin* in the protracted conflagration of the Cold War, the catastrophic results of which form the basis of Afghanistan's problems today.

The Afghan government's decision to grant blanket amnesty and legal protection for war crimes in the name of the National Stability and Reconciliation Bill has made it possible for onetime warlords to occupy positions of unchallenged and uncontrollable power.[4] What has unified these warlords since the war against the Soviets is a threefold dynamic: their active engagement in the modern global capitalist economy (e.g., through drug trafficking), their purported religious orthodoxy, and their particularly reactionary policies towards women. That which remains is a caricature of the East/West dialectic. A loose reactionary ideology inherited at once from the *mujahedin* and the Taliban is presented as the sole alternative to dominant Western democratic-liberal economic discourse embedded in reconstruction politics in Kabul. Much of the clout behind this reactionary force draws on the perception of Western options as a failure to address Afghan cultural values.

The gap between women's theoretical constitutional rights and their daily reality—especially in Afghanistan's rural areas—has been one of the main consequences of this situation. Despite visible improvements in some urban areas, the standard of Afghan women's lives (that is to say, 85 percent of the population) may well be sinking. The most relevant indicator is the rate of maternal mortality, still the highest in the world, especially in the Badakhshan region. Neither U.S.-directed policies with huge accompanying aid packages nor the Afghan religious conservatives and Taliban supporters seem to have made a dent in the dismal condition of Afghan women's health. As far as health choices are concerned (which includes the right to be examined by a doctor), women remain entirely at the mercy of fathers and husbands.

Extremist violence against women goes unpunished as patriarchal privilege continues to dominate any kind of state or religious legislation.

This chapter explores four key areas of inquiry. First, I examine those wartime changes in gendered cultural norms that traditional rural Afghan populations have used to define themselves during exile and after. These cultural references are duplicated on both sides of the Durand line, a porous and artificial frontier inhabited by a population numbering 22 million.[5] This population is referred to as Pathan on the Pakistani side and Pashtun across the Afghan border. Second, I examine how radical Islam emerged and triumphed in refugee camps, having been previously a marginal force in Afghanistan, limited to a sector of Kabul university students. The camps provided ideal conditions for experimenting with social forms of women's repression, creating a social model handily imported back into Afghanistan after the demise of the pro-Communist government. Third, I address the changes (and resistance to change) affecting female Afghan refugees living in camps along the NWFP from the late 1970s to 2006. These are the years of major foreign military interventions, first by the Soviet Union (1979) and then by the U.S.-led coalition (2001). Finally, I explore the consequences such changes have had on the lives of women living in Pakistan's refugee camps and inside the NWFP, as well as in Afghanistan.

This chapter is based on fieldwork conducted in Pakistan and Afghanistan between December 2001 and June 2006, including Afghan enclaves within Pakistani cities, namely Islamabad, Rawalpindi, and Peshawar. Brief comments were added after a trip to Afghanistan in May 2008. Fieldwork also took place in several Afghan camps situated along the NWFP in Pakistan, including Jalozai, Kobobian, Nazir Bagh, Katcha Gari, Shamshatoo, and Akkora Hattak and the smaller camps, Sharwali and Khewa. In addition, interviews were conducted with Afghan individuals in Kabul, Herat, and Farah all of whom were returnees from camps.[6]

A FOUNDATION OF SCHOLARSHIP

Apart from journalistic and partisan narratives glorifying the so-called Afghan freedom fighters,[7] most research on the refugee camps in question dates from the early 1980s. Until now, gendered research conducted in regard to these refugees has been scant, with the exception of a few articles by Micheline Demont-Centlivres, Inger Boesen, and Nancy Hatch-Dupree. Hatch-Dupree's publications and resource center in Peshawar have proven invaluable, as has Valentine M. Moghadam's critical approach to recent Afghan history, before the arrival of the Taliban. The anthropological milestones produced by veterans in the Pathan field have provided an essential basis, such as the writings of Fredrik Barth, Charles Lindholm, Akbar Ahmed, and Benedicte Grima. Equally important are those works on Afghanistan by Pierre Cent-livres, Louis Dupree, Olivier Roy, Nancy Tapper, and David B. Edwards.[8] The feminist approach to the British Raj by Meredith Borthwick, Geraldine Forbes, and Dagmar Engels was especially helpful in comprehending models of "progress" applied by Afghan rulers and problems encountered by humani-tarian aid workers. The writings of Lila Abu-Lughod, Leila Ahmed, and Deniz Kandiyoti were essential for putting all these readings in a wider context of non-Western feminist thinking and to challenge culturalist assumptions em-bedded in most of the standard references about Islamic society, such as those by Bernard Lewis. I have chosen to follow Mahmood Mamdani's definitions regarding Islamism — such as "political movements that speak the language of religion" — as opposed to Fundamentalism, which Mamdami presents as a purely religious ethic.[9] Nevertheless, I do not subscribe to the uncritical cul-tural relativism occasionally implied in some of these texts, having witnessed firsthand the consequences of ideologically driven misogynistic excesses on the health and well-being of Afghan women.

PASHTUNS IN PATHAN TERRITORY:
EXODUS TO PAKISTAN

Starting with the social consequences of the pro-Communist revolution known as the Saur (April) Revolution of 1978 and reinforced by the Soviet intervention (December 1979), rural populations fled from Afghanistan to the NWFP, crossing the Khyber Pass into nearby frontier regions. Pashtun clans and extended families were allied on both sides and initially welcomed their brethren. The flood of refugees settled into camps set up by the UNHCR through its Pakistani representation.

What united these Pashto-speaking populations and how these popula-tions continue to define themselves merits careful analysis. One could argue that attachment to and indeed the ossification of certain cultural traits rep-resent a deliberate effort to counter foreign influence, both in colonial times and today.

Although the Pashtun and Pathan rural populations are devout Muslims, they conform (to varying degrees) to an unwritten pre-Islamic code that pro-vides identity and ethical guidelines.[10] This framework, enforced by councils of village elders (*jirgas*), continues to take precedence over any kind of state-imposed law or Sharia. Variations of this honor-based code are also practiced by once-nomadic societies, such as Bedouins, Nuers, and the neighboring Balutch. The systematic control of women is the most salient feature of the Pashtun version and has allowed them to dominate other ethnic groups of refugees within the camps, primarily because this unwritten code (Pashtunwali) efficiently vouchsafes family honor. Pashtun norms incorporate extreme forms of classic patriarchy with built-in hierarchies and opposing male/female values. Male honor is proactive and expressed through exacerbated virility, whereas female honor is necessarily passive, submissive, and based on avoidance of shame. These norms are acted out in different ways, according to the social class and education of the families concerned.

Whatever the milieu, male domination is never questioned; indeed, male authority is viewed as God-given even by the women themselves, who regard marital brutality as a normal part of marriage.[11] Pashtun proverbs eloquently support abusive male attitudes. For example, consider the following: "A woman's place is in the home or in the grave." Another proverb insists, "Women have no noses; they eat shit." And yet another: "One's own mother and sister are disgusting."[12]

Nevertheless, historically, women have negotiated their place in traditional settings. Older women were respected, and the eldest daughter was often the father's favorite. Like other patriarchal societies in the West (Jewish and Christian) until the end of the eighteenth century, although women were never particularly favored, neither were they incessantly oppressed.

Despite their ritual seclusion (*purdah*), Pashtun women have not always been regarded as passive. Afghanistan's national hero is a Joan of Arc figure, the Pashtun woman Malalai, killed in battle during the Anglo-Afghan war (1878–1880). Today, any such latitude for female heroism has unquestionably been banned from Afghan society.

Cultures, however stolid they may seem, are hardly monolithic, static entities. The circumstances in which Pashtun honor is expressed are continually shifting with the times. Male honor, as Fredrik Barth has explained in detail, was traditionally expressed through physical courage and compliance to rules of hospitality and solidarity in a particularly antimaterialistic society. But as the U.S. "war on terror" continues to have an impact on Afghan and Pakistani populations, wealth and financial success in those regions have become the markers of some kind of nouveau riche honor, bolstered by the wartime economy and the warlords' direct handling of massive U.S. financial aid.

At the same time, expectations regarding gender norms persist. Some researchers, including Bernt Glatzer, have noted that *purdah* was especially strict in the refugee camps during wartime, despite a dominantly female population.[13] Glatzer suggests that in peacetime traditional male authority is asserted naturally without any outside constraint, whereas during periods of war existing male institutions are threatened. Thus, when men left to participate in war, women continued to seclude themselves, symbolically preserving family honor and maintaining their daughters' economic worth on the marriage market. This custom is especially important in a society that operates through bride-price (i.e., money given by the groom's family to the bride's father) rather than according to a dowry system.

War against the Soviet Union, civil war, and continuing conflict today have resulted in a significant increase in revenge killings, enforced marriages, and disproportionate marital exchanges (between old men and prenubile girls, for instance). The reliance on some form of tradition to justify such transactions confers a fraudulent legitimacy on those transactions, a fraudulence noted by the local populace. Women continue to be victims of multiple forms of escalating oppression; it is misleading to place the blame solely on intractable cultural customs. Doing so detracts from the many ways that war, strife, extreme poverty, and the globalized drug trade have negatively affected women and girls in Afghanistan.[14]

RESISTANCE TO CHANGE: A HISTORICAL PERSPECTIVE

Beginning in the late nineteenth century, the Western model of progress became the established paradigm in British India and still remains influential in the entire region. Progress has translated into medical and technological advances, as well as the implementation of necessary infrastructure such as schools, hospitals, post offices, and roads. Reforms were instituted to bring the colonized areas up to Western standards of propriety and morality. Social legislation aimed at improving the living conditions of women included raising the age of marriage and introducing educational opportunities. During the Raj, educated urban dwellers, whether in Afghanistan or India, always associated with Western modernity, a choice that permitted access to privilege and power.

By comparison, though Afghanistan was not colonized, many members of its ruling class were educated in the frontier region of the Raj and inherited some of its ideals. Paradoxically, British colonial Realpolitik supported Pashtun tribal clans in their opposition to Kabul.

In Afghanistan today, rural populations are the ones most strongly resisting Allied occupation, the presence of international organizations, and control by the Kabul government. Large segments of the rural poor, always excluded from the elitist process, have retaliated by setting themselves up as the sole champions of ethnic tradition and authentic religion. They have defended this tradition with an orthodox zeal, as evidenced by the riots that took place against the Raj in Peshawar and, today, by the riots against aid agencies in rural Afghanistan.

Muslim fundamentalist reform movements—mid-nineteenth century onwards (especially the rigorous Deoband mosque)—associated any form of Western progress, including secular education, with infidel propaganda emanating from colonial powers. Today this attitude in Pakistan is sustained and championed by the powerful ultra-conservative Mutahidda Majlis-e-Amal (MMA) coalition in Pakistan's NWFP, formed after the beginning of the U.S. bombings of Afghanistan. This coalition has grown out of the right-wing political Islamist-Taliban ethic and remains the main support for armed struggle against President Karzai and the coalition forces in Afghanistan.

Again, historically, it was the rural Muslim populations of British India who were reluctant to attend English schools in the NWFP and Baluchistan, both frontier regions.[15] A similar reaction occurred in Afghanistan. When Afghan's King Amanullah (1919–1923) tried to implement an English style of education in the 1920s, the general population resisted. King Amanullah had been inspired by the radical secularizing reforms imposed by Ataturk. However, unlike his much-admired Turkish counterpart, the Afghan king lacked the necessary backup forces to implement reforms effectively.

The absence of open communication and mutual sympathy between Afghanistan's Dari-speaking ruling elite and the vast rural Pashtun majority created instant rejection of any measures coming from the capital. Many felt threatened and alienated by these new cultural norms; the reactionary backlash was extreme and long lasting.

A similar dynamic occurred when the Marxist-leaning elite started to exert its influence within the government beginning in the mid-1960s. When the People's Democratic Party of Afghanistan (PDPA) took over (1978–1979), measures put forward to improve the status of women proved too radically secular for such a deeply conservative Islamic population. Although much more progressive reforms had been successfully adopted by earlier rulers, their methods of implementation had not been nearly as abrasive. The reconfiguration of Afghan identity with Western-style aspirations under British, Turkish, then Soviet authority did nothing to help unite the Afghan population. In fact, the opposite outcome ensued. President Karzai is encountering a similar reaction, even though his government's efforts at gender equality seem timid in comparison to previous efforts.

All would-be reformers have encountered the same obstacle in this region: a profound suspicion of the Western notion of progress, one that transfers responsibility for women from the male's province to the state. This history of mistrust and suspicion regarding the Western model (British colonial, Soviet inspired, or U.S. aid) explains, in part, why UNHCR encountered such resistance when setting up schools in the refugee camps. Despite the official reinstatement of girls' education, Afghanistan has experienced a significant resurgence of extreme violence: girls' schools have been torched and teachers killed by Taliban elements. To date, over three hundred schools have been destroyed, representing at least a quarter of all girls' schools in Afghanistan. As a result, parents are reticent about sending their daughters to school, and it is estimated that about half of all Afghan children (approximately 7 million) do not receive any kind of formal education, despite the fivefold increase in enrollment since the fall of the Taliban.

Meanwhile, the Taliban has been promising to spend $1 million to open schools in fourteen regions of Afghanistan under their control. Their intention is to use the same Qur'an-based curriculum that they did from 1996 to 2001. An Al-Jazeera online article quotes Taliban spokesperson Abdul Hai Mutmaen as saying that it is "not clear if they [the schools] would be open to boys and girls, or just boys."[16]

POLITICAL ISLAM IN THE REFUGEE CAMPS

The very first refugee camps in Pakistan were likely built as extensions of military training camps designed to house and train Afghan insurgents. Their origins can be traced to 1973, when Mohammad Daoud deposed his uncle King Zahir Shah in a bloodless coup and established a republic. The Pakistani government was alarmed by Daoud's nationalist politics supporting the Pashtunistan ideal—a cross-border rapprochement that indeed threatened Pakistan's integrity. That same year (nearly six years before Soviet intervention), the antinationalist and antisecular Hekmatyar, Massoud, and Rabbani all opposed Daoud,[17] fleeing to Peshawar where they met with support from President Bhutto. With Pakistani assistance, military camps were constructed as training environments for Islamist insurgents, then converted to refugee camps during the era of Soviet intervention. After the 1978 Communist coup, help arrived from the United States to reinforce massive Pakistani aid to the Islamist insurgents in their anti-Soviet struggle. From the start, it would appear that these camps were never destined to be neutral gathering places for refugees.[18]

Each camp became a village with idiosyncratic characteristics under the administration of a ruling camp chief, generally a former high-ranking *mujahedin* or insurgent combatant affiliated with one of seven official fundamentalist parties that had resisted the Soviets. These chiefs fell into one of two political categories: traditional nationalists and Islamist ideologues.

The social structure within refugee camps was modeled on the ruling authority in the adjacent autonomous Federally Administered Tribal Areas (FATA). Each camp turned into a self-sufficient citadel ruled by a strict hierarchy (contrary to egalitarian Pashtun norms), allied with FATA chieftains. These FATA chieftains remain responsible for much of the heroin and arms trade between Afghanistan and Pakistan. During the years of exile, a powerful solidarity was established among a hybrid local ruling class that included FATA barons, top-level NWFP politicians, Afghan anti-Communist politicians and warlords, and their representatives in the various refugee camps. Today, they provide the backing necessary for successful Taliban operations.

In the early days of war against the Soviets, combatants and tribal elders competed for power within the refugee camps. Cashing in on the kudos of heroism and warfare, *mujahedin* skillfully managed to redefine their roles. They became tribal chiefs boldly leading their troops, bolstered by warrior tradition and a mission of *jihad,* one legitimating the other. Their influence was far more important in exile than at home. Indeed, on home turf they were not always able to ingratiate themselves with the larger Afghan population, which, according to Olivier Roy (1985), did not trust them to defend Islam.

Influence and power in these regions depend on exchange and the possibility of building support through a system of retribution. This served as an ideal context for guerrillas evolving into full-fledged warlords and posing as legitimate representatives of the Afghan people. Not only did they benefit from U.S. military assistance, but they also handily managed to step into roles of directing humanitarian aid and overseeing the narcotics trade—all the while protected by the CIA and Pakistan's secret service, the ISI.

Clearly the war against the Soviets provided a focal point for all opposition and helped unite people who previously had very little in common. This coalition included secular leftist Kabul intellectuals, peasants, mullahs, and radical Islamists. It was as military commanders that the newly emerging leaders managed to rally support and ultimately came to represent all levels of opposition to the Soviet invasion. This maneuvering continued what had been initiated in Kabul on the university campus, even before the Soviet-backed PDPA took over.

Insurgent commanders wanted to pose as the only entities representing organized opposition to the Communist threat—thereby ensuring their status as sole recipients of the massive aid pouring into the region. Initially this was by no means an obvious process. Indeed, the founder of the Revolutionary Association of the Women of Afghanistan (RAWA), Mina Kheshwar Kamal, was invited to attend a major Socialist conference in France as the official representative of the Afghan resistance. Yet it was Gulbedin Hekmatyar—warlord and drug dealer and trafficker, supported by the United States—who would control the Afghan situation in Peshawar.

Barnett Rubin, quoted by Mahmood Mamdani, cited a UN refugee worker who described Hekmatyar's rule as "a reign of terror."[19] The ISI not only permitted Hekmatyar control of the refugee camps, but also that of the urban refugee population in Peshawar, leading to the elimination of dissident intellectuals who also happened to oppose the *mujahedin* groups.[20] This purposeful eradication of any alternative secular opposition to radical Islamist ideology had catastrophic effects on women's rights. In short, when the pro-Communist government and its supporters fell, no organized political groups were left to defend the attempts that had been made to improve Afghan women's lives. As the sole visible remnant of the left-wing secular opposition actively working on behalf of women, RAWA was forced to function in a clandestine, underground manner—this despite the fact that the organization had achieved worldwide recognition.

In 1978 the dictator General Zia-Ul-Haq ushered in an Islamic system in Pakistan that brought legal, social, economic, and political institutions into alignment with the most rigorous interpretations of the Qur'an and Sunnah. One measure Zia-Ul-Haq used to convert Pakistan to an Islamic state was the introduction of certain offenses into the criminal law. One of these provisions included the infamously misogynistic Hudood Ordinance.[21] Ideological affinities gave him ethical reasons to support the Afghan insurgency (relocated in Peshawar) and sponsor what turned into a full-fledged international armed *jihad* against the Soviet Union. Zia-Ul-Haq built thousands of *madrasas* in the vicinity of refugee camps, with financing from Saudi Arabia and under the control of the ultra-virulent Maulana Sami-ul-Haq.

Reassured by the promise of regular meals and a minimum education,[22] many desperate widows eagerly sent their sons to what became Taliban and Al-Qaeda training centers. Herded into decrepit boardinghouses, cut off from contact with mothers and sisters, these boys were fed a simplified messianic Islam of Deobandi inspiration that became the Taliban creed.

Whereas the struggle against Soviet intervention provided a means for external unification, inner cohesiveness was achieved through Islam. Moreover, the treatment of women served to bridge any differences between pre-Quranic tribal codes and modern political Islamism. Patriarchy was deliberately re-formulated into a fundamentalist religious ethic, misogynistic in ways that even the most traditionalist patriarchs had never imagined. Under *mujahedin* control, the camps provided laboratory conditions to experiment with modern forms of gendered repression. The rigorous separation of genders made the moral and psychological divide more acute: women were rooted in the camps, whereas men operated in army formations, virtually estranged from their own families, often with only the company of young boys as solace.[23]

It is highly significant that unlike other revolutionary and resistance movements in the world (including Muslim Iran, Algeria, Eritrea, and Oman), women were totally excluded from any participation in the anti-Soviet struggle, military or civilian (Moghadam 2003). Valentine M. Moghadam compared and contrasted Afghan women's lives in Kabul under the Communist PDPA rule in 1989 and in Peshawar, site of one of Pakistan's main refugee communities. Whereas women were present and visible in Kabul at practically every level of society, from social organizations to airlines and offices, in Peshawar they were completely absent. The refugee Resistance movement in Peshawar did not even have a female spokesperson, as gender segregation had become the official way of life, even in urban settings. Yet as Kandiyoti has noted, a number of independent women's NGOs were set up in exile by educated women.[24]

In Pakistan's refugee community, educated and peasant women alike were removed from the public sphere, confined instead to the home and enforced domesticity. Female teachers and physicians continued to work for the exiled urban Afghan community in private organizations, but former female civil servants and students found themselves cut off not only from all means of subsistence but also from the social life they had enjoyed in Afghan cities before the war. During the Taliban era, professional women were no longer allowed to exercise their skills; as a result, the entire society suffered, especially in the fields of health and education in which 70 percent of employees had been female.

In 1992, when Islamist warlords came to power in Kabul under President Rabbani's rule, they imported an ideological mix from exile. Legitimized by the narrowest sectarian interpretations of Islam, this virulent ideology proved the ideal foundation on which to build an idiosyncratic set of rigid rules and regulations. These included decrees (fatwas) restricting women's mobility and dress in a context of escalating human rights violations that included rape, abduction, and forced marriages. Yet somehow these events went unnoticed in the public arena, as criticism would have called into question the massive U.S. support for the onetime *mujahedin* controlling Afghanistan at that time.

Their abuses scarred the memories of Kabulis to a far greater extent than those of the Taliban. Had the world reacted earlier to warlord-perpetrated abuses, it is possible that neither the Taliban nor events and politics leading to 9/11 would ever have taken place.

Western intellectuals bear a heavy responsibility for this outcome, in that they refused to support the Afghan secular left resisting the Soviets and championed instead the warlords—without questioning American imperialist motivations. The sentimental intellectual West, led by such prominent figures as novelist Doris Lessing and French salon philosopher Bernard Henri Levy, provided ideal propaganda and incomprehensible moral justification for U.S. policy. Bolstered by Sylvester Stallone aiding Afghan freedom fighters (*Rambo III*, 1988), they promoted an image of rugged (and photogenic) resistance fighters, without pausing to consider the attitude of these individuals towards women. Indeed, foreign aid channeled through these warlords helped to finance fundamentalist Afghan politics and, subsequently, supported the ineffably cruel, relentless oppression of women. This is a phenomenon similar to the one described by David Rieff in his discussion of Live Aid and its consequences on the Ethiopian famine as "an exercise in deadly compassion."[25]

The situation in Afghanistan today represents continuity in terms of the post-*jihad* warlords, hardly a surprising circumstance since the self-same commanders are in power, fifteen years older and shrewder politically. Women certainly are nominally present in an official capacity, but their real power is minimal. In Kabul in May 20008 there were a growing number of female students at the university and an increasing female workforce in peripheral government offices and especially in foreign NGOs. Nevertheless, theirs is a precarious situation, given that a woman's mobility remains inevitably dependent on personal negotiation with her family. The very notion of women's social rights enshrined in Muslim texts is totally nonexistent in Afghanistan. By contrast, in Egypt and especially Iran, for example, even the most devout Islamic sector of society provides a measure of advancement and creativity for its female citizens.

REFUGEE CAMPS AND TALIBAN RULE

The rule of the Taliban had direct consequences for the refugee camps; many of them continued to act as outlets, indeed regional offices, for every kind of political representation (official and unofficial) within Afghanistan. What all these political factions shared was an interest in reconfiguring religion and cultural mores into a rigidly reactionary mold. The Taliban took this

FIGURE 3.1
Afghan women in Kabul (photo by Carol Mann, 2003)

ideology further, upholding a perception of women as unnecessary at best, dangerous temptations at worst. Ahmed Rashid explains, "They [the Taliban] felt threatened by that half of the human race which they had never known and it was much easier to lock that half away, especially if it was ordained by mullahs who invoked primitive Islamic injunctions which had no basis in Islamic law."[26]

The Taliban (all of whom are ethnic Pashtun) exacerbated traditional Pashtun custom, especially regarding the seclusion of women. They did so by disregarding traditional life observed in the village (where compromise was ultimately possible) in favor of rigid structures of the refugee camps where they themselves grew up. Here, the practice of female seclusion previously described as a marker for the family's respectability was transmuted into veritable incarceration. As a result, only men and boys were allowed to shop for food or to have any interaction with the outside world. Traditional female social customs such as exchanging visits and sharing conversations were drastically curtailed, making life even more difficult and lonely for women in their narrow compounds. These women had come from villages where extended

FIGURE 3.2
Afghan women strolling with children (photo by Carol Mann, 2003)

families occupied large spaces, giving rise to frequent social interaction. The refugee camps put an end to this dynamic. Only rarely could any woman leave her compound, and then she had to be forcibly shrouded in the anonymity of a *burqa,* the sartorial equivalent of her enclosure.

At the same time, opportunities for men expanded considerably, as they sought work in distant cities or abroad, leaving young sons or old men in charge. From the start, men enjoyed new possibilities in these camps, whereas women were locked into their makeshift homes. Although most men had previously been farm laborers, they were able to find work in local bazaars and small towns, in local brick or textile factories; a number of them were even hired by the oil-rich Gulf states. That they provided cheaper labor than the local workforce contributed to the erosion of sympathy between populations, even those related by ethnic identity.

Women in the camps remained locked in a grid of multiple forms of repression, what Foucault calls "schémas de docilité."[27] At the Jalozai camp in December 2001, I personally observed aged male guards swinging rifle butts in the direction of women who attempted to walk away from their makeshift tents. These were refugees who had fled the U.S. bombings in their region. This goes well beyond customary *purdah,* even in the harsh Pashtun context.

AFGHAN REFUGEES:
RURAL VERSUS URBAN EXPERIENCES

According to the UN census data from March 2005, the NWFP area in Pakistan hosted about 1.8 million refugees, living in approximately 150 camps.[28] The UNHCR estimated at the time that 3.5 million refugees remained outside Afghanistan, despite massive repatriation efforts and much coercion from the hosting countries, especially Pakistan. Eighty percent of these represent longtime settlers (over twenty years), and at least 50 percent were born in exile.[29]

Many Pashtun refugees openly travel between Afghanistan and their settled areas. This follows a centuries-old custom, a kind of seasonal behavior characteristic of the entire rural Pashtun seminomadic population. Shared ethnicity (and, at present, politics and ideology) has created a strong political interdependence between Pashtun refugees and hosting communities. Taliban forces operating in Afghanistan continue to receive support from the equally conservative Pakistani provinces across the border, especially in the NWFP region and in Baluchistan. Their combined efforts constitute the major threat to any real democratic future for Afghanistan and Pakistan.

Afghan refugees settling in cities have received far less assistance and humanitarian aid than those in the camps. Essentially urban dwellers have been obliged to fend for themselves. Liisa Malkki, researching another group of refugees, the Hutus in Tanzania, found numerous differences between urban and rural refugees, differences that may also be applied to the Afghan population. Refugees in camps tend to cultivate their tribal identity and traditions, whereas city dwellers are more permeable to change and more vulnerable to integration into the local society.[30] Urban-dwelling refugees from Afghanistan largely avoided camps and settled in Pakistani cities and shantytowns — which were turned into veritable Afghan ghettos. Even though urban living conditions were often inferior to those in the refugee villages, it was important to these former city dwellers, in terms of image and status, to escape the humiliation of living in a camp environment. As refugees, urban professionals had virtually no access to official employment, health care, or education for their children. Whole families have been crammed into tiny shuttered apartments overlooking open sewers. The only links between different members of the refugee communities resulted from previous relationships and affiliations. The abysmal conditions explain why urban refugees were the first to attempt a return, as soon as the situation in Afghanistan appeared to improve.

Audrey Shalinsky, in her study of Afghan Uzbek migrants in Pakistani cities, describes the inward-looking mind-set of these families solely preoccupied with piecing together a coherent lifestyle from salvaged scraps of their past. The powerful patriarchal mold, even in educated families, remains a staunch barrier to change in girls' lives. Even in the most privileged circles—such as the wealthy migrant families living in the Hayatabad quarter of Peshawar—boys (and increasingly girls) are sent to top private schools with a British curriculum. However, at home the strictest restrictions prevail. In most other comparable war and refugee situations, single men manage to break away from the status quo and help introduce change. This is less the case here; unmarried men are generally housed with members of their extended families. Only to a limited extent are they able to cultivate socio-professional contacts with their contemporaries in the workplace, at the mosque, or at school. This dynamic is unthinkable for young women, who remain far more secluded than they ever were in their native Afghan environments.

In Iran, female Afghan refugees have experienced a different situation. Many have been able to take advantage of educational opportunities, all within a uniquely Islamic framework—which is therefore acceptable to their families. In Pakistan, the women who have developed this level of independence make up a tiny minority and are primarily urban, educated widows or wives of men living abroad. Some receive a modicum of support, allowing them to take advantage of opportunities the city affords, usually health care and schooling for their children. As in the camps, RAWA has been particularly active in empowering widows—individuals who would be repressed by their own contemporary society, as well as by a hostile Pakistani environment. Likewise, the daughters of these relatively few urban families remaining in exile have been able to achieve a much higher level of education than that which would be available to them in Afghanistan. Hence, the regrets of many young returnees.

THE REALITY BEHIND REFUGEE CAMPS

Since the 1989 Soviet retreat, refugee camps have offered an alternative lifestyle to nearly two million Afghans who are unwilling or unable to face harsh conditions in their devastated homeland. As I have stated, refugee camps gradually evolved into self-contained tribal enclaves. Until the last big camp, Jalozai, officially closed (April 2008), each camp was a fortress run by a chief who maintained specific political allegiances to local politicians and to other tribal chieftains. According to Ahmed Rashid, the whole region has been thriving on illicit economy, what he calls the "heroin pipeline," which may well include some of the camps, since a number of the heroin pipeline officials can be linked to local tribal chiefs.[31] The camps operated largely as unofficial embassies for politically active groups inside Afghanistan, all the while maintaining facilities generally associated with refugee camps, facilities such as schools and dispensaries provided and paid for by international humanitarian agencies. The duality of these structures and the tribal chiefs' multiple allegiances require closer scrutiny by the media and reevaluation by their donors.

Despite the now-fashionable deconstruction of humanitarian aid into strategies of control by the capitalist world,[32] aid agencies have nevertheless created some advantages for women living in the camps. Certain structures were donated in the 1980s by UNHCR: that is to say, camps usually had a modest dispensary, a school, and perhaps a workshop area nominally accessible to women. Also available were water, electricity, and, sometimes, a public telephone. Television and videocassettes brought access to global media. Women became far more aware of the outside world, with the availability (conditioned by electricity) of television or radio: Pakistani television became a staple, and cassette rental stores multiplied in every bazaar used by Afghans. These stores generally rent old Afghan Pakistani or Iranian films rather than Western ones, but Western XXX-rated films are also shown in secluded booths, for a male clientele only. The Pashtun-language BBC series, *New Home, New Life,* broadcast since 1994, has brought women new awareness of problems and solutions, with themes such as vaccinations, drug addiction, and female literacy woven into the stories. RAWA's publication, *Payam-e-Zan,* has also been instrumental in bringing news to even the remotest refugee camp.

Living conditions in the old established camps were distinctly better than in neighboring Pakistani villages, and, in fact, infant mortality was lower among the refugees than among the local rural Pakistani population.[33] Indeed, refugees in the camps received preferential treatment from humanitarian agencies; for instance, rudimentary clinics were built in the camps while virtually no health care facilities existed in surrounding villages. One easily understands the reticence of many refugees to return to their destroyed homes in Afghanistan, bereft of even the most basic necessities. The presence of modern medical institutions (however paltry and underequipped in most cases) in the camps alongside more traditional ones has been instrumental in effecting a measure of change. The constant friction between physicians and mullahs over the respective merits, for example, of rituals against the evil eye versus modern medication provided new options to women. In their husbands' absence, these women became primary decision makers regarding their children's health. By addressing women specifically, health programs have challenged the inevitability of pain and suffering and introduced a notion of personal well-being, which entails the even more novel concept of self-worth.

Nevertheless, as Lila Abu-Lughod has pointed out,[34] it is difficult to speak in terms of human rights in a Western sense, as they are totally irrelevant in a context where notions of personhood are so different. The notion of the individual is absent as much for men as for women: identity is expressed in terms of relation (to parents, spouse, children, clan, group). Empowerment here means positively reinforcing a function within that relationship. For instance, women in the refugee camps have gradually assumed the socially acceptable role of educators, as well as nurturers, which is why they were increasingly involved with their children's schooling. Literacy programs could function if they were able to demonstrate that women and girls attending them would necessarily become better wives and mothers (rather than independent women). The failure of program administrators to acknowledge and address this traditional value has meant the failure of many educational programs. Unfortunately, literacy levels remain very low in camps, and without the backup of minimal reading material, any skill acquired through a literacy course is generally doomed to rapid failure.[35]

As in other war zones, humanitarian agencies attempted to set up handicrafts centers, enabling refugee women to use their skills to generate direct income. This notion was alien to traditional rural Muslim villages, where men are usually paid for whatever labor or task their women and children accomplish. In Afghanistan, the beautiful art of embroidery and similar handicrafts have always been restricted to family use only. With the expansion of worldwide fashion and a growing taste for folk art, however, these crafts have entered the global market. Nancy Hatch-Dupree claims that Afghan men began to acknowledge that many women ensured the survival of their families in exile, even though in reality the money was (and is) still handled by the males of the family.

THE REFUGEE CAMP LEGACY

Communities that have developed in Pakistan's refugee camps over the past twenty-five years have left an indelible mark, both in Pakistan and in Afghanistan. The Pakistani Pathans have undergone notable radicalization, resulting from ideological spill-off from the camps and the influence of the ruling religious alliance MMA. The MMA was ousted by a resounding PPA victory in the Pakistani general elections of 2008; however, this represents an urban victory only, as the rural areas continue strict adherence to conservatism. In 2006, posters in Peshawar depicting female faces were either obscured with black paint or torn up; cinemas and their brightly painted posters have almost entirely disappeared, and the *burqa* is ubiquitous, worn at present by the local population today as much as the refugees. In local elections, despite official Pakistani constitutional rights, women were forbidden to vote by decree (fatwas) of village elders.[36]

Many rural Pashtuns today pride themselves on codes of behavior expressly forbidden by Islam, practices that were on the wane before radical Islam took over the camps. These practices include the levirate (widows being obliged to marry their deceased husband's brother), refusal of inheritance for women, the giving of daughters to compensate for a murder committed by a son of the family, "honor" killings, blood feuds, and stoning women on suspicion of dalliance (as opposed to proof required by Islamic courts).

In Afghanistan, the hybrid Constitution now unites orthodox Sharia and conventional democratic forms. These two forms are completely at odds with the reality of equal rights within an Islamic state—even given that Afghanistan has signed the Convention on the Elimination of all Forms of Discrimination against Women (CEDAW), adopted in 1979 by the UN.

Against this backdrop stands a solitary figure representing the new generation of women entering Afghan politics. She is Malalai Joya, a twenty-eight-year-old elected representative of Farah province, whose outspoken manner and systematic opposition to the warlords have made her popular with a large segment of the public. Nevertheless, Joya's life is continually threatened, and, as an outspoken opposition figure, she is obliged to sleep in a different location every night.

At the other end of the political spectrum is the chief justice minister in Afghanistan (until 2007), Fazul Hadi Shinwari, whose office was said to be decorated only with a Qur'an and a whip. Versed exclusively in Islamic (rather than constitutional) law, he attempted to legislate systematic repression of women by banning female singers, opposing co-education and publicly stating his lack of reticence regarding stoning of "adulterous" women (i.e., those who have had sex outside marriage, including rape victims). Shinwari has been responsible for naming judges throughout the country, none of whom have been trained in constitutional law. These powerful figures are bound to exert far greater influence than any human rights effort attempted by foreign NGOs working on short to midterm projects out of their offices in Kabul.

The general outlook is very bleak indeed, even as the bravest among Afghan women attempt to fight back. One of these courageous young women, Shaima Rezayee, a twenty-four-year-old producer of a youth music show on independent Tolo TV, was shot dead in May 2005. Her liberal (albeit veiled) manner was considered anti-Islamic, as was the genre of music she presented. Since this tragic murder, the *ulama* have been intent on removing every female presence from Afghan television.

The first female attorney in Afghanistan, Maria Bashir, works from the court of Herat. In a 2006 interview, she explained that her greatest challenge is defending women against marital violence: "Whenever I manage to put one of these brutal husbands away, he generally finds a way to buy himself out of jail. Judges are never on the side of women, and it is getting worse." Bashir has refused to accept offers from foreign NGOs to work for them, preferring her low-paying job in a spartan, poorly equipped environment. "Otherwise, there would be no one to defend these women," she explained.

One of the brighter developments for young Afghan women results from a new social order established in the refugee camps, that is, the reconfiguration of families. The patriarchal scheme outlined earlier in this chapter, while remaining the reference and the ideal, has in practice been transformed. Afghan camps, like most refugee camps throughout the world, have been comprised primarily of women and young children, as men participate in war or seek employment in the outside world. New configurations have evolved as a result, the most interesting of which is the decision to keep at least one educated unmarried daughter at home. This new dynamic is establishing itself in the camps, in refugee urban dwellings in Pakistan, and in Kabul. Traditionally, in Afghan villages, girls would be married off between the ages of thirteen and fifteen.

The privileged daughter, her mother's favorite (the Khub Dokhtar),[37] now carries the family's honor not through passivity and submission but rather through her achievements—going to school or getting work with an NGO, for example. Her illiterate married sister-in-law (the wife of her elder brother) is left with all the housework while the educated Khub Dokhtar attends to her studies. A comparable process has been observed in Palestinian refugee camps in Lebanon, where educated single girls have become emblematic of their families' respectability.[38]

For educated young refugees returning to major Afghan cities, there does seem to be a brighter future. After the fall of the Taliban, when more middle-class families returned to Afghanistan, many young males attempted to obtain employment with one of the numerous foreign NGOs that offered far larger salaries than did government jobs. Today these NGO positions are gradually being taken over by young female returnees who have learned English in Pakistan, especially in the provinces. Other young Afghan women, who have benefited from education abroad (outside of Pakistan) and who can now speak English, are securing good positions with foreign NGOS. Some of these women are choosing to forgo marriage, preferring to keep wages for their own families. In some cases involving widows or daughters of widows, young Afghan women are proudly assuming the role of breadwinner. This decision minimizes their need (and, in some cases, opportunity) to marry. Potential husbands are often reluctant to take over full financial responsibility for their bride's family—a phenomenon Anila Daulatzai notes in her 2005 research.[39] The situation has indeed brought about a shift in social recognition, financial success, and new forms of respectability.

CONCLUSION

In Kabul today, crowds thronging the markets no longer wear turbans and beards. Instead, one finds clean-shaven men in Western anoraks and sport jackets. Women too have returned to urban spaces. Until 2008, they were more heavily veiled than at any time in modern Afghan history, except during the Taliban era. A change is occurring in Kabul: the *burqa* is fast becoming a class marker, principally indicating poverty and unemployment, distinguishing the vast majority of illiterate women from those literate few who are studying to attain a profession or are already employed.

The trappings of Western-style modernity bring consumer goods for sale in bazaars, generally Chinese replicas of Western fashions. In 2005, in a very conservative refugee camp, I interviewed a fashion-conscious young woman who wore a replica designer scarf under her *burqa* and had multiple piercings in her ears. She rationalized her fashion choices by claiming they were designed to please her husband. That year, a neon-lit shopping mall opened in Kabul, offering Chinese and Turkish clothing and toiletries to admiring groups of mostly veiled women who could not afford them. By 2008 some of these facilities have expanded as financial opportunities multiply for educated women whose only permissible manifestation of independence, with regard to their family, seems to be a modest shopping spree. At best, these are facile manifestations of a consumerist form of modernity rather than indicators of any true social change. For instance, one of the posters put out by the Kabul Bank to attract female customers shows two women in *burqas:* one is holding out a credit card, and the slogan purports to be quoting her as saying, "Tut-tut, aren't you with the Kabul Bank yet?" At best, access to Western consumer goods introduces new patterns of behavior vis-à-vis communication or hygiene; at worst, the new availability of items intensifies the frustration of those who cannot afford the glitzy commodities.

For the majority of Afghan women, especially those living outside Kabul, the situation is grievously difficult, as women continue to be deprived of any autonomy, including, as previously mentioned, the choice to receive available health care. This has led to a spate of suicides by self-immolation, especially in western Afghanistan, by women who have returned from Iran.[40] In this region, new awareness of validated modern Muslim alternative lifestyles, based on media exposure or firsthand experience in Iran, has made life even more intolerable for female urbanized, literate returnees, forced to live in Afghan rural areas under conditions of unabated patriarchal violence. As one informant, an elderly woman in a remote village in the Farah region, told me when discussing the suicides, "In the olden days, we were beaten by husbands and mothers-in-law who made us work like slaves, even as we gave birth to one child after the next. We were unhappy, we suffered, but we didn't know it. Life was just like that for women. Now girls are learning through TV, school, and travel that is not normal, and it has made matters worse for them. They cannot put up with traditional hardship, so they set themselves on fire."

In Afghanistan, perhaps Asia's most tribal and patriarchal society, resistance to the notion of health care, education, and personal autonomy for women as a set of basic human rights remains fierce. The defeat of positive reform has produced a uniquely reactionary environment in Afghanistan, not regression to some kind of archaic past. Contrary to other models, in which enduring transformations emerge from the capital and then radiate out to the rest of the nation, the opposite has taken place in Afghanistan. This has been possible only because the power of the state remains weak and therefore cannot enforce any kind of legislation to supersede private patriarchal authority. Rural tribal populations, commanding and strong, are united in their claims against state intervention, especially any legislation regarding women. This is where the Taliban influence exerts itself maximally.

The new generation of Taliban, unlike the previous one, is heavily involved in the opium and heroin trade, so there is a potent commercial stake in present politics that goes well beyond religious ideology. Taliban influence now stretches into the large NWFP area in Pakistan (which Afghanistan has always claimed as its own). Restrictive practices towards women, both in Afghanistan and in the NWFP area of Pakistan, have played a key role in creating an extreme female Islamist stereotype. This modern reactionary paradigm seeks to be representative of Afghanistan as a whole. It relies on a unique formulaic ideology, fraudulently traditional and religiously compounded from the prototype evolved in refugee camps in Pakistan, molded by a now-globalized individualistic liberal economic ideal, at the cost, as ever, of women's lives.

NOTES

1. The subject is still under debate. See *Encyclopedia Iranica,* vol. 4 (New York, 1995), 385.

2. The NWFP is one of the four main provinces of Pakistan.

3. Edward W. Said, "The Clash of Definitions," in *Reflections on Exile and Other Essays* (Cambridge, MA: Harvard University Press, 2000), 581.

4. Dan Noorani, "Amnesty Law Condones Warlords' Past Abuse," Inter Press Service News Agency, March 23, 2007. http://ipsnews.net/news.asp?idnews=37056.

5. Most of these 22 million belong to the same ethnic Pashto-speaking group.

6. Staying in Khewa camp and traveling in the area was made possible through humanitarian work undertaken by the author, through the NGO FemAid—a Paris-based charity (www.femaid.org) established in July 2001. FemAid works alongside RAWA, the only secular women's organization in Afghanistan.

7. For example, Doris Lessing wrote, "If heroism has been your chief weapon for seven years, then heroism is what you value most. . . . Yes they're a flamboyant lot, but they break your heart, they are so brave and they have so little: even now, most of their weapons have been captured from the Russians." *The Wind Blows Away Our Words* (London: Picador, 1987), 47–48.

8. See bibliography.

9. Mahmood Mamdani, *Good Muslim, Bad Muslim: America, the Cold War and the Roots of Terror* (New York: Doubleday, 2005), 37.

10. This honor code, or concept of living, is referred to as "Pashtunwali" among the Pashtun people.

11. While researching the issue of violence, I frequently heard women in different camps say, "It is normal; my husband is allowed to beat me when he is not happy. The Qur'an says so."

12. Charles Lindholm, *Generosity and Jealousy: The Swat Pukhtun of Northern Pakistan* (New York: Columbia University Press, 1982), 113.

13. Bernt Glatzer, "Sword and Reason among Pashtuns: Notions of Individual Honour and Social Responsibility in Afghanistan," paper presented at the 14th European Conference on Modern South Asian Studies, Copenhagen, August 1996.

14. Deniz Kandiyoti, *The Politics of Gender and Reconstruction in Afghanistan*, Occasional Paper 4 (New York: United Nations Research Institute for Social Development, 2005).

15. "So far as the Musalmans had shown an indifference to the education offered them, that was ascribed by the Government to the disproportionate attention given by them to religious studies, to a preference, as more practical, for the course of study in indigenous schools." *Hunter Education Commission Report 1882* (Calcutta: Superintendent of Government Printing, 1883), 482.

16. "Taliban to Open Schools," Al-Jazeera.net, January 21, 2007. http://english .aljazeera.net/NR/exeres/64E67830-5B5B-4303-8B31-0877CF632311.htm.

17. All three were to fight over control of Kabul in the early 1990s, thereby destroying the city and killing tens of thousands of its inhabitants.

18. Nobody seems to have noticed that all the major refugee camps were built around Cherat, a virtually undocumented military camp in the NWFP that the United States built in the 1950s for training elite units. This is where Massoud and other Afghan anti-Soviet leaders were trained in the mid-1970s. Osama bin Laden probably trained at Cherat. This author suggests that it is likely that the United States may have been active in Afghan politics well before the first rumblings of Soviet tanks. (Information accessed from journalists at *The Nation,* daily newspaper in Peshawar in October 2003 and from the following remarkably well-informed Web site: www.specialoperations.com/Foreign/ Pakistan/SSG.htm.)

19. Mamdani, *Good Muslim, Bad Muslim.*

20. His most well-known targets include Sholay's leader Saydal Sukhandan (1972); Faiz Ahmad, leader of the Afghan Liberation Organization (ALO) (1986); and his wife, RAWA's founder, Mina (1987); as well as the internationally acclaimed poet Sayed Bahauddin Majrooh (1988).

21. Law enacted in Pakistan in 1979 by Zia-Ul-Haq's military ruler and revised in 2006. The law followed punishments prescribed by the Qu'ran and the Sunnah for extramarital sex and other proscribed behavior.

22. The reality of these *madrasas* frequently reveals appalling conditions and mistreatment of children. See Amnesty International, "Children in South Asia: Securing Their Rights," April 22, 1998. http://web.amnesty.org/library/index/engASA040011998.

23. Homosexual relationships involving adult men and young boys are well known in the camps and discreetly condoned. See "Kandahar's Lightly Veiled Homosexual Habits," *Los Angeles Times,* April 3, 2002.

24. Kandiyoti, *Politics of Gender and Reconstruction in Afghanistan.*

25. David Rieff, "Did Live Aid Do More Harm than Good?" *Guardian* (London), June 24, 2005.

26. Rashid 2000.

27. Michel Foucault, *Surveiller et punir* (Paris: Gallimard, 1975), 161.

28. National census conducted by the government of Pakistan with financial and technical assistance from the UNHCR, February 5, 2005.

29. UNHCR: Afghanistan, Operational Update, September 2006. http://www.unhcr .org/cgi-bin/texis/vtx/home/opendoc.pdf?tbl=SUBSITES&id=451a47ec2.

30. Liisa Malkki, *Purity and Exile: Violence, Memory and National Cosmology among Hutu Refugees in Tanzania* (Chicago: University of Chicago Press, 1995).

31. Rashid 2000.

32. Viz. David Rieff, Michael Ignatieff, David Chandler, and many others.

33. Linda A. Bartlett, "Maternal Mortality among Afghan Refugees in Pakistan, 1999– 2000," *Lancet* 359, no. 9307 (2002).

34. Lila Abu-Lughod, "Feminist Longings and Post-Colonial Conditions," in *Remaking Women: Feminism and Modernity in the Middle East* (Princeton: Princeton University Press, 1998), 8.

35. An excellent point made by Margaret Mills, "One Size Doesn't Fit All: Addressing Diversity in the Needs and Development Capacities of Afghan Women, Short and Long-Term," Social Science Research Council, New York, 2002. www.ssrc.org/sept11/essays/ mills.htm.

36. To quote a local English-language Peshawar newspaper article, "Earlier, as per decision of the tribal elders, the women voters were barred from casting vote in the by-election to NA-26 constituency of Bannu district on Thursday. Except for a few polling stations, located in the limits of Bannu city, all other polling stations gave a deserted look, as there were neither female voters nor any female polling agents of any candidate. However, the female polling staff along with required election material was present, locking the doors of booths from inside. All the tribal elders, irrespective of their political affiliation, ideology and party manifesto regarding women's rights, had agreed in a meeting that no woman would be allowed to cast her vote in the election, the polling agents and other people informed the journalists." Excerpted from "Durrani Welcomes Victory of MMA Candidate F. P. Report," *Frontier Post* (Peshawar and Quetta), March 30, 2007.

37. Translation: "the good girl/daughter."

38. Rosemary Sayigh, "Remembering Mothers, Forming Daughters: Palestinian Women's Narratives in Refugee Camps in Lebanon," in *Women and the Politics of Military Confrontation: Palestinian and Israeli Gendered Narratives of Location,* ed. N. Abdo and R. Lentin (Oxford: Berghahn, 2002).

39. Anila Daulatzai, "Acknowledging Afghanistan: Notes and Queries on an Occupation," *Cultural Dynamics* 18(3): 293–311.

40. See C. Mann, "Les shahidé du monde traditionnel: Le suicide des jeunes filles afghanes," TERRA Travaux, Etudes, Recherches sur les Réfugiés et l'Asile. http://terra .rezo.net/article.php3?id_article=404. February 2006. Also see Medica Mondiale, "Study of Suicides among Afghan Women." www.medicamondiale.org/_en/presse/pm/aktuelles/ mm-pm06-11-17.html. December 2006.

4

GENDERED AID INTERVENTIONS
AND AFGHAN WOMEN

Images versus Realities

LINA ABIRAFEH

Gender policies do not operate in a sociopolitical vacuum. In the wake of the U.S. invasion of Afghanistan, women's issues have become highly contested and politicized, yet there is a dearth of research and analysis on the formulation, intent, implementation, and effects of gender-focused aid. It may be argued that Afghanistan's particularly high-profile focus on women in the aftermath of conflict has remained at the level of rhetoric and has failed to translate into funding and significant gains for Afghan women. The current political project in Afghanistan is not unlike previous projects in that it demonstrates the gendered nature of conflict and the potential resistance to externally enforced social change. The case of Afghanistan presents a unique opportunity to critically rethink so-called gender-focused aid interventions.

Data that inform this work were collected from 2002 to 2006 and include the perspectives and experiences of gender policy makers and practitioners,[1] as well as Afghan women and men.

A GENDERED HISTORY

Afghan history is one of gender politics. Women's rights have always been highly politicized terrain, amplified by twenty-three years of conflict. Attempts at modernization have been made in several critical stages throughout modern Afghan history.[2] Each time, these modernizations carried the *perception* that reforms were imported and artificially imposed.[3] And each time these reforms, especially those relating to women's rights, were met with strong resistance.

In the 1880s the Afghan ruler Amir Abd al-Rahman Khan (and later his son Amir Habibullah) launched one of the earliest attempts at women's emancipation and social reform in the Muslim world. Women's emancipation thus began to play a prominent role in the nationalist ideology of modernization (Hans 2004). During the 1920s King Amanullah sought to drastically transform gender relations by enforcing Western norms for women,[4] measures that were in turn met with violent opposition and swiftly replaced by more conservative policy. King Nadir Shah's brief reign (1929–1933) saw the closing of girls' schools and the revival of veiling and segregation. Indeed, although modernization attempts were made by rulers that followed, these attempts were invariably met with strong opposition from conservative forces. Despite incremental changes, women's rights vacillated between enforced modernization and conservative backlash. Following the Saur (April) Revolution of 1978 and its program for social change, Afghan women once again found themselves at the center of a conflict between Western concepts of modernization and Afghan codes of culture (Hans 2004). Opposition to Soviet occupation–enforced reforms for women fueled the fundamentalist movement that took hold in refugee camps. This in turn served as grounds for the Mujaheddin opposition to expel the Soviets and regain control both of women and of Afghanistan.[5]

Despite these vacillations, the international aid community and the Western media's attention turned to Afghanistan—and Afghan women—only when the Taliban secured control. The Taliban's crimes against women became well documented and acknowledged, yet Afghan women suffered under *all* the regimes in Afghanistan. Today the country enjoys a democratically elected government and relative stability (mostly confined to Kabul). In this period of alleged liberation, history repeats itself. Once again Afghan women face another period of imported and imposed social change. As Afghan history has aptly demonstrated, a conservative backlash inevitably follows.

GENDERED INTERVENTIONS

In any postwar region, it is not unusual for aid agencies to be under great pressure to achieve immediate results. Unfortunately, in the case of Afghanistan, aid programs were designed and instituted before gender analyses could be thoroughly conducted. As a result, these aid programs have been unable to adequately integrate women—and men—in their efforts. A report to this effect states that Afghan "women have traditionally been viewed as a target group distinct from the socio-political, economic and cultural context, and humanitarian and development programmes are often based on unfounded assumptions and preconceptions" (Afghanistan Research and Evaluation Unit 2005). To this end, activists working on behalf of Afghan women frequently advocate that aid interventions should focus on the perspectives of

Afghan women and men, as those voices and viewpoints are for the most part absent in the international arena (Skaine 2002).

Until the fall of Kabul on September 27, 1996, the so-called international community and the Western media hardly took notice of Afghan women. Ironically, it was the Taliban that first brought attention to the need for Afghan women to be "liberated." The general consensus was that once the Taliban had been ousted, their stringent restrictions would vanish as well (Johnson and Leslie 2004). Such facile assumptions reflected the inattention to flagrant abuses of basic human rights suffered by Afghan women under previous regimes—and ignorance of Afghan women's history in general.

As the U.S. bombing campaign intensified in Afghanistan, violations of Afghan women's rights began to take on an increasingly prominent role (Charlesworth and Chinkin 2002; Clark 2004; Rawi 2004). Rhetoric used during the invasion period emphasized liberating, or saving, Afghan women (Abu-Lughod 2002). This focus on liberation became rife with controversy. Afghan women who were themselves engaged in aid activities felt uncomfortable with the high international visibility and felt that they were not being consulted regarding campaigns on their behalf (Benjamin 2000).

PERCEPTIONS OF LIBERATION

During the mid-1970s, as in other periods in Afghanistan's history, attempts were made to introduce "economic development and reform." At this time many Afghans were flush with optimism; women's rights became an imperative: "For the next couple of years, the words *economic development* and *reform* danced on a lot of lips in Kabul. . . . For a while, a sense of rejuvenation and purpose swept across the land. People spoke of women's rights and modern technology" (Hosseini 2003: 38). This initial euphoria ultimately faded, as regressive policies towards women were slowly reinstituted.

During the post-Taliban period, similar attempts at reform have been made. This agenda of reform is perceived by Afghans to be an externally imported and imposed ideological occupation. It has been aided in part by the media and its images of Afghan women.

Because media attention influences the way aid institutions approach gender issues during conflict and in its aftermath (Mertus 2000), Afghanistan presents an especially interesting case. An analysis of the media's perspective on Afghan women reveals a specific rhetoric that has informed public perception and in turn has informed the design of aid interventions for Afghan women. Select images of Afghan women in the media have served different purposes at various stages of conflict and afterwards. During conflict, they were portrayed as victims of a *chaddari*-obsessed archaic patriarchal order.[6] In the immediate aftermath, they were presented as having eagerly embraced their (Western-bestowed) gift of liberation.

Periodically, the media has been peppered with images and stereotypes of Afghan women, in particular in the context of Islam. Media images have variously portrayed Afghan men as resistance fighters, bellicose warlords, and every image in between—depending on the prevailing political winds. Such varied perceptions undoubtedly have influenced policy, especially regarding the degree to which international aid agencies sense an obligation to "save" Afghanistan. In terms of media images, an international aid worker in Afghanistan had this to say: "There is no doubt that the media has played a huge role in shaping people's perceptions of the plight of women in Afghanistan. For most, this is the only exposure that people have to Afghanistan."

A gender adviser with an international organization also expressed strong views about media images:

> I guess if we say that media and donor portrayals of Afghan women are negative it is in part because we conflate those portrayals with all Afghan women, which is in itself a problem. I think aid agencies and the media must walk a very fine line between depicting the struggles that so many women face on a daily basis and portraying Afghan women as helpless victims, often of a barbaric culture. This seems to push women into a corner of defending themselves or their culture, religion, nation. That's a tough place to be in and one that seems to happen in many places.

Media attention—even if inaccurate—can serve strategic purposes. For example, it can generate new interest and bolster increased funding for certain causes. According to the senior gender officer of a UN agency:

> In the case of Afghan women, the media definitely played on the image of the bourka, raising a lot of awareness about and sympathy for their [the women's] situation. At the same time, women were portrayed only as victims, anonymous, hidden away. They were rarely portrayed with the kind of strength and courage that they really have, despite the bourka. As a result, some of the assistance offered them may not have been appropriate.

A similar comment was made by yet another gender officer, who is also a longtime Afghanistan activist: "I think we have failed to see Afghan women as possible active participants in their own futures." Indeed, Afghan women

FIGURE 4.1
Three girls on Chicken Street in Kabul, Afghanistan, 2002. (photo by Lina Abirafeh)

have always been active participants, demonstrating agency and cultivating their own feminist self-identity. And yet their perspectives have been sidelined by the pervasive images in the Western media.

AGENCY DENIED

In the context of conflict and postwar experience, it is not unusual for generalizations and stereotypes to prevail. Thoughtful analyses of context and understandings of local agency require time and commitment. Unfortunately, humanitarian crises do not usually allow for such careful consideration. As a result, the aid apparatus often comes armed with preconceived notions and facile analyses that do little to accommodate local realities.

Again, there is no denying that rhetoric has the power to convey particular images and, in doing so, often denies agency. For example, rhetoric that focuses on "saving" and "liberating" women in Afghanistan implies that Afghan women need to be saved, that they cannot save themselves. Furthermore, it suggests that they must be saved *from* something. This is problematic in two

FIGURE 4.2
Woman in makeshift housing on outskirts of Kabul, Afghanistan, in 2003.
(photo by Lina Abirafeh)

FIGURE 4.3
Woman in Khairkhana, Kabul, Afghanistan, in 2003. (photo by Lina Abirafeh)

FIGURE 4.4
Election poster encouraging women to vote in Pashtun-Afghanistan in 2005
(photo by Lina Abirafeh)

ways: first, it may fail to achieve the promise of "liberation"; and second, it may result in more damage than benefit. The rhetoric surrounding Afghan women is inundated with contradictory images of survivor/victim, empowerment/vulnerability, dependent aid/independent change (Bouta, Ferks et al. 2005). Furthermore, it often succumbs to sensationalism and fails to do justice to the complexities involved. An Afghan man working with a nongovernmental organization (NGO) explained, "For us to judge Afghanistan as a backward society where women have no say is totally wrong."

A gender adviser for an aid institution explained that facile labels—such as "backward"—are mistakenly applied to Afghan women who opt for a slower pace of change than that offered by a fast-paced aid apparatus. This adviser had worked closely with an Afghan women's NGO and discovered an "internal struggle [experienced by] many women between wanting to broaden the role they played in society and their desire to be proud Afghan and Muslim women and good wives and mothers." She explained that pushing too abruptly for change not only negates these women's ability to act on their own behalf but also comes across as a harsh criticism of the "Afghan way."

Value judgements by aid agencies are in part justified by the myriad "myths created and perpetrated by the Western world"—the most powerful of which has been the idea that Afghan women are victims and *need* to be saved (Wali 2002). This perception is strengthened by the assumption that Afghan women are a homogeneous group. According to Western myth, Afghan women come in one of two forms: as part of a long line of anonymous *chaddaris* waiting for aid or as the occasional young emancipated woman.

AFGHAN WOMEN'S IDENTITIES

The majority of Afghan women I interviewed live in rural areas (63 percent), are married (55 percent), and have no education (59 percent). They are all participants in aid programs and represent diverse ethnic and age groups.[7] In aid interventions, Afghan women have been characterized as a uniform group based on their shared oppression. To this end, I began my research by analyzing identity markers in order to challenge the assumption that gender

FIGURE 4.5
Khala Jan ("Dear Auntie"). This woman used to clean the office I was running. Photo taken in Qalai Fatullah, Kabul, Afghanistan, 2003. (photo by Lina Abirafeh)

self-identity was the most important category of analysis for Afghan women. I asked participants to rank five aspects of their identity in order of importance: national identity, religious identity, ethnic/tribal identity, gender identity, and family identity. The rationale for this exercise was to achieve a better understanding of how Afghans themselves value certain aspects of their identities. In asking respondents to prioritize a single identity as most important, I had no intention of negating the existence of multiple identities, nor did I intend to ignore the fact that identities and affiliations change over time and in different contexts. My objective was simply to demonstrate that in aid programming artificial divisions based on sex may not be valid for some participants.

THE IMPORTANCE OF ISLAM

The majority of women ranked religion as the primary social category within which they chose to identify themselves. This reflects the prominence Islam enjoys in Afghanistan—and the impending consequences of Islam being sidelined, as Afghan history aptly demonstrates.

In conversation with Afghan women regarding the role of religion in their lives, I noticed how frequently they stated that they were Muslim. They were adamant about defining themselves in the context of Islam and its prescribed roles for women. An eighteen-year-old single female pointed out that "religion is an important part of our society. Without it, there cannot be progress." Many respondents expressed sentiments of duty to safeguard their religion and voiced concern that Islam could once again be threatened by "occupying regimes." Many evoked a historical responsibility to defend and protect the religion from "outside interference." One young woman in rural Afghanistan explained, "Our ancestors have always struggled to receive this religion, and we are responsible for saving it."

The importance of their operating first and foremost in the context of Islam cannot be overstated. In fact, many respondents felt that aid interventions "failed to operate in the Muslim context" and, more seriously, "lured Afghans away from Islam." One woman explained that the general perception of aid institutions as un-Islamic was sufficient reason to avoid them. Many women were quick to blame "invading cultures and customs" for polluting the Afghan version of Islam. The women strongly expressed a dislike for foreign intervention and a desire to regain Afghan autonomy.

OTHER IDENTITY MARKERS

The majority of women interviewed placed their Afghan national identity as second in importance, with ethnic background rated third. Gender and family ranked at the lower end of the spectrum. A few of the women who selected national identity also connected their role as women to their role as keepers of men's honor—and therefore as safeguards of national honor. In their own words, they are expected to be "obedient" and to be the "keeper of the family and the [family's] honor." A widow of rural origins believed that "women's behavior represents the family and the motherland. If she is good, people will think well of the family and the nation."

Those few interviewees who placed importance on gender as an identifying marker all acknowledged that this distinction had become important only after the war. One married woman in her early thirties put it this way: "This has become the most important thing in our new time of peace." Another woman who shared this perspective claimed, "Being a woman is now important in Afghanistan, before it was not." A woman from Kabul with ten years of education insisted (tongue-in-cheek) that if she were a man, she would surely have selected sex as the most important identity marker—but since she is female, she easily refrained.

The notable difference I discovered between men and women was in their ranking of family identity. Men viewed family as the second most important aspect of their identity. Surprisingly, women ranked family last.

NANG: WOMEN'S HONOR[8]

Most of the women I interviewed—regardless of age, marital status, educational level, and place of origin—felt that Afghan women do suffer under a patriarchal system but that slowly women are beginning to exert their rights. Many of these women are seeing themselves through the eyes of the world for the first time, and in doing so, they have become conscious of their own suffering. One woman called attention to the global perception of Afghan women as "weak creatures." Another explained that through the presence of the aid apparatus and its interventions to support Afghan women, she has learned that "a woman is not very respected [in Afghanistan] as she is in other countries." One married respondent put it this way:

> The view of the world regarding the women in Afghanistan is as slaves of men and prisoners in the home. The meaning of woman in Afghanistan

has come to be "being deprived of all kinds of rights." As a result, Afghan women are synonymous with guilt and shame. The men are afraid and so do not let the women have an education or take part in the socioeconomic spheres of the community because they think it is very bad work and it is very shameful for them to be in the public sphere and with the foreigners.

Almost without exception women voiced a desire to be the ones governing those changes taking place in their lives. A middle-aged married woman from the countryside explained that "women in Afghanistan must give position to *themselves;* they have to struggle for their *own* rights in society." She emphasized the italicized words to indicate that Afghan women have the necessary ability to make changes that are important to their well-being. The interviewees recognized that they have agency and acknowledged being perfectly competent to act on their own behalf, despite the challenges they might face.

Many women affirmed that change is taking place, and, as a result, men fear losing power and control. A thirty-year-old woman from southern Afghanistan observed, "Men are unsure of their role today. They want to bring back the old ways." Other women felt comfortable operating within traditional roles and stated that men should shoulder a greater responsibility than women, as is their place. "Men are not only responsible for themselves, but they have a responsibility to their wives, too," a thirty-four-year-old married woman explained. The theme of power and honor also came up repeatedly, with the notable difference being that women *represent* honor, whereas men *defend* it. Many women preferred that men take on public roles and felt that this gave women more freedom and room to maneuver. A married woman in her early twenties said, "Men have the full right and control over women in the family. It is their role to give their wives and daughters permission to do their tasks." She was not alone in these sentiments. Many preferred that the man represent the "public face of the family and the defender of the family."

A twenty-seven-year-old married woman with a primary school education defended men, declaring that they were neglected and had good reason to be angry. She explained, "The position of women is better than men in society today. Priority is given to women in every aspect of opportunities." Most of the women agreed that they received a larger share of attention from the aid apparatus; clearly, they were uncomfortable with the imbalance.

However, the general consensus among interviewees was that men's fears about losing power were unfounded. None of the women were seeking to usurp power or restructure traditional roles. Rather, what they envisioned was an equal sharing of resources, all the while respecting traditional boundaries.

Yet they also voiced frustration that this vision seemed unlikely given the current political agenda to "liberate" women.

Women across all age levels and educational backgrounds made statements like the following:

- Some men think that women are being taken care of by international organizations, while men are receiving significantly less attention. But the reality is that both men and women have suffered.

- My brother-in-law believes that everyone in the present government pays more attention to women than to men; therefore, he encourages my husband to forbid my attending literacy training classes.

- My husband has not behaved well with me. His anger at not having a job caused him to leave me forever. The best times for men and women are long past.

- We have not seen any good outcome from aid organizations. Men are feeling that they have been tricked into accepting women's authority.

Afghan women and men both felt that in the rhetoric of women's liberation women's honor had been compromised and their voices sidelined. In short, Afghan women are activists, seeking structural change appropriate to their own contexts and engaging in movement towards change at their own pace.

IMPLICATIONS FOR AID INTERVENTIONS

Catapulted onto the global stage and into the media's limelight, most of the respondents felt distinctly uneasy about being the focus of international pity. They also held fast to the belief that their new visibility would be short lived. From the interviews, I learned that although lofty promises had been made to Afghan women, few of them had been realized. This view—espoused by women of all ages and backgrounds—reflects a general frustration with programs implemented by aid institutions, programs that have failed to bring about real change.

Many women echoed the sentiment that the "changes are on paper, not in real lives." Indeed, initial expectations and high hopes—based on the rhetoric of aid institutions—were never met. Others pointed out that the aid apparatus supported and promoted only a few Afghan women, mostly those frequently in the public eye. These were the seemingly liberated "success stories." One woman suggested that the aid schemes have "led one woman to a comfortable life and have led thousands of other women to disaster."

Many interviewees felt obliged to acknowledge new rights for women. At the same time, although these rights were expressed on paper, one woman posed the question: "But what will [we] do with them?" An older woman from Kabul said, "I am told that we are equal now, but I am not sure yet." A widow in her forties put it this way: "In general, women have been given rights and freedom. But in my mind, women expected more rights because that was what was promised to them. Most of the women are illiterate and they cannot analyze and understand what freedom is."

Given the fast pace of the aid apparatus, Afghan women have not been given an opportunity to set their own agendas, negotiate changing identities, and struggle for their rights in a manner appropriate to their circumstances.

CONCLUSION

Afghan women have long-established mechanisms by which they have achieved gains in the past. Projecting images of Afghan women as victims may serve a strategic purpose; however, this strategy reveals little about women's realities and serves only to dislocate them as historical and political actors. Research has demonstrated that feminism does not need to be imported. It has always existed in Afghanistan.[9]

Afghan feminism—while perhaps eschewing this specific label—is indeed responding to the conditions of Afghan women. It is beyond the scope of this work to address the myriad examples of how this is happening. Nevertheless, in my estimation, it is important to understand that the nature of Afghan "feminism" may not necessarily resemble a Western model. From what I have observed, Afghan women—even those in the most difficult circumstances— rightfully claim that they are strong, countering pervasive images of public passivity.[10]

Many policy makers and practitioners admitted to a lack of understanding where Afghan women are concerned. This gap of understanding translated to failure in terms of how best to assist these women. The officials I interviewed also felt overwhelmed by stereotypes, many of which they had themselves adopted. The senior gender officer of a UN agency warned, "It behooves us not to project from our own perspective and assume that their lives are restrictive." She continued:

Empowering women is not a self-evident process. Many observers assumed that Afghan women would throw off their bourkas the moment the Taliban were deposed. That has not been the case. Inquiries with local women indicate that, for them, the bourka does not necessarily mean that they are oppressed. Instead, for many, the bourka actually protects them and gives them a freedom they feel they could not have without it. We as Westerners and development agents need to learn to disassociate the bourkas from oppression, need to acknowledge emotionally that Afghanistan is not the West, and need to support Afghan women in a manner meaningful to them, whatever that is.

Afghan women have repeatedly demonstrated that "meaningful support" does not need to correspond to Western models of democracy, human rights, and women's liberation. Despite the rhetoric and images, Afghan feminism continues to express itself across a broad spectrum of women's agency.

NOTES

1. By "gender policy makers and practitioners," I mean those Afghan and expatriate women and men who serve in the following capacities: heads of international agencies, gender program implementers, heads of Afghan women's NGOs, and others.

2. This section on Afghan women's history has been adapted from Abirafeh's 2005 report. See www.fes.org.af/AFGHANISTAN0905ABIRAFEHGENDER.pdf.

3. It is crucial to understand how Afghans *perceived* the modernization. Perception often holds more sway over the citizenry than the actual goal of modernization.

4. Amanullah was influenced and inspired by Western notions of modernity and progress. He sought to model Afghanistan after Western nations and saw the liberation of women as integral to this agenda. Examples of Amanullah's enforced emancipation include abolition of the veil and *purdah* (seclusion of women).

5. The Mujaheddin period is known for its violence towards women in the form of rape, abduction, and restrictions on mobility.

6. The Dari-Persian term *chaddari* refers to a full-body traditional covering worn by Pashtun women in Afghanistan to mark the symbolic segregation of men's and women's spheres. Among non-Afghans, the Arabic-Urdu term *bourka* is used.

7. Ethnic groups in Afghanistan include Pashtun, Tajik, Uzbek, Hazara, Aymaq, Turkmen, Baluchi, Nuristani, and Pashai.

8. *Nang* is defined as "honor," in particular, the honor resulting from a woman's behavior.

9. RAWA, the Revolutionary Association of the Women of Afghanistan, is an often-cited example (www.rawa.org), although there are many others.

10. For more information, see N. H. Dupree, "A Socio-Cultural Dimension: Afghan Women Refugees in Pakistan," in The Cultural Basis of Afghan Nationalism, ed. E. W. Anderson and N. H. Dupree (London: Pinter Publishers, 1990).

5

"BLACK WIDOWS" IN THE *NEW YORK TIMES*

Images of Chechen Women Rebels

SARA STRUCKMAN

The Chechen struggle for independence from the Russian Federation has resulted in a seemingly new brand of terrorist: the "black widow." This term, coined by the news media, is used to describe Chechen women who carry out suicide bombings and other violent acts to avenge lost husbands, fathers, sons, and brothers. Several sources claim that the Russian media developed the term to sensationalize female suicide bombings.[1] Unlike other terrorist or separatist movements, including the Palestinian struggle in the West Bank, women make up a majority of suicide bombers in the Chechen struggle. Since 2000 Chechen women have carried out over 65 percent of the twenty-three suicide attacks charged to the Chechen movement.[2]

The American media have to some extent adopted the "black widow" label in an attempt to explain Chechen women's violent involvement. This chapter examines how the *New York Times* attempted to challenge this facile explanation in its coverage of Russia and Chechnya between 1994 and 2004, when most of the violence between the two countries occurred and was reported in the U.S. media. However, because the *Times* questioned the black widow explanation, it was forced to offer other culturally suitable reasons to account for women's motivation in carrying out suicide bombings or other violent attacks. In doing so, it simultaneously broke away from and remained faithful to the media's role as a "circuit of culture,"[3] skillfully disseminating acceptable feminine—especially acceptable Western feminine—gender roles.[4] A critical analysis of how it accomplished this feat demonstrates the ways in which violent women fit into the media's representation of women—especially non-Western Muslim women.

CHECHNYA'S CHECKERED HISTORY

Chechnya is a small republic with geographic borders that embrace the Caucus Mountains near the Caspian Sea on the southeastern limits of the Russian Federation. A majority of Chechnya's population is Muslim, although they are often described as practicing moderate rather than fundamentalist Islam. The relationship between Chechnya and the larger Soviet and Russian republics has long been strained due to religious and cultural differences. Joseph Stalin forced the deportation of over 400,000 Chechens from their homeland after World War II, claiming that they had conspired with the Nazis. The exiled population was permitted to return to the Chechen-Ingush Autonomous Republic in 1953 after Stalin's death.[5]

Following the Soviet Union's collapse in 1991, Chechnya declared independence from the new Russian Federation and attempted to build a democratic state and society.[6] In December 1994 then–Russian Federation President Boris Yeltsin directed an assault on Chechnya that led to the first Russo-Chechen War. After a ceasefire, Chechnya became a "common economic space" within the Russian Federation, and Russia provided funds for the reconstruction of the war-ravaged republic. However, the situation in Chechnya remained unstable as separatists continued to fight for true autonomy from Russia. In 1999 the war between Russia and Chechnya resumed under the leadership of Russian Federation President Vladimir Putin and continues to the present day. Since 1999 Russian soldiers have carried out "mopping up" campaigns to find and punish Chechen rebels. These campaigns have led to accusations of human rights abuses against Chechen civilians. Putin has attempted to tie the separatist movement to international terrorism and often claims that Chechen separatists are funded and trained by terrorist organizations in the Middle East and Afghanistan.

After Russia launched its second attack on Chechnya, Chechen separatists increasingly turned to guerrilla warfare against the Russian military, government officials, and civilians. On June 6, 2000, a woman carried out the first suicide bombing in the conflict's history by driving a truck filled with explosives into a temporary Russian special services detachment in Chechnya. Since the attack, women have been involved in numerous attacks against Russia, both in suicide bombings and in hostage situations that have been covered by the news media, including the *New York Times*. Most notably, the *Times* covered hostage situations at a Moscow theater in 2002 and at a school in Beslan in southern Russia in 2004. Chechen women rebels were involved in both scenarios.

IMAGES OF WOMEN IN THE MEDIA

The Chechen women involved in violent actions represent a direct contradiction to the dominant images of women that have pervaded American media for over a century. Stereotypical images of women as passive, wholesome, and pretty are often represented in the limited dichotomies virgin/vamp or sex goddess/mother; this is especially the case for white women.[7] Sherrie Inness argues that these media images may be opening up to a newer, tougher image of women in the media, especially the popular media.[8] As films and television increasingly cast buff, tough women as heroes, they suggest that there are a greater variety of acceptable gender roles for women. However, Inness does not attach too much hope to this revolution as the "tough" girl's "tough image is often mitigated by her femininity, which American culture associates with weakness."[9]

In the case of mediated images of violent, or potentially violent, women, representations are gathered and assembled "from a reservoir of images that already exist; that is why it is possible, through analyzing the repeated use of certain images, to speak of cultural obsessions that shape, feed and articulate shared identities."[10] Media images of women warriors, whether they are defined as soldiers or terrorists, rely heavily on assertions of feminine characteristics to uphold their socially defined positions as nurturers needing protection. These images could depend on feminine appearances,[11] gender dualisms,[12] and/or mythical archetypes.[13]

Rhiannon Talbot characterizes representations in the history of female terrorists (a history dating back at least to the eighteenth century) as fitting into five myths: (1) extreme feminists; (2) women bound to terrorism only through relationships with men; (3) women acting only in supporting roles; (4) women who are mentally inept and/or (5) unfeminine in some way.[14] Some research on female terrorists supports these myths. Representations are often hyperfeminine, focusing on women's appearance,[15] which relates to Inness's interpretations of the new "tough" female characters on television and film.[16] In the specific case of Palestinian female suicide bombers, Frances Hasso's analysis argues that women's use of violence undermines the dominant notion of male-perpetrated violence, especially in a male-dominated society. Hasso's nuanced analysis acknowledges that this form of female political agency can complicate the patriarchal understandings of gender in a culture where women, in general, do not have political agency.[17] In addition, the media tends to explain women's motivations for carrying out suicide bombings as emotional (feminine) rather than ideological (masculine),[18] a dualism that John Howard III and Laura Prividera note in the coverage of women terrorists.[19]

Given that the media use mythical archetypes and ideological gender stereotypes to construct images of women terrorists,[20] in this case, how do the U.S. media construct news at the international level, especially when from a "remote" area of the world where the United States has relatively minor influence? Embedded in this question is yet another: how is gender constructed in the news, and how are these constructions situated within society and culture? Also, does the fact that Chechens are Muslim affect coverage of them?

As the media industry assumes an increasingly prominent role as producer of cultural messages and a dominant ideological framework that shapes the way people think and act, modern culture has gone through a process of "mediazation." This means that the media have substantive power to define the boundaries of acceptability and deviance.[21]

The concept of ideology helps provide a framework for understanding how images of females in the media follow a certain prescribed notion of femininity. It can be applied to Gaye Tuchman's observation that the media provide us with social guidelines for gender.[22] The media produce meanings that "regulate and organize our conduct and practices—they help to set the rules, norms, and conventions by which social life is ordered and governed" in what Stuart Hall calls the "circuit of culture."[23]

For Hall, media representations within the "circuit of culture" are the production of meaning through language. These representations both make up the circuit of culture and are influenced by it. They are representations that not only reflect societal and cultural norms but also instruct us how to act with respect to our gendered and other identities. Certainly media representations contribute to our understanding, or misperception, of people in other parts of the world.

To demonstrate how the *New York Times* constructed images of Chechen women rebels and to understand this process in relation to the larger ideological process of negotiating femininity when representing violent women, I focus on news coverage about the conflict between Chechnya and Russia. The time frame begins in 1994, when the first Russo-Chechen War began, and ends in 2004, when Chechen militants staged their most recent high-profile attack at a school in Beslan, North Ossetia, a republic in southern Russia.

As Chechen women seemed to gain more agency in the struggle, the *Times* used a series of themes to cover them: (1) passive victims (especially before reports about women participating in violence surfaced), (2) vengeful actors, and (3) female terrorists as a new, unnerving trend. A broader theme emerged when journalists began to report the gender of the separatists carrying out terrorist attacks but omitted that information when women were not involved. I examine how these representations of women rebels and constructed coverage fit into theoretical positions of the media as circuits of culture.

This chapter uses media texts about a specific group of "unfeminine" women to examine how they fit into media representations of women. As gender is understood as unstable based on a definition that is socially and culturally constructed, this analysis is well situated to ask, "how [is] gender discourse constructed in the various moments of mediated meaning production" and "which meanings are available in media texts and from which discourses do they draw?"[24]

THE PASSIVE VICTIM

When Chechen rebels seized a Russian hospital in June 1995, more than two hundred Chechen rebels participated. Presumably, the participants in the siege were male, but the *Times* did not report their gender. Russian women hostages were victims of the siege, holding that position in common with Chechen women, who figured largely as victims or as background characters in the *Times'* coverage. Prior to the reporting of a suicide bombing in Urus-Martan, journalists referred to women mostly as victims, either refugees or prisoners.

The following excerpt is a striking example of how Chechen women were represented as passive characters in this political war.

> As the men talked of war and Allah, the women vanished to the basement kitchen to cook huge pots of meat, rice and potatoes. . . . Wearing chador-like scarves and ankle-length robes, the women served in silence, disappearing into separate rooms when the men sat down at the table to eat. The women had little to say about the war that has taken away sons, uncles, cousins and husbands. One young woman finally shrugged. "We are worried, of course, but we are used to it," she murmured. But the women are not entirely preoccupied with the war—one young cousin had the Russian translation of an Italian romance, "Marianna," hidden in her nightstand.[25]

Women and children were often lumped together as refugees or portrayed in a domestic capacity, providing services to men who were fighting, similar to this reporter's description of a scene at a Chechen home: "While Mr. Yel-tsin spoke [on the television], local Chechen women cooked and served tea to the men, who were sitting in a big room plastered with portraits of Mr. Duda-yev and other Chechen leaders."[26] The link between the Chechen movement and Islam remained relatively weak in many of of the stories reported in the *Times*. While Yeltsin and Putin both tried to connect the Chechen struggle with international Muslim terrorist groups, reporters often challenged this connection by pointing out how Chechen attacks were different from attacks in the Middle East. However, when women and religion were discussed, re-porters often noted women's passive character. For example, when a Muslim sect took over Urus-Martan and replaced the local militia, girls were removed from schools and forced to wear veils. Even when women were involved in attacks, reporters noted the deviant nature of their actions. After the Moscow theater attack, reporters noted, "The use of women, veiled or not, was an-other departure from strict Islamic practice";[27] and "another [female terrorist] seemed to regret having taken part in the capture, forgot about her gun and prayed 24 hours a day."[28]

THE VENGEFUL ACTOR: "BLACK WIDOWS"

It was not until December 2001, nearly a year and a half after the first female suicide bomber had attacked a Russian military installment in Chechnya, that the *New York Times* acknowledged that women were actively involved in the struggle. Michael Wines reported that a "young woman strapped with explosives blew herself up outside the Urus-Martan's military headquarters. The woman's husband . . . died in a mountain battle last year."[29]

In this first *New York Times* report of a woman suicide bomber, Wines relied on the "black widow" explanation. He did so without explicitly using the label, explaining her motivation to become a suicide bomber as a cultural-religious one: "In Chechen culture, survivors are honor-bound to exact a blood revenge for a relative's killing."[30] However, as more women became violently involved in the struggle, the *Times* reporters were forced to negotiate between violence and femininity.

Although there are indications in the news coverage that women were actively involved prior to the first suicide bombing in 2000, the *Times* did not in fact begin addressing women's involvement until after a series of at-tacks between 2002 and 2004. Images of Chechen women shifted dramati-cally from victims and passive supporters to potentially active participants, especially after the Moscow theater attack in October 2002, when a group of Chechen rebels held seven hundred members of the audience hostage. Coverage during this period encompasses two major themes: an attempt to understand women's involvement under the general moniker "black widow" and a discussion of violent women as an unnerving but effective "new trend" in the Chechen struggle. Both themes point to women as potentially active subjects in the struggle.

The newspaper's coverage, rather than rely on the "black widow" explanation, delves further into the issue; the result is a nuanced account of the women who were involved. The need to explain women's uncharacteristic violent behavior suggests, at the very least, that it is unnatural for women to be violent.

Before 2001 the *New York Times* did attempt to make sense of Chechen rebels' (both male and female) participation in the struggle as motivated largely by the years of cruelty they suffered at the hands of the Russian military stationed in Chechnya. Halfway through the first war, journalists quoted Chechen men discussing their involvement in the struggle as unsatisfactory but necessary, given the conditions of their country.

In the midst of the Moscow theater crisis in 2002, a Russian government official who met with the rebels compared their involvement to Hitler Youth, which Sabrina Tavernise described as "fanatically devoted to a cause" and "a young, completely new type of militant who grew up not under Soviet control, but in a brutal war."[31] Their only goal: to get Russian troops out of Chechnya. In this case, men and women seem to have the same political motivation—to contribute to the movement to secure Chechnya's independence.

It was the female suicide attacks following the Moscow theater siege that seemed to be the catalyst for the coverage of gender. Reporters often did not interview Chechens involved in the cause. Rather, they merely speculated about why women would join the cause, mostly with the assistance of Russian officials or the Russian media. And it was after this point that the term "black widow" began to appear consistently in the coverage of Chechnya. Reporters would often cite "official sources" without naming them specifically but rather attaching these sources to government bodies or law enforcement organizations. For example, Stephen Lee Myers alluded to a "Russian official" who identified two women as Chechen by documents found on their persons after the attack and claimed that one woman's husband had died when the war in Chechnya began.[32]

Although reporters often included information about dead relatives in stories about female suicide bombers and wrote about black widows, they also qualified these details with statements such as the following:

Russian news media, echoing officials, have dubbed the perpetrators "black widows," women prepared to kill and to die to avenge the deaths of fathers, husbands, brothers, and sons at the hands of Russian troops.[33]

The women, whom the news media here call "black widows," are said to be avenging the deaths of husbands, sons, fathers and brothers who have died in the grueling conflict with Chechnya, though little is known about the women's lives.[34]

In Russia, such women are known as shakhidki, the feminine Russian variant for the Arabic word meaning holy warriors who sacrifice their lives. In the media, they are known more luridly as black widows, prepared to kill and to die to avenge the deaths of fathers, husbands, brothers and sons in Chechnya.[35]

Instead of accepting the category "black widow," Myers attributed its source to the Russian news media or Russian officials. Anne Nivat, journalist and author of a book detailing her experience in Chechnya, explains that the Russian government restricted news coverage of Chechnya so that outsiders would have little idea of what was actually happening there.[36]

Although Myers does not explicitly address the problems with the Russian media, he does not accept the suggestion that women are simply avenging the deaths of loved ones and searches for more complex explanations. In the case of one woman who blew herself up outside a rock concert in Moscow, Myers notes that "little seemed to explain" why she did it; she had no dead father, husband, brother, or son to motivate her. Here Myers uses interviews with officials who attributed Chechen women's involvement to Islamic extremists who had "co-opted 'black widows' against their will to become suicide bombers"—drugging them or raping them on video so they would have no option but to blow themselves up.[37]

Toward the end of the spate of female suicide bombings in 2004, Myers and other *Times* reporters explained women's violent involvement as a "retaliation for the suffering that has accompanied the Chechen war."[38] Myers writes, "Some people here say a decade of war and destruction, including atrocities by Russian forces, have driven women to desperate acts."[39] Women's participation—"despite Chechnya's deeply patriarchal society—reflects a radicalization of a war that began as a separatist struggle but has turned increasingly nihilistic."[40]

Interestingly, journalists did not attempt to understand why men were involved in the struggle to gain Chechnya's independence. In an article that detailed where, when, and why women were involved, Myers reported, "The only recent attack not carried out by a woman was the truck bombing of a military hospital in Mozdok on Friday, which left 50 dead at last count."[41] Myers stopped there. He did not attempt to explain why the (presumed) man drove a truck to a military hospital and exploded it.

A NEW UNNERVING TREND

Clearly reporters for the *Times* attempted to understand and explain the behavior of women rebels, especially those who carried out suicide attacks. At the same time, reporters were describing these women as part of a "new trend," although evidence showed that women had been involved in the rebellious movement since at least 2000.[42] Yet in 2003 reporters began to search for explanations as to why women would be involved, describing this "new trend" of attacks as especially effective and therefore unnerving to authorities.

In reporting about an unsuccessful attack at a Moscow restaurant, Tavernise writes, "Officials here have said the incident fit a pattern of suicide bombings by women, which began in the Chechnya region last year."[43] Similarly, in a critical report of the Russian military's difficulties containing separatist attacks, Nivat suggests, "The soldiers have also been forced to contend with a new trend, suicide bombings and other attacks committed by young Chechen women."[44]

Because gender roles are so restricted to masculine and feminine and because violence is not a female trait, Russian security forces were not prepared to deal with female suicide bombers. In fact, "The suicide attacks by women have particularly unnerved Russian authorities, in part because Chechen women had been able to move more freely than Chechen men, who are routinely harassed by Russia's police and security services."[45]

At the end of one article, Myers lists suicide attacks in and around Russia carried out in 2003. "The Dark Shadows of Chechnya," as the list is titled, only mentions the gender of a suicide attack if a woman was involved.[46] Myers labels these "dark shadows" (female suicide bombers) part of one of the "deadliest waves of terror ever in Russia."[47]

In its coverage, the *Times* offers no single explanation for why Chechen women have turned to suicide bombing. When journalists interview local Chechens about female suicide bombers, many Chechens respond, "How could she?" Interviews suggested that female suicide bombers are not celebrated in their society, potentially ruling out the motivation for women to become martyrs, as is often the case with female suicide bombers in Palestine.[48]

Indeed, Myers reported that most Chechens do not embrace martyrdom; there are no posters or graffiti celebrating suicide bombings, as often occurs after a woman's suicide attack in Palestine. One female suicide bomber's grandmother expressed shock and horror and asked, "How can a person who kills someone get to heaven?"[49] Another Chechen woman exclaimed about a female suicide bomber she knew, "'We were so shocked.' Her eyes reddened with tears. 'How could she?'"[50] Others expressed the same disbelief, indicating that it was unfathomable for women, givers of life, to take life away.

MANIPULATING MOTIVES: THE MEDIA'S ROLE

Since the Beslan school siege in 2004, all has been mostly quiet on the Chechen front, at least according to the *New York Times'* coverage. Rebel Chechen forces did stage a raid in Nalchick, Russia, in October 2005, but according to the news coverage, women were not involved. The "deadly wave of terror" seems to be quelled for the moment, but that does not lessen the importance of gender coverage in this war.

The *Times'* representations of women during the first war—as passive victims and disinterested characters in the Chechen struggle for independence—align with other media images of women as passive during wartime. The quality of being a refugee and indifferent to the politics surrounding a conflict fits into the dominant ideology that females are weak and apolitical.

However, even if a woman is a violent actor, the media can force her into passive status, as the *New York Times* did with descriptions of the "black widow" phenomenon. The *Times* never addressed the possibility that women could be avenging the death of a female family member or that men were involved in the movement to seek revenge for a dead or missing family member.

The motives of black widows, along with other explanations for Chechen women's involvement in the violent movement, can also be classified as emotional rather than political, as Patkin suggests happens in the media coverage of Palestinian female suicide bombers.[51] The *New York Times* provided other potential reasons for women to become involved in the struggle other than vengeance. These included coercion through drugs or videotaping rapes of the women,[52] retaliation for suffering at the hands of the Russian military,[53] and even the nihilistic perspective that the conflict will never end.[54] Myers almost completely rules out the possibility that martyrdom is a motivation, even though the Russian government claims there has been a "Palestinization" of the war with the use of suicide bombers.[55] Only once did the stories

about Chechen women rebels mention the possibility that women's motivation was political — to gain independence from Russia — though this very
motivation is often assumed in stories that do not mention gender (and thus
assumed to refer to male combatants). In addition, during the spate of female
suicide bombings, the *Times* represented these women as at once "unnerving
and effective" — because the violent actions they were carrying out were unexpected for Chechen women.

These attempts to represent even the most violent women as passive actors
illustrate the media's role in defining gender roles based on the dominant
ideology. Similar to research on the media's representations of U.S. female
soldiers, who occupy roles outside the normative feminine boundaries and
complicate what it means to be a woman, the question arises, are they protectors or protected? In the case under discussion here, are violent Chechen
women rebels actively choosing to be involved in a separatist movement? Or
are they victims of a long-drawn-out war?

The dominant ideological message inherent in the coverage of Chechen
women suggests that if women do break out of gender norms, the media
will negotiate their actions. Further, the media will attempt to ameliorate
those actions with explanations that remain consistent with femininity. This
is precisely what the *Times* has done with Chechen women rebels and is also
the case with media representations of violent women, tough women, and
women in general. Religion, in this case, was used to strengthen the link
between passivity and femininity, especially when used to explain women's
roles in the struggle.

Does this mean that Chechen women rebels were never active subjects in
the *New York Times*' representations of them? Not necessarily. When reporters interviewed Chechen women, rather than rely on official Russian sources
who often classified women rebels as "black widows," the messages diverged
from the dominant idea of passive women warriors. This coverage is more
consistent with Hasso's analysis of the discourse surrounding female suicide
bombers in Palestine, which indicated that some Palestinian female suicide
bombers understood their actions as political.[56]

Anne Nivat spoke to the sister of one of the women involved in the Moscow theater siege and reported this conversation:

> "My sister went for her own jihad," explained a 19-year-old girl, conser-
> vatively dressed in a headscarf and cloak, whose sibling was a perpetrator
> of the theater attack. We spoke in the kitchen of a relative's house, as her
> family has lived as nomads since their house in a village southwest of

Grozny was dynamited by Russians in revenge for her sister's actions. "She sought revenge by escaping to paradise," the girl told me. "And I am willing to do the same if nothing changes." Her friend, 21-year-old Tamara, added: "We women are now acting because nobody else is reacting and no one cares about Chechnya."[57]

While this passage indicates that Chechen women may get involved for religious or even nihilistic reasons, consistent with the *Times*' explanations, it also indicates that women have different motivations for carrying out violence. Because Nivat spoke directly with women, she provided a more credible representation of these women, credibility that was lacking in most of the stories about Chechen women rebels.

CONCLUSION

Using a textual analysis, I have attempted to provide a detailed examination of how the *New York Times* has covered Chechen women rebels. While the *Times* offers a few examples of Chechen women actively making their own choices, most of the coverage suggests that men are warriors with political motivations and women are drawn into violence or terrorism only through their relationships with men. Although reporters questioned the black widow motivation for carrying out vengeance, their coverage relied heavily on other feminine explanations that stripped women of agency, effectively robbing them of a desire on political grounds to fight for the Chechen cause. In addition, gender was not mentioned when only men were involved in an attack, whereas gender served as a focal point when women were the perpetrators. Also, it was not until large numbers of women became involved in the Chechen struggle that the *Times* began seriously to cover their role, despite the fact that there was evidence that women had been involved for some time.

By using primarily official sources, specifically, Russian ones, the *Times* was able to support the dominant ideology of women as weak and needing protection and men as warriors fighting for a cause. In the few instances that reporters were able to interview Chechen rebels, their reports offered alternative explanations as to why both males and females entered the struggle. Within the "circuit of culture," the *Times* was able to negotiate femininity and violence in the case of Chechen women rebels and arrive at a socially acceptable motivation for their violent actions, even while challenging the black widow explanation.

NOTES

1. John Reuter, "Chechnya's Suicide Bombers: Desperate, Devout, or Deceived?" (report for the American Committee for Peace in Chechnya, 2004); Paul Murphy, *The Wolves of Islam: Russia and the Faces of Chechen Terror* (Washington, DC: Brassey's, 2004).

2. Reuter, "Chechnya's Suicide Bombers."

3. Stuart Hall, *Representations: Cultural Representations and Signifying Practices* (London: Sage, 1997).

4. Gaye Tuchman, "Introduction: The Symbolic Annihilation of Women by the Mass Media," in *Hearth and Home: Images of Women in the Mass Media,* ed. Gaye Tuchman, Arlene Kaplan Daniels, and James Benet (New York: Oxford University Press, 1978).

5. Brian Glyn Williams, "Commemorating 'The Deportation' in Post-Soviet Chechnya: The Role of Memorialization and Collective Memory in the 1994–1996 and 1999–2000 Russo-Chechen Wars," *History and Memory* 12, no. 1 (2000): 101–134.

6. Anatoly V. Isaenko and Peter W. Petschauer, "A Failure That Transformed Russia: The 1991–1994 Democratic State-Building Experiment in Chechnya," *International Social Science Review* 75, no. 1–2 (2000): 3–15.

7. Carolyn Kitch, "Changing Theoretical Perspectives on Women's Media Images: The Emergence of Patterns in a New Area of Historical Scholarship," *Journalism and Mass Communication Quarterly* 14, no. 3 (1997): 477–489.

8. Sherrie A. Inness, *Tough Girls: Women Warriors and Wonder Women in Popular Culture* (Philadelphia: University of Pennsylvania Press, 1999); Sherrie A. Inness, "'Boxing Gloves and Bustiers': New Images of Tough Women," in *Action Chicks: New Images of Tough Women in Popular Culture,* ed. Sherrie A. Inness (New York: Palgrave Macmillan, 2004).

9. Inness, *Tough Girls,* 5.

10. Jayne Steel, "Vampira: Representations of the Irish Female Terrorist," *Irish Studies Review* 6, no. 3 (1998): 276.

11. Ibid.

12. Terri Toles Patkin, "Explosive Baggage: Female Palestinian Suicide Bombers and the Rhetoric of Emotion," *Women and Language* 27, no. 2 (2004): 79–99.

13. Dan Berkowitz, "Suicide Bombers as Women Warriors: Making News Stories through Mythical Archetypes," *Journalism and Mass Communication Quarterly* 82, no. 3 (2005): 607–622.

14. Rhiannon Talbot, "Myths and the Representation of Women Terrorists," *Eire-Ireland* 35, no. 3–4 (2000): 165–186.

15. Berkowitz, "Suicide Bombers as Women Warriors"; Steel, "Vampira."

16. Inness, *Tough Girls;* Inness, "Boxing Gloves and Bustiers."

17. Frances S. Hasso, "Discursive and Political Deployments by/of the 2002 Palestinian Women Suicide Bombers/Martyrs," *Feminist Review* 81, no. 1 (2005): 23–51.

18. Patkin, "Explosive Baggage."

19. John Howard III and Laura Prividera, "Rescuing Patriarchy or Saving 'Jessica

Lynch': The Rhetorical Construction of the American Woman Soldier," *Women and Language* 27, no. 2 (2004): 89–97.

20. Berkowitz, "Suicide Bombers as Women Warriors"; Patkin, "Explosive Baggage."

21. John Thompson, *Ideology and Modern Culture: Critical Social Theory in the Era of Mass Communication* (Stanford, CA: Stanford University Press, 1990).

22. Tuchman, "Introduction."

23. Hall, *Representations,* 4.

24. Liesbet van Zoonen, *Feminist Media Studies* (Thousand Oaks, CA: Sage, 1999), 131.

25. Alessandra Stanley, "As Chechens Take to Hills, Clans Gird for Long Fight," *New York Times,* January 22, 1995, 6.

26. "Wary Chechens Scorn Plan by Yeltsin," *New York Times,* April 1, 1996, A8.

27. Serge Schmemann, "The Chechens Holy War: How Global Is It?" *New York Times,* October 27, 2002, 3.

28. Sabrina Tavernise, "Terrifying Nights in a Theater Where Lights Never Dimmed," *New York Times,* October 26, 2002, A6.

29. Michael Wines, "War on Terror Casts Chechen Conflict in New Light," *New York Times,* December 9, 2001, A6.

30. Ibid.

31. Sabrina Tavernise, "Bomb Kills Russian Security Agent in Moscow," *New York Times,* July 11, 2003, 6.

32. Stephen Lee Myers, "Russia Finds No Corner Safe from Chechen's War," *New York Times,* July 20, 2003, A3.

33. Stephen Lee Myers, "Suicide Bombings on Russian Train Near Chechnya Kills 42," *New York Times,* December 6, 2003, A3.

34. Stephen Lee Myers, "Suicide Bomber Kills 5 in Moscow near Red Square," *New York Times,* December 10, 2003, A3.

35. Stephen Lee Myers, "Suicide Bomber Kills 9 at Moscow Subway Station," *New York Times,* September 9, 2004, A1.

36. Anne Nivat, "A War Russia Loses by Winning," *New York Times,* August 5, 2003, A5.

37. Stephen Lee Myers, "Female Suicide Bombers Unnerve Russians," *New York Times,* August 17, 2003, A1.

38. C. J. Chivers, "Russian Forces Kill Last Rebels to End Standoff," *New York Times,* October 15, 2005, A8.

39. Stephen Lee Myers, "Insurgents Seize School in Russia and Hold Scores," *New York Times,* September 10, 2004, A1.

40. Ibid.

41. Myers, "Female Suicide Bombers."

42. Reuter, "Chechnya's Suicide Bombers."

43. Tavernise, "Bomb Kills Russian Security Agent."

44. Nivat, "A War Russia Loses."

45. Myers, "Female Suicide Bombers."

46. Myers, "Suicide Bomber Kills 5."

47. Myers, "Insurgents Seize Russian School."

48. Dan Berkowitz and Sarah Burke-Odland, "'My Mum's a Suicide Bomber': Motherhood, Terrorism, News and Ideological Repair," paper presented at the Association for Education in Journalism and Mass Communication, Toronto, Canada, 2004.

49. Myers, "Female Suicide Bombers."

50. Ibid.

51. Patkin, "Explosive Baggage."

52. Myers, "Female Suicide Bombers."

53. Chivers, "Russian Security Forces"; Myers, "Insurgents Seize School."

54. Myers, "Insurgents Seize School."

55. Myers, "Female Suicide Bombers"; Stephen Lee Myers, "Second Bombing This Week in Chechnya Kills 15 at Festival," *New York Times,* August 7, 2003, 16.

56. Hasso, "Discursive and Political Deployments."

57. Nivat, "A War Russia Loses."

PART TWO

THE MIDDLE EAST AND
NORTH AFRICA

6

THE ISLAMIC REPUBLIC OF IRAN
AND WOMEN'S IMAGES

Masters of Exploitation

FAEGHEH SHIRAZI

He who controls images controls thought, belief, and ideology.

— ROXANNE VARZI, *WARRING SOULS, YOUTH, MEDIA,*
AND MARTYRDOM IN POST-REVOLUTION IRAN

Since the birth of the Islamic Republic of Iran in 1979, all graphic representations of women have had to comply with strict rules and adhere to rigid regulations established by the late Ayatollah Khomeini. During the Iran-Iraq war (1980–1988), Ayatollah Khomeini consolidated power and mobilized his troops to defend Iran's territory and religion. At this same time, the public image of Iranian women assumed unprecedented importance. Posters, banners, even postage stamps instructed women in appropriate social and ethical behaviors, including public dress and veiling. Over time, political and religious events gave rise to the creation of high-quality graphic arts, and ultimately, Iran's artists found increasingly innovative ways to represent the ideal Iranian woman. This chapter explores the political agenda behind posters, banners, and stamps created in the 1980s and analyzes the purposeful semantic fusion of *hejab* (veiling) and *jihad* (holy war), especially in the context of martyrdom.

MESSAGES THROUGH ART

One of the most remarkable aspects of the Islamic Revolution in Iran was an ability to imbue specific images with religious-political messages. For example, according to Roxanne Varzi:

> Khomeini projected his own image as that of the nation, and thus to love the nation was to love Khomeini. Hidden in every image that portends

freedom was the ideology of subordination to a leader and to death: the absolute masters.[1]

Khomeini's image was plastered throughout Iran, and, as a result, "his photographic image played as important a political role as did the man himself."[2]

Especially in the decade 1978 to 1988, Iranian artists took the merging of image and text to its highest expression, relying heavily on ancient myths and symbols drawn from Iranian sacred history. Their artistic endeavors mobilized an entire nation to respond effectively to the Islamic Revolution and the Iran-Iraq war. In both instances the services of graphic artists and painters were employed to create posters celebrating nationalism—posters that evoked a deeply emotional response. Graphic representations fusing compelling images of familiar religious symbols with written messages also appeared on murals and in graffiti and slogans on public buildings. This type of art became ubiquitous, reflected in banners, poems, audio- and videocassettes, bank notes, postage stamps, and even on retail merchandise such as chewing gum and boxed candies. The artistic designs were shrewdly contrived, constantly reminding Iranian citizens of their duty to revolution and war. As noted by the International Institute of Social History (Amsterdam) in its Web site publication "War between Iran and Iraq Collection 1980–1988":

> During the war the Islamic Republic of Iran launched widespread propaganda in various areas, particularly [aware] that the language of art and documentary films, photos and paintings, pictorial mummeries . . . are the effective, attractive, and understandable language to the majority of the people.
>
> [All these artistic images] reflected one message: the correctness of war, [the importance of] attracting public support, and [the necessity of] encouraging warriors.[3]

The well-orchestrated semiological, dramaturgical dimensions of these images make a fascinating topic, one that deserves in-depth study from a sociological and psychological perspective. Peter Chelkowski and Hamid Dabashi, in their book, *Staging a Revolution,* state, "A reading of the constellation of revolutionary images is indispensable in comprehending the more compelling question of how public sentiments and collectively held symbolics are used to mobilize a people for radical and revolutionary purposes."[4] Chelkowski and Dabashi suggest that this wealth of print and recorded information produced by the Islamic Republic Revolution and necessitated by the Iran-Iraq war would not have been possible without delicately balancing

Shi'i faith and Persian history. The central message in many of the images underscores the ideology of a God-centered, rather than human-centered, worldview. Such pictorial designs have left an indelible legacy and serve as a vibrant contribution to Iranian contemporary art.[5] Chelkowski and Dabashi refer to this genre of art as self-exhibition, the product of a nation turning "itself into a museum of—if not so 'fine' then at least—furious art. 'The Museum of Furious Art'—that is the Iran of the 1980s, a nation engaged in a revolution and a war, relentlessly remaking itself in images and forms, shapes and colors, frames of angers and anxieties."[6]

In my opinion, what is of particular interest is the manner in which images of women were used (and continue to be used today) to further the Islamic message of revolution and patriotism. According to Meyda Yegenoglu, some feminist theorists posit that power "takes the [female] body as its target, the object, the medium to extract information so as to transform, remake, re-inscribe, and subject it to the functioning of power."[7] The powerful Islamic Republic of Iran mastered this act of subjecting and exploiting women, adeptly disguising it as the promotion of patriotic piety.

In the decade of war and revolution, Iranian artists were charged with seamlessly combining and overlapping socialist, nationalist, and religious ideas. They portrayed women attending to daily domestic duties while also celebrating them as mothers of the young and revolutionary Islamic Army soldiers. Iranian artists, charged with the responsibility of promoting a state-owned and controlled media, followed the pattern discussed by Hamid Naficy, who wrote about media influence and power: "The influence and authority [of media] stems from its wide circulation and commodification of only selected, partial, atypical highly cathexted truths and representations of the other that are made to stand for the totality of the other."[8]

In the context to which I refer, the "other" is the Iranian woman. *All* women, therefore, are represented as mothers sacrificing their children to the front lines of war. *All* women are the dutiful daughters, bidding good-bye to their revolutionary fathers who, despite advanced age, volunteer to fight for Islam.

Following the example of Fatima al-Zahra, beloved daughter of the Prophet of Islam, the ideal Iranian woman is represented as dedicating herself to domestic life and piety. She is fortunate indeed to walk in the footsteps of Zaynab, the brave lion[9] of Karbala,[10] granddaughter of the Prophet Mohammad and sister to Imam Hossain, the Sayyed al-Shohada, or Master of Martyrs. Taking full advantage of Zaynab's symbolic value, the Islamic Republic shrewdly created a female commando network called the Sisters of Zaynab (Khaharan e Zaynab) to patrol streets and target women dressed "immodestly." Punishments ranged from scolding and name calling to jail sentences and fines. More zealous members of the Zaynab commando units would wipe off women's lipstick with a razor blade hidden in a handkerchief. In 1983 an amendment was added to the Iranian constitution stating that women who harmed public chastity by appearing without religiously sanctioned veiling in streets and in public view would be subject to receiving up to seventy-four lashes.[11]

In short, the Islamic Revolution of 1979 ushered in a new era of violence against women in the name of religious morality. It also expanded the Iranian woman's roles and assigned to her new duties, all of which were literally spelled out in publicly displayed images and words. According to Kamran S. Aghaie, with the establishment of the Islamic Republic, "the traditionalist model of womanhood became the dominant state-supported model."[12]

As Iran's religious leaders attempted to rally a significant portion of the population—in both Iran and Iraq[13]—around Shi'i ideology, a new semantic dimension of the *hejab* emerged. Posters, billboards, and stamps not only promoted the war but also projected images of the "ideal" woman. Ayatollah Khomeini pointedly described the duties of this perfect woman in a sermon delivered on April 25, 1981—a date designated as "Woman's Day" in Iran. He stated:

> You, respected ladies, are charged with bringing up pious children. Your job is to rear pious children and deliver them to society.... [Y]ou should bring up children who will safeguard the Prophet's wishes and aspirations.
>
> The assistance of the women is many times more valuable than that of men. May God protect you in bringing up human beings, the job of the Prophets.[14]

This pronouncement was later used as a constant reminder to women in terms of how to behave in traditional Islamic society. Armed with this description, graphic artists rushed to translate the Ayatollah's vision into appropriate visual images. Iran was soon plastered with posters of Ayatollah Khomeini's ideal woman promoting the war with Iraq.

It should be noted here that the preamble to the Iranian constitution expressly forbids any private sector to use a woman's image in commercial ads for services and/or goods. However, the Islamic Republic of Iran managed, effortlessly and without resistance, to use images of veiled women to further very specific ideological agendas.

Suddenly images of veiled women sprang up everywhere, seemingly infinite variations on a theme. In every Iranian city, on every building, inside all businesses, outside and inside public transportation facilities, and in every educational institution, the private and "sacred" woman of Iranian culture was transformed into a public image for all to view. Indeed, Iran's government sanctioned the public's right and duty to gaze upon these images of women, all of which were calling men to war, demonstrating strong support of the war, and/or modeling the proper style of *hejab*. During this era, the *hejab* became a universal symbol of the chaste and pious Iranian daughter, sister, wife, and/or mother.

When posters praising Fatima al-Zahra failed to curb the loss of Iranian territory to Iraq, the government introduced new public images and messages describing the "Tragedy of Karbala." This shift from Fatima to her daughter, Zaynab, represented a shift away from revolution (against the Pahlavi regime) to focus on the war with Iraq, a shift from internal crisis to external threat. The revolutionary movement had associated Fatima with piety, patience, pain, and suffering—an archetypal figure with limited economic resources. This model fit the mass of Iran's population resisting the shah's "tyranny." As stated by Aghaie:

> Khomeini often referred to the active involvement of women in the struggle against the shah, [although] when women were referred to in texts written by male religious leaders . . . they were usually placed outside the discussion in the sense that men were the speakers and they were speaking about women rather than to them.[15]

The figure of Zaynab, and all that she symbolized in terms of sacrifice, bravery, and martyrdom, proved more appropriate in postrevolutionary Iran when the populace fought against Iraqi invaders. In fact, paramount among the Karbala themes was the concept of martyrdom, an integral part of Shi'i Islam. Consider Ayatollah Khomeini's musings on the subject of martyrs and martyrdom:

> Think about the fact that the best people of His own time, His Holiness the Lord of the Martyrs [Imam Hossain], peace be upon Him, and the best youths of Bani-Hashim [the tribe of the Prophet Muhammad and Imam Hossain], and his best followers were martyred, leaving this world through martyrdom. Yet, when the family of Imam Hossain was taken to the evil presence of Yazid, Her Holiness Zaynab, peace be upon Her, said: "What we experienced was nothing but beautiful."[16]

The motif of martyrdom as a "beautiful experience" was glorified in an infinite number of ways, both visually and textually. One might agree with Varzi, who suggested that in the Islamic Republic of Iran the visual image "was born in death." According to Varzi, "The space of death needs two things in war-era Iran: a martyr and a photograph. Martyrdom is meaningless without memorialization, and memorialization is not possible without a photograph."[17]

The Islamic government repeatedly used images of women as propaganda tools. Photographs displayed on posters and postage stamps represented women as the quintessential martyrs, sending beloved husbands, sons, fathers, and brothers off to certain slaughter. This agenda exacted an inexpressibly heavy emotional toll on Iranian women, who were expected to remain calm and controlled, especially when receiving news of a loved one's "martyrdom." Although the government rewarded martyrs' families with material goods and services and other forms of privileges, the unfathomable loss of life became too burdensome for women — especially for those women who had to grieve the loss of multiple family members.

WOMEN'S IMAGES SUPPORTING THE WAR

In short, the most honorable way an Iranian woman could contribute to the Iran-Iraq conflict was by sending her beloved family member to the front lines. For a woman to commit a husband or son to certain death to further glorious victory against Iraq was presented (by the government) as a completely logical notion.

One finds evidence of this propaganda on a postage stamp introduced in 1988 on the occasion of the "Eighth Anniversary of Sacred Defense" (fig. 6.1). This stamp portrays a veiled woman standing behind three men who appear to be her son, father, and husband.[18] The military uniforms worn by the men indicate their readiness to go to war. Their red-and-green headbands read "Ya Hussein"(Oh Hussein) and "La ilaha illa Allah" (There is no God except Allah).[19]

This image originally appeared on a poster designed by the graphic artist Jamal Khorrami Nejad. The poster version, titled *Moghavemat*, or Resistance, includes the following text:

Standing Tall and Firm to Offer Our Martyrdom.
Shouting Fight, Fight until Victory

FIGURE 6.1

Postage stamp introduced in 1988 on the occasion of the Eighth Anniversary of Sacred Defense

This is an excellent example of how Iranian women were represented as major supporters of the war. Images such as this were meant to influence all Iranian women who had eligible men still living at home. Notice how the artist strategically placed the woman *behind* the three men, indicating both physical and moral support. Indeed, although the "glorified" figures in this composition are men, it is the woman behind them who blesses and supports their action as soldiers. This moral support theme appears in posters throughout the war era. Without fail, a veiled woman is placed behind men of all ages, especially behind young men preparing for war. It should be noted that the Islamic Republic of Iran recruited and drafted boys as young as thirteen. Furthermore, volunteering for war became almost a religious obligation for Iran's adolescents. All eligible young men were drafted and had no choice but to serve. Numerous men, age fifty and older, also volunteered.

In the wartime posters, then, messages to women were crystal clear: it was the religious duty of all mothers and wives to send husbands and sons to war and not to expect them to return alive. Newspaper clippings, as well as audio and visual documentaries from the 1980s, serve as testimonials to the incredible pressure exerted on Iran's youth to fight the war. In addition, insurmountable feelings of guilt experienced by those who did not become "martyrs" made many young men wish that they *had* died a martyr's death. In Iranian newspapers from that era, one also finds records of letters written by "martyrs," individuals who left letters behind addressed to their parents asking forgiveness for their unpardonable sins. This reflects the Iranian cultural belief that the blessing of one's parents is imperative—as demonstrated by a popular Persian proverb:

Parvardegar az kasi razi ast ke pedar va madarash az ou razi bashand
(God is happy with those whose parents are happy with them.)

In other words, to please God, one must first please one's parents. Thus letters written to parents served as an effort to secure forgiveness and receive those blessings requisite for entering paradise—even though these individuals had already been classified by the Islamic Republic as martyrs, a classification that automatically guaranteed a ticket there.

One especially startling image from 1980 published by the *hameh bà ham jehad-e sazandegi*[20] organization shows a very young girl, approximately seven, posing in a full black *hejab* and holding a military rifle with a red carnation in its barrel (fig. 6.2). In the background are young soldiers, some with their backs to the camera and others directly facing it. A message from Ayatollah

FIGURE 6.2
Young girl with rifle

Taleqani, written in both English and Persian, is printed on the right-hand corner of this poster. The message reads:

> Our army does not belong only to our brothers in the armed forces. Men and women, young and old in our country are the members of Islamic Army, and are guardians of Islam.[21]

The image of this young girl can be interpreted in several ways. In contrast to Ayatollah Taleqani's statement, interpretation may be based solely on the visual impact, aside from the written text. The young female figure in a full adult *hejab* suggests that even at a tender age every Iranian girl is expected to step into adult roles. She must exhibit adult moral behavior, demonstrating her chastity through adoption of an adult *hejab* and aligning herself with Zaynab by becoming a courageous warrior. She is part of the next great generation of Iranian women safeguarding Islam by supporting and contributing to the war.

IN ZAYNAB'S FOOTSTEPS

The two paintings, shown in figures 6.3 and 6.4, by Naser Palangi,[22] both titled *Az Tabar-e Zaynab*, "Zaynab's Progeny," use the same model—a woman with large and emotionally expressive eyes. She seems fearless and is engaged in some kind of military activity. She holds a rifle with her left hand, and the flow of her scarf and fluid movement in each fold of her garment suggest hurried action. In the second painting, the same woman is depicted with a similar facial expression, again completing some type of military activity. She carries a wooden box replete with rows of unused bullets, even as her face reflects a furtive anxiety and concern. As in the previous image, the painting suggests hurried movements and the woman's face shows determination.

Zaynab's reputation for fearlessness has contributed to the centuries-old tradition of public eulogy and lamentation so sacred to the Shi'i community, and her image is often used to mobilize women during wartime.

The Islamic Republic Party, or Hezb-e Jumhuri-e Eslami, published a commemorative poster on the anniversary of Zaynab's death (fig. 6.5). Chelkowski and Dabashi describe the poster's significance in terms of religious symbolism and also point to parallels between Yazid (the Umayyad caliph who fought against the Prophet's grandson at Karbala) and the shah:

> The clenched fist of a silhouetted woman is controlled by the "relay" of the linguistic message referring to Zaynab, Imam Hussein's sister, and to her revolutionary eloquence. A second iconic "relay," the multitude of women from contemporary Iran, narrows the field of interpretation to the immediacy of the Islamic Revolution. The smashed crown, as a result, is as much Yazid's as the Shah's.[23]

The poster depicts Zaynab as an eloquent orator,[24] as well as a maternal figure. It was Zaynab, known as the protector of orphans, who took respon-

FIGURE 6.3
Naser Palangi's Az Tabar-e Zaynab, *or "Zaynab's Progeny #1"*

FIGURE 6.4
Naser Palangi's Az Tabar-e Zaynab, *or "Zaynab's Progeny #2"*

FIGURE 6.5
Commemorative poster of Zaynab

sibility for her brother's orphaned daughters, Roghayah and Sokaynah (great-granddaughters of the Prophet Mohammad). On the poster's right-hand side, multiple figures garbed in white *hejab* ride camels toward a palace, all the while holding a small child. The palace they face, constructed with Ionic columns and arches, is a familiar example of Islamic architecture and suggests the court of Yazid in Damascus. The captive female figures being led to court have assumed the role of mother for the orphans of Karbala, the same role played by Zaynab. The following message appears in the lower right-hand corner: "Zaynab, Eay zaban-e Ali dar kaam," or Zaynab, who has Ali's tongue. This message not only makes reference to Zaynab's eloquence and brazen tendency to speak the truth but also gives credit to Imam Ali for teaching his daughter well. The literal translation, "Ali's tongue in Zaynab's mouth," perhaps suggests that Imam Ali is speaking through his daughter, which some might argue diminishes Zaynab's stature.

A poster designed by Mostafa Goodarzi, *Varesan-e Zaynab* (The Heirs of Zaynab), celebrates Zaynab's militant nature, symbolized by a group of women assembled in the background who are ready to sacrifice their lives (fig. 6.6). The dominant image of a militant woman with a single red tulip superimposed over her head, while countless women support her in the background, signals the invaluable contribution of martyrdom, whether in a personal or a collective sense.[25]

THE IDEAL OF PIETY: FATIMA AL-ZAHRA

Many posters designed in the 1980s were accompanied by slogans praising the virtue of *hejab* and celebrating the piety of Fatima al-Zahra. In Shi'i hierology, Fatima al-Zahra represents the ideal pious woman. As wife of the first Shi'i imam, Ali ibn-Abi Talib, and mother of both Imam Hassan and Imam Hossain (the Master of Martyrs), she exemplifies the highest example of the good wife and mother. In the 1980s posters praising Fatima al-Zahra usually did so through written expression rather than by depicting her in human form. In these posters the words themselves are visually appealing, their exquisite calligraphy attracting the viewer's eye.

Ahad Yary Rad created the poster titled *Eay zan be tou az Fatemh ingoneh khatab ast* (O' Woman, This Is Fatimah's Advice to You) in a strikingly provocative way (fig. 6.7).[26] A large group of women wearing black *hejabs* weep openly and grieve deeply against a background of gloom. They appear to be slowly sinking into water. Beneath the water are images of foreign/Western luxury commodities such as makeup, cologne and perfume, and American-

FIGURE 6.6
Poster by Mostafa Goodarzi: Varesan-e Zaynab, *"The Heirs of Zaynab"*

FIGURE 6.7
Poster by Ahad Yary Rad: Eay zan be tou az Fatemh ingoneh khatab ast,
"O' Woman, This Is Fatimah's Advice to You"

FIGURE 6.8
Postage stamp of militant woman, titled Hejab

brand cigarettes. Although this poster is devoid of text, the message is clear: Women of Islamic Iran! Whoever follows Western ways is doomed to disaster and despair! This implied message (of Fatima al-Zahra) reflects the sentiments of a famous speech by Ayatollah Sharyati during the early stages of the Islamic Revolution in which he warns Iranian women against emulating "Western painted dolls."

The 1980s postage stamp in figure 6.8 displays the central figure of a woman against a red and white background. Some would suggest that red symbolizes blood, while white signifies peace and tranquility, a condition achieved only through sacrifice and martyrdom. The figure is wearing a conservative, Iranian-style *hejab* known as *maghnaeh,* a garment that gained popularity only after the Islamic Republic took control. On the woman's right side, the barrel of a gun is visible. In the lower left-hand corner of the stamp, the word *hejab* is clearly inscribed, neatly fusing the concepts of *hejab* and *jihad*.

The same effort to fuse *hejab* and *jihad* is demonstrated in another stamp, this one published in 1988 commemorating the birth of the Prophet's daughter, Fatima al-Zahra (fig. 6.9). On the stamp, a banner in the background reads *Ya Zahra,* Oh Zahra. A shapeless, faceless figure wrapped in a large

FIGURE 6.9
Postage stamp, 1988, commemorating birth of Fatima al-Zahra

FIGURE 6.10
Painting by Hamid Ghadirian, titled Behesht-e Zahra, *"Zahra's Heaven"*

flowing *chador* wields a machine gun in her right hand, which is crossed over her body to the left. Certainly Iranian women were honored to celebrated Fatima al-Zahra's birth and viewed it as a joyous occasion. However, from the government's viewpoint, the occasion was to be exploited fully by reminding women of the compatible nature of militancy and *hejab*.

Historically, Fatima al-Zahra has never been associated with war or violence. On the contrary, the figure of Fatima al-Zahra is described by both Islamic medieval and contemporary historians as a pious beloved daughter to the Prophet, a loving wife to Imam Ali, and an affectionate mother to her children. Thus the military motif associated with Fatima al-Zahra emerges as yet another propaganda tool developed by the Islamic Republic of Iran.

If she had lived long enough, Fatima al-Zahra (as a devoted mother) would have experienced the painful loss of her beloved son Imam Hossain, who died a martyr. In this context, Fatima assumes the role of faithful companion to all Shi'i women who sacrifice family members as martyrs. The painting by Hamid Ghadirian, titled *Behesht-e Zahra* (Zahra's Heaven), evokes a strong emotional response from the viewer (fig. 6.10).[27] Behesht-e Zahra is the largest cemetery in Tehran province. In the poster version of this painting, five female mourners in dark *hejabs* gather to place freshly cut red gladiolas at a gravesite. Another faceless female figure, presumably Fatima al-Zahra, appears in a white *chador* and radiates heavenly light. The artist has strategically positioned her at the head of the tombstone to signal a maternal gesture, as if she is holding a small child's head on her lap for comfort and security. The background accurately reflects what a visitor to the Behesht-e Zahra cemetery would see — rows of graves with photos of fallen soldiers attached to tombstones. This area is designated exclusively for the martyrs of the Iran-Iraq war.[28] Thus there is no doubt that the women in the poster are mourning the loss of a martyr, and Fatima al-Zahra is with them in spirit, grieving alongside. After all, she too had lost her warrior son Hossain, martyred in the battle at Karbala. The poster's message to the families of martyrs is unmistakable: You are not alone, as Fatima al-Zahra shares your pain and sorrow.

IMAGES OF WOMEN JUXTAPOSED TO MARTYRS

The graphic artist Mohammad Khazai offers two additional posters depicting women mourning the loss of a martyr.[29] The first, titled *Defa-e Moghadas* (Sacred Defense), portrays a woman next to a dead soldier, gently holding his head. The background is an intense blood-red color with shades of black (fig. 6.11). Four tall red tulips — the traditional symbol of a martyr's blood — have been placed next to the figures of the woman and the dead soldier. The second poster, *Bar Mazar-e Shahidan-e Khaneyeh-e Khoda* (On the Grave of Hajj Martyrs), depicts a woman gazing off in the distance while seated on a floor holding a tall branch of red gladiolas (fig. 6.12).[30] Behind her is a small image of the Ka'ba covered in black cloth.[31] The Ka'ba seems to be swimming or floating in a sea of blood, which may be interpreted as the blood of martyrdom. In the left-hand corner are a few stems of white tuberoses,[32] also dripping with blood. The poster's title implies that all Iranian martyrs of war have died for the sake of Islam. The Ka'ba motif especially suggests a Muslim's last earthly journey. The white tuberoses symbolize white shrouds soaked in the blood of martyrs. That the martyr has sacrificed his blood is clear, first as indicated by the seated female image below the Ka'ba and second by the red drops from the white tuberoses. Although the artist has eschewed the use of literal images of a cemetery or tombstone, his intention is clearly conveyed through the use of religious and cultural symbols.

The poster by Mostafa Goodarzi, *Daricheh-ei be Khold-e Barin* (Window to Paradise), reveals a woman garbed in *chador* (fig. 6.13).[33] With her right

FIGURE 6.11
Mohammad Khazai's poster titled Defa-e Moghadas, *"Sacred Defense"*

hand the woman has covered part of her face with a corner of her veil. In her left hand are four red tulips. She stands in front of an open window, beyond which four white doves gracefully fly across a blue sky. Although the wall framing the woman's figure is green, it gradually changes to orange and then to red. Behind the woman mourning the loss of her beloved is a field of red tulips. Perhaps the four red tulips in hand symbolize individual family members who have been martyred, while the expansive field of tulips represents countless young men who have also died as martyrs for Islam.

Another 1980s poster designed by Ahad Yary Rad, titled *Raftanat Az Ghafas-e Khak Mobarak Bada* (Congratulations on Departing the Worldly Cage), emphasizes the benefits of martyrdom (fig. 6.14).[34] The central focus of the poster is a black-and-white photo of an Iranian mother saying farewell to her young son leaving for war. Chelkowski and Dabashi state, "The artist Ahad Yari transformed this farewell black and white photograph, which ended in the death of the young hero at the front, into a compelling icon of maternal love and youthful sacrifice, framed and separated from the human realm."[35] Once again, the thematic intertwining of maternal love and martyrdom recalls Fatima al-Zahra and her prominent role as mother of the martyred Hossain. Also, using the name *Behesht-e Zahra* (Zahra's Heaven) for one of the largest cemeteries where war casualties (*shahid,* martyrs) are buried is no coincidence or accident. Rather, it is a carefully considered choice, especially in cultural and religious contexts understood by Iran's Shi'i population.

The proverb "Behesht zir-e pay-e madaran ast" (Heaven is spread beneath the feet of mothers) is what an Iranian child hears during its first year of school and throughout its life. The cultural respect for the sacrifices a mother

FIGURE 6.12
Mohammad Khazai's poster titled Bar Mazar-e Shahidan-e Khaneyeh-e Khoda,
"On the Grave of Hajj Martyrs"

FIGURE 6.13
Poster by Mostafa Goodarzi: Daricheh-ei be Khold-e Barin, *"Window to Paradise"*

FIGURE 6.14

1980s poster designed by Ahad Yary Rad, titled Raftanat Az Ghafas-e Khak
Mobarak Bada, *"Congratulations on Departing the Worldly Cage"*

makes and the important role she plays in the lives of her children create a strong lifetime bond between mother and child. This experience translates to the acknowledgment that although a son is born to an earthly mother, when he departs this earth he will join his heavenly mother, Fatima al-Zahra.

After the Islamic Republic of Iran was established, many Iranian cemeteries were completely transformed from dry, barren environments to lush green gardens. This too was no accident. Just as ancient Iranian landscaping and architectural design incorporated lush gardens and water fountains (two important motifs associated with Heaven), the newly lush cemetery environments effectively remind visitors that a martyr's soul finds lasting peace in a real Heaven. Furthermore, the beloved martyrs rest eternally with their heavenly mother, Fatima al-Zahra.

I have personally visited the Behesht-e Zahra cemetery on many occasions. At the entrance gate is an impressive tile mural with a large female image in a flowing head-to-toe white veil. Her hands are open at her sides, positioned to indicate that she is collecting or gathering (what turns out to be souls). This figure is set against a lush blue sky with an arched gate in the background, representing the gateway to Heaven. At the feet of this faceless figure are multiple images of men in military fatigues wearing red and green headbands similar to those worn by soldiers in Ayatollah Khomeini's army during the war with Iraq. Their headbands are inscribed with phrases such as "Allah Akbar" (God is Great) and "Ya thar Allah" (Oh, Revenge of God). These are the martyrs who gave their lives defending nation and Islam. In the mural, they arise from earth to their mother Fatima al-Zahra in Heaven. This mural at Behesht-e Zahra is one of the best examples of the purposeful use of symbolic iconography to convey an intended message.

Ali Shariati (1933–1977), an Iranian social activist, wrote extensively about Fatima and her significance — not only in the Prophet's life but also as the true archetype of the ideal Shi'a woman. Shariati describes Fatima's extraordinary devotion, especially after her mother's death:

> [After Khadijah died], she [Fatima] acted as a mother to her father who was now very much alone. She devoted love, faith, and all the moments of her life to her father. Through her kindness, the feelings of her father were satisfied. Through her devotion and faith in the mission of her father, she gave him energy and honor.[36]

Shariati also commends Fatima for loyalty to her husband, as she remained devoted despite Ali's poverty. Here is a woman who, although she died at the young age of twenty-eight, left a legacy that Shariati describes thus: "She was stronger than life, purer than will and faith[,] . . . [a soul] joined with the spirit of her father."[37] Shariati died before the Iranian Revolution began. Had he survived long enough to witness revolutionary events, the Iran-Iraq war, and finally the postwar period, he would have observed a subtle shift in the Iranian government's focus from Fatima to Zaynab and back to Fatima, depending on the desired political outcome. In contemporary Iran, then, especially in civil and social affairs, Fatima remains the sacred Shi'i role model for all Iranian women. One need only refer to posters held high in religious processions, posters that echo Khomeini's sentiments:

Agar Fatema mard bud nabi bud.[38]
(Fatima, had she been a man, would have been a prophet.)

Because Fatima's image is entirely sacred, even the highest clerics have carefully avoided associating her name with war or aggression, while her daughter, Zaynab, can fulfill that very purpose since she was physically present at the Battle of Karbala.

Iran's regime is currently developing a new strategy to acknowledge and honor the central role of female martyrs—beginning with the emergence of Islam (ostensibly Fatima and Zaynab) and continuing to the present day. Construction on a new project, the Museum of Women Martyrs of War, began in Tehran in mid-September 2008. Farahnaz Fatehi, secretary-general of the International Congress of Women Martyrs of War, announced plans for this new museum.[39] One wonders how many Iranian women were consulted in the museum's initial conception and design. It would be unwise to underestimate the clever guile of the Iranian government in manipulating women behind a facade of honoring them. Available information suggests that no expense will be spared in implementing modern methods and technologies to project images promoting the culture of martyrdom. I borrow the term "culture of martyrdom" from the Shohada (Martyrs) Museum of Behesht-e Zahra Web site.[40] Situated between the cities of Tehran and Qom, the Behesht-e Zahra cemetery doubles as a museum and celebrates male martyrs only. Another existing and well-known martyr museum is the Martyr Mohammad-Ali Rajai Museum located in Tehran, which houses Rajai's personal belongings and works. As an architect of the Islamic Cultural Revolution and assassinated after only fourteen days (in 1981) as president of Iran, Rajai was immediately designated a martyr.

Two aspects of the projected martyrs museum seem extraordinary. First, it is the only museum of its kind to specifically honor female martyrs, representing a new effort at political correctness by the Ahmadinejad regime. Second, the new museum, sponsored by Iran's Cultural Heritage, Handicrafts and Tourism Organization (ICHHTO), is clearly an effort to interweave bloodshed, the horrors of war, and women's sacrifice with notions of "cultural heritage," "handicrafts," and "tourism." To my knowledge, this unlikely juxtaposition has no precedent, at least in Iran. According to Wikipedia, of the fourteen major listings of ICHHTO museums in Iran, none has ever been dedicated to war or war-related experiences.[41] Although administered and funded by the government of Iran, the ICHHTO—equivalent in focus and activities to the Smithsonian Institution in Washington, D.C.—is traditionally engaged in educational and artistic projects, often in collaboration with foreign museums. ICHHTO's sponsorship of the martyrs museum represents an unexpected shift away from academic and aesthetic concerns to the marketplace of propaganda.

CONCLUSION

Graphic artists hired by the Islamic Republic of Iran contributed greatly to the efforts of revolution and war. These artists were charged with the task of revealing a spiritual relationship between symbolic, allegorical worlds and the modern-day struggle to promote a particular brand of Islam. Whether opposing the shah or opposing Iraq, the challenge lay in presenting convincing ideas using familiar cultural and religious themes. To engage viewers and to win support for the Islamic Republic, the artists, hired by the government, creatively incorporated poetry and calligraphy—key elements in Iranian culture. They designed and produced unique works by building on existing religious, mystical, mythological, and poetic foundations.

Women played a significant role in this process. Images of the Iranian woman were explored and exploited, always to serve a political agenda and to communicate the government's intended messages. Glorifying a woman's domestic and maternal roles translated to unquestioning support for an especially brutal war. Through the manipulation of women's images, the Islamic Republic presented a convincing argument: by sacrificing the people they loved, Iranian women too would be considered martyrs. Such profound sacrifice was expected from the "daughters" of fearless warriors such as Zaynab. In addition, the Iranian woman was expected to follow the path of Fatima al-Zahra, whose perfect example of loving mother, obedient wife, selfless daughter, and compassionate woman was nearly impossible to emulate.

As if that were not enough, the Iranian woman's image was broadcast internationally as a sort of public ambassador.[42] All images had to suggest religious piety, and all behaviors reflect honor and chastity, especially in public arenas. Both tasks required *hejab,* a dress code instituted by the Islamic Republic and single-mindedly enforced without once consulting the women themselves.[43] Within the confines of that narrow role, the Iranian woman of the 1980s became a familiar image worldwide. In short, her fate was determined by a nation in crisis.

NOTES

1. Roxanne Varzi, *Warring Souls: Youth, Media, and Martyrdom in Post-Revolution Iran* (Durham, NC: Duke University Press, 2006), 26.

2. Ibid., 26–27.

3. www.iisg.nl/archives/pdf/10930603.pdf.

4. Peter Chelkowski and Hamid Dabashi, eds., *Staging a Revolution: The Art of Persuasion in the Islamic Republic of Iran* (New York: New York University Press, 1999), 9.

5. Michael Fischer and Mehdi Abedi, "Revolutionary Posters and Cultural Signs," *Middle East Report,* no. 159, *Popular Culture* (July–August, 1989), 30.

6. Ibid., 10.

7. Meyda Yegenoglu, *Colonial Fantasies: Towards a Feminist Reading of Orientalism* (Cambridge: Cambridge University Press, 1998), 113.

8. Hamid Naficy, "Mediating the Other: American Pop Culture Representation of Postrevolutionary Iran," in *The U.S. Media and the Middle East: Image and Perception,* ed. Yahya R. Kamalipur (Westport, CT: Greenwood Press, 1995), 86.

9. Faegheh Shirazi, "The Daughters of Karbala: Images of Women in Popular Shi'i Culture in Iran," in *The Women of Karbala: Ritual Performance and Symbolic Discourses in Modern Shi'i Islam,* ed. Kamran S. Aghaie (Austin: University of Texas Press, 2005), 93–118. Note the masculine reference to lion rather than lioness. In the late twentieth and early twenty-first century, Iranian eulogies and lamentation poetry designate Zaynab the "King" of Karbala rather than the "Queen" of Karbala. Zaynab's piety is a direct reflection of her mother, Fatima al-Zahra. However, Zaynab's wisdom and knowledge are associated with her father, Ali, and her loyalty and bravery are associated with her brother, Hossain. These masculine qualities overlaid on Zaynab do nothing to promote her value as a woman. On the surface, her image is glorified, but a more in-depth analysis leaves one questioning the true intention of these eulogies. Is there a purposeful effort to diminish Zaynab's value as a woman whose worth emanates primarily from her own feminine merit?

10. According to the Muslim calendar, the Battle of Karbala occurred in the month of Muharram 10, 61 AH (October 9 or 10, 680 c.e.) in Karbala, present-day Iraq. On the one side were supporters and relatives of Imam Hossain, grandson of the Prophet Mohammad and son of Ali ibn Talib, the first Shi'i imam. Ali ibn Talib was Mohammad's son-in-law and first cousin. On the opposing side were the forces of Yazid I, the Umayyad

caliph who ruled the Muslim world at that time. Yazid's forces reportedly numbered over several thousand, while Imam Hossain's group consisted of approximately seventy-five of Mohammad's family members, including men and women, some of whom were very old, and others, very young. The battlefield was a desert region located near a branch of the Euphrates. Imam Hossain was defeated. Most of his men were slain and the women and children taken captive. For Shi'i Muslims, the Battle of Karbala stands as one of the most significant battles in history. It is commemorated annually for ten days during the month of Muharram and culminates on the tenth day, known as Ashura, the day when Imam Hossain reportedly died of his wounds.

11. I found these notes in a booklet titled *Simaye Hijab* (Face of the Veil) (Tehran: Ma'avenate Mobareze ba mafasede ijtima'iye naja [Ministry of Fight against Immorality], 1373 H.), 17.

12. Kamran Schot Aghaie, *The Martyrs of Karbala: Shi'i Symbols and Rituals in Modern Iran* (Seattle: University of Washington Press, 2004), 115.

13. A large segment of Iraq's Muslim population belongs to the Shi'i sect.

14. Faegheh Shirazi, *The Veil Unveiled: The Hejab in Modern Culture* (Gainesville: University Press of Florida, 2003), 95.

15. Kamran Scot Aghaie, "Gendered Aspects of the Emergence and Historical Development of Shi'i Symbols and Rituals," in *The Martyrs of Karbala*, 13–14.

16. Ibid., 97.

17. Ibid., 62.

18. The identity of the background images is unmistakable. The young boy's face lacks facial hair, indicating adolescence. The white-bearded man is clearly an elderly figure, while the figure closest to the foreground could be a husband. Note the direction of the woman's gaze. She appears anxious and is communicating this anxiety directly to the spectator with her eyes.

19. Shirazi, *The Veil Unveiled*, 97–98.

20. The translation of *hameh ba ham jehad-e sazandegi* is "together move forward to rebuild."

21. The poster is reprinted in Chelkowski and Dabashi, *Staging a Revolution*, 10.

22. Mostafa Goodarzi, comp., *A Decade with Painters of the Islamic Revolution, 1979–1989* (Tehran: Art Centre of the Islamic Propagation Organization, 1989). Naser Palangi's art is presented and discussed on pp. 180 and 182.

23. Chelkowski and Dabashi, *Staging a Revolution*, 102.

24. While being led to Yazid's court as a prisoner of war, Zaynab publicly recited the tragic events of the Battle of Karbala. This eloquent recitation resulted in great public sympathy for the death of her brother Imam Hossain and the alleged seventy-five other individuals who died in the historic battle.

25. Abolfazl Aliy, comp., *A Decade with the Graphists of the Islamic Revolution, 1979–1989* (Tehran: Art Centre of the Islamic Propagation Organization, 1989).

26. Ibid., 161.

27. Goodarzi, *A Decade with Painters of the Islamic Revolution*, 85–86.

28. Since the beginning of the Islamic Republic Revolution every cemetery in Iran has

reserved exclusive plots for those given the title *shahid,* or martyr. These martyrs are buried free of charge, and the plots are maintained and guarded by the government.

29. Aliy, *A Decade with the Graphists of the Islamic Revolution.*

30. In Iran the red gladiola is traditionally placed on Islamic grave sites to honor the dead.

31. The Ka'ba is the holiest site in Islam. The *qibla,* or direction that Muslims face during daily prayer, is oriented toward the Ka'ba. It is around the Ka'ba that Muslims perform the ritual of circling seven times—during the Hajj (pilgrimage) season, as well as during the Umrah (lesser pilgrimage).

32. The white tuberose is another flower traditionally used to adorn grave sites in Iran.

33. The artwork discussed in this reference is printed on p. 131.

34. Aliy, *A Decade with the Graphists of the Islamic Revolution.*

35. Chelkowski and Dabashi, *Staging a Revolution,* 235.

36. Ali Shariati, *Shariati on Shariati and the Muslim Woman,* trans. Laleh Bakhtiar (Chicago: ABC Group International, 1996), 205.

37. Ibid.

38. See color photo in Aghaie's *The Martyrs of Karbala,* n.p. The caption reads: "Women participating in the central procession holding banners with political and religious slogans. They also carry jars of water, to quench symbolically the thirst of Hoseyn and his followers, and shovels to bury symbolically the martyrs."

39. www.tehrantimes.com/index_View.asp?code=172605.

40. www.persiatours.com/museums_tehran_behesht_zahra.htm.

41. http://en.wikipedia.org/wiki/Iran_Cultural_Heritage_Organization#Some_ICHO_Museums_and_Palaces.

42. Numerous postage stamps with images of veiled Iranian women were published exclusively for international use. It is in this context that I refer to the Iranian woman as a foreign ambassador presenting a "pious" image of Iran to the world.

43. See Shirazi, "Iranian Politics and the Hijab," in *The Veil Unveiled,* 88–109.

7

WIDOWS' DOOMSDAY
Women and War in the Poetry of Hassan al-Nassar

ABBAS KADHIM

I don't hear the women,
I only hear the screaming of their wombs.

— HASSAN AL-NASSAR

Two wars and a decade of economic sanctions define the generation of Iraqi poets to which Hassan al-Nassar belongs. The initial four decades of his lifetime signaled profound changes in Iraq: the pains of poverty in the 1960s, the relative economic prosperity in the 1970s, the 1980s wartime era, and finally, the economic sanctions in the 1990s. These years left an indelible mark on his generation; however, it was the 1980s and 1990s especially that strongly influenced Al-Nassar and his fellow poets.

From the early days of the Iraq-Iran war (1980–1988), the regime of Saddam Hussein recognized that poetry and song could play a significant role in terms of manipulating the masses. Musicians and singers were expected to "produce" songs for every occasion and every battle—often with only a single day's notice.[1]

One group that was drafted to support the war effort included poets who wrote in the vernacular Iraqi Arabic. Ironically, the Iraqi regime had denied those poets permission to form an association prior to the war. However, as soon as their potential contribution to the war effort became clear, Saddam Hussein designated them—along with the entire war-song industry—the Eighth Division in Iraq's army. With this recognition came a plethora of perks and privileges, including generous salaries, bonuses, cars, farms, and handguns. These privileges were often earned at a high price. For example, Hadi al-ʿAkayshi, one of the rising stars among Saddam's poets, was stabbed more than a hundred times by pro-Iranian religious activists in the holy city of Najaf.

Al-ʿAkayshi, a Shiʿi from Najaf, crossed the sectarian lines by making Ayatullah Khomeini the subject of his sharp satire. Another talented poet, who sold his soul to the regime, was Falah ʿAskar, a Shiʿi from Hilla. ʿAskar, a true sycophant, praised Saddam for having the influence of Al-ʿAbbas (the son of Imam Ali and one of the most revered icons of Shiʿism). ʿAskar was captured during the 1991 uprising and met a dreadful fate at the hands of an angry crowd.

Hassan al-Nassar belonged to a distinctly unique group of intellectuals, poets who wrote in standard Arabic. For the most part, Saddam's propaganda experts deemed their poetry too sophisticated and, therefore, less valuable in mobilizing the masses. The majority of this group saw the regime's lack of interest in their work as a blessing in disguise. Because these poets wrote and published poetry on virtually every topic except war, quite a number of them faced the potential wrath of a police state. Indeed, neutrality was viewed as merely another form of opposition. In this tenuous environment of mutual distrust between the regime and the intellectuals who professed neutrality, poetry was nevertheless created, and served as a reflection of the 1980s era. After Saddam's fall, some individuals charged the war generation with "taking refuge in the language," accusing them of averting risk by not addressing the tangible aspects of daily life.[2] In fact, many poets led a double life; they were the regime's mouthpieces in broad daylight and revolutionary poets in private. Only a handful of trusted confidants knew of their clandestine efforts. In the words of a leading Iraqi critic:

> A cursory look at the poetic experience in the 1980s should cause us to be shocked by the obsession with experimentation, the testing of the aspects of modernist poetry and the preoccupation with the crafting of the potency of the prose poem. But no one spared a moment to examine the hundreds of thousands of burnt bodies at the borders.[3]

No one could make this type of accusation against Hassan al-Nassar, whose contributions are unquestionable. It should be noted that, aside from his remarkable talent, he possessed all the necessary tools of a well-educated poet, overcoming the general curse of his generation of poets, which was that many of them lacked rigorous training in classical Arabic. Al-Nassar engaged in arduous study of the Arabic language at the University of Baghdad, from which he graduated in 1994. Afterwards he taught Arabic language and literature for a living.

Controversy swirled around Al-Nassar, primarily for two reasons. First, his collection *Widows' Doomsday* was selected (along with two other works) from fifty-eight manuscripts for the coveted Abd al-Wahhab al-Bayyati Award in

1999.[4] Second, he chose an unconventional topic for his poetry: it was dedicated almost entirely to the hopes and sorrows of the Iraqi women whose lives were changed irrevocably by war.

In 1994 the regime placed Hassan al-Nassar under surveillance after he submitted his poetry collection, *Dark Poems,* for publication in Baghdad. Al-Nassar recalled being summoned before the officer in charge of reviewing such manuscripts prior to their release and receiving a lecture on the need to write poetry supporting the war effort and Saddam Hussein. The not so subtle message was clearly conveyed; Al-Nassar had to prove to the authorities that his failure to write on these topics was merely an oversight, not intentional. The remedy for this "oversight" was prescribed: a plethora of poems written for various state occasions that, of course, Al-Nassar had no intention of writing.[5] Prudently, he took the warning seriously and departed Iraq for Libya, where, in exile, he taught Arabic, wrote poetry, and published freely without fear of censorship by or retaliation from the Iraqi regime. His mind was already made up; no number of words could possibly defeat Saddam's totalitarian stranglehold, as he had hoped when writing the following:

Always . . .
We imagine the scorpion
bigger than its real size.
That is why we step on it
with words.[6]

The Abd al-Wahhab al-Bayyati Award was named for the poet Abd al-Wahhab al-Bayyati, a founder of the free verse movement in Arabic poetry—along with his fellow Iraqi poets, Badr Shakir al-Sayyab and Nazik al-Mala'ika. At this point, Al-Nassar came under attack from a number of Iraqi papers, including a weekly publication whose editor in chief was Saddam Hussein's son. This newspaper published an editorial titled "Hassan al-Nassar: From Black Poems to a Disreputable Award." The article states in part:

It seems that the poet, Hassan al-Nassar, is the most recent joiner of this group of poets who look for petty gains and the wonders of "new homelands." We heard that the aforementioned poet has spent five years in the dark caves of Africa, during which period he did everything but be an excellent and patriotic poet. . . . Finally, we heard that Al-Nassar has won a disreputable literary award (Al-Bayyati Award) for his most recent poetry collection (*The Widows*). It is self-evident that this award is indecent and financed by groups that have no relation to literature whatsoever. Thus, dry leaves fall one after the other without affecting the tree of Iraqi poetry. Indeed, this fall is a healthy sign of the vivacious tree of Iraqi poetry.[7]

The editorial's jingoism reflects an era of inverted values during which no citizen was allowed to question the state, and no morality was held above state morality. Patriotism, for the regime's henchmen, meant loyalty to Saddam and his destructive policies and unconditional support for his war effort. Eight editorials from five different countries came to Al-Nassar's defense, underscoring his merit and prodigious talent.

The editorial reference to the collection's title as merely *The Widows* is telling. It attempts to trivialize the collection and implies insignificance of the subject—the widow. In Iraqi parlance, a widow signifies extreme vulnerability, someone surely deserving of pity. This is precisely what Al-Nassar's poetry calls into question. In a stern outburst, he writes:

> When the night fails
> darkness stands—fully awake
> at the feet of the widows
> This is what happened in Baghdad . . .
> And before their eyes—
> the eyes of the new widows
> my eyes blink in defeat.

Al-Nassar's widows are strong and resilient, in spite of their suffering. They tame fear (darkness), which stands "fully awake" at their feet like a watchdog. Furthermore, their gaze is steadfast, with eyes that never blink first. Defeating pity and inverting the social paradigm with a powerfully stoic acceptance, these are the widows who meet adversity with unique resourcefulness:

> the widows are bridges
> under them flow the rivers of sorrow.

Only the widows can stretch like bridges over "the rivers of sorrow." The widows themselves do not pass across the bridge but rather help others to cross. While these individuals continue on their life journeys untouched by sorrow, the widows alone continue to define sorrow's beginning and end. With a Messianic touch, Al-Nassar seems to suggest that the widows suffer that which is unbearable, so that the rest of us may be spared. Sorrow cannot distract them from the flow of life, since they are the guardians of the future and the means of continuity:

for every bullet fired,
a widow of fire is born
and armless orphans
We strap them with school rucksacks
they read about towns whose borders are drawn by guns
and write fear along some shuddering lines
in their shadows hides the homeland!

As the following lines suggest, Iraqi women miss the touch of their warrior-husbands. Al-Nassar hears the screams of unfulfilled wombs crying out for the seeds of life. Their cries are lost in the wilderness, however, and crushed under images of destruction. Hearing the screams of these wombs, the poet's heart opens:

I used to love pregnant women and my wife
they supplied our sidewalks with
little girls carrying school bags
and little boys who scratch the skin of our childhood
    with their teasing . . .
the war is over
catastrophes are over
but lazy women are still all over the country's sidewalks

and fill our nostrils with the smell of their flesh,
burned by the blazes of lust
they still swallow their saliva and the residue of a kiss.[8]

It goes without saying that Al-Nassar's imagery entirely contradicts that promulgated by Saddam's regime: the image of widows as honorary warriors. The propaganda machine insisted that widows participated in battle by proxy, sending their loved ones (and, especially, their sons) to the front. Death for one's country was to be glorified and celebrated, as the following 1980s song illustrates:

The mother of the martyr says,
"I put henna on my hands,
I wish I had a hundred sons
[to sacrifice] for the homeland."

Compare these lyrics with Al-Nassar's protest against the catastrophic consequences of an endlessly brutal war that changes everything and spares no one. Al-Nassar's women are not offering sacrifices for their homeland but rather offering prayers to God, asking that their men return home alive:

> The hearts of our women are graveyards
> and their hands are empty baskets
> A million breasts seduce the Heavens
> and offer sacrifices:
> Our breasts have no chests
> And the river that went dry
> They drape it with black flesh—
> as black as the Sun-disk in the homes of the widows
> They drape its glory with downfall

Saddam's regime carefully manipulated women, making a show of them as symbols of the nation's solidarity—then conveniently dispensing with them once the state's objectives had been achieved. Women in the military and in the Ba'ath militia (the Popular Army) were especially well trained in how to participate appropriately in every ceremonial parade.

As one author noted, combatant women did not make it into the novels and stories of the war.[9] Women represented an auxiliary symbol to be invoked by the state, whenever it became necessary to do so, but the war remained essentially a man's concern. The heroes, generals, and warriors were all men, as were the nation's writers and poets. Even the few women who wrote fiction and poetry during these decades were preoccupied with the deeds of warriors rather than with the grief of women.[10] It is precisely for this reason that Hassan al-Nassar represents a unique and exceedingly important phenomenon. He dedicated his entire poetic experience to the endless sorrow of the widow, and not just any widow, as he makes clear in the following poem:

> O Widows—
> I mean only the widows of war
> Know that the dirtiest fires
> are the fires that mix with lust,
> and the most naked streets
> are those that took off their asphalt
> and wore Lead

The widows of war are unique in the untimely tragedies that befall them and the shocking circumstances of their loss. The stereotype of the widow of war is the one whose husband leaves after the wedding and never returns. Al-Nassar coins a new term in reference to these women, "virgin widows." He uses this term in all his collections; each time, in compelling and shocking contexts. Consider this passage, for example:

> What an almost endless Autumn in this pseudo-city!
> What a special language!
> Who can understand it, other than migrating birds?
> And who will inherit the pain?
> Injuries . . . reproducing for centuries
> in the streets of Lead
> I descend . . .
> I descend to your height, to continue one half of the scene
> At a half wall,
> a virgin widow is cutting from the gown of the night . . .
> to hide in it her tears
> and on inflated wounds like her breasts . . . she leans
> counting on her fingers the centuries of suffering
> in the heart of Zainab . . .

Zainab is the sister of Hussein, the third imam of the Shiʿa Muslims. She is also the granddaughter of the Prophet and the central figure in the tragedy of Karbala. The poet is invoking Zainab's memory not only to stress the tragedy of the situation but also to present several layers of meaning, the most important of which is Zainab's legacy—tragedy passed down through generations of Shiʿa women (Al-Nassar's widows are predominantly Shiʿa). The war disproportionately claimed the lives of their men and thus left them heartbroken:

> War is poverty
> and the bus goes by . . .
> But . . .
> It has not the fare to depart from our town
> War is affluence
> Heads are its gain
> as well as the hearts of virgin widows

Their hearts, like budding roses, are destroyed even before they blossom, open to love. Widows of war are paralyzed by the thin line separating the girl from the woman; hence the brilliance of Al-Nassar's reference to them as "virgin widows" and his use of the powerful image of "wives who are still learning how to kiss":

When the homeland becomes a human torso
pointed at with a pistol
gun powder inhales us
it inhales us . . .
while we are kneeling down
it inhales us in
while we are caught among the lips of our wives
who are still learning how to kiss

Al-Nassar dwells on this same theme in another collection, *And Said Some Women* (2001). Indeed, he dedicated the collection as follows: "To you alone, O Virgin Widow." Again, the Shi'i identity of the women is made apparent by the invocation of the Seventh Imam of the Shi'a, Musa al-Kadhim, who is known among the community by his honorific title, Abu al-Jawadayn (literally, "the father of two generous imams"). Al-Nassar places his young widows at the shrine of Musa al-Kadhim and presents a list of grievances on their behalf. Their husbands have been sent away, to prisons or to forced exile, making the women de facto widows:

O Abu al-Jawadayn!
Those who made widows of us before their death,
divorced us before the marriage
and made the unborn children, in our wombs, orphans[11]

Because the war is everlasting, vicious, and all-consuming, soldiers are doomed to experience only virtual marriages. In the next excerpt, the poet-soldier mixes love and war. His young heart, terrified by mortar shells in an incessant war, gives up all hope and does the unthinkable:

my heart, like a little puppy, stares at you
a mortar's bomb just landed next to it
Who can drape my heart with tranquility?
Guns are yawning on the shoulders of soldiers
and the war is an ever-lit Cuban cigar
I bought for it alone
the Mediterranean clouds, and the Two Rivers

and clothed it with the beaches of the Dead Sea
and the moment I entered a truce with the wind
and kissed the sun's boot
I sold my wife's virginity

In Al-Nassar's third collection, *Stand Up! Sit Down!!* one of the poems is again titled "The Virgin Widow." However, the reference here is actually to Baghdad, that ultimate female presence capturing the imagination of Arab poets for thirteen centuries. Like the consummate virgin widow, Baghdad has lost her heart over the centuries, trampled beneath the feet of invading soldiers and oppressive rulers. In a sense, this poem was Al-Nassar's prophecy of the ineffable tragedy that lay in store for Baghdad. He portrays the city as the confluence of Two Rivers and heir to Iraq's seven-thousand-year history:

Baghdad . . . the virgin
Your quiet secret grows with ease
The lips of my beloved woman at the dawn,
as they recite the prayer
It is said that everything helps create the general
The homeland . . . the people . . . the war
the city itself . . .
even the land participates in the making of a general
and with every general, a new graveyard is born . . .
I say: it is impossible for me to forget you [. . .]
O virgin widow![12]

In conclusion, it must be noted that the poetry of Hassan al-Nassar stands out as a unique phenomenon in modern Iraqi culture—for three reasons. First, Al-Nassar resisted the coercive, alluring incentives to glorify Saddam Hussein's brutal regime. While other Iraqi poets were unable to withstand the temptation of rewards and state patronage and unwilling to face the risk of severe punishment, Al-Nassar stood firm and refused to defend the indefensible. Second, as one of the few poets who managed to successfully evade pursuit by the Iraqi literary police, Al-Nassar courageously continued to "produce poems that had nothing in common with the concurrent war, except for their length," as one literary critic eloquently stated.[13] Al-Nassar drew his poetic experience from the most deeply felt, yet least acknowledged aspects of life: the pains of a prolonged war as they were experienced by the most vulnerable hearts, the widows of war and their orphaned children. Finally, he stepped outside the customary paradigm of Arabic poetry by lending his poetic voice to the widows of war. He did so in defiance, as an act of dissent against a regime that tried to transform these women into symbols of manufactured patriotism. His poetry itself stands as an impeachment of the intellectual callousness of social patriarchy.

NOTES

1. Ja'far al-Khaffaf, a talented composer, who produced more songs for the war than any of his colleagues, told the interviewer for Iraq's state television that he prepared one of his songs on the way to the TV station using the windshield wipers of his car as rhythm.

2. The first to identify this phenomenon was the Iraqi critic Hassan Nadhem in his article, "Phantom Texts and the Violence of Reality," in *Al-Nass wa al Hayat* (The Text and the Life), ed. Hassan Nadhem (Damascus: Dar al mada Press, 2008), 3 ff.

3. Nadhem, *Al-Nass wa al Hayat*, 29.

4. For a biography of Al-Bayyati, see Hassan Nadhem, "Abd al-Wahhab al-Bayyati, in *Biographical Encyclopedia of the Modern Middle East and North Africa,* ed. Michael R. Fischbach (Farmington Hills: Gale Cengage, 2007).

5. Hassan al-Nassar, personal interview, April 24, 2007.

6. Hassan al-Nassar, *Widows' Doomsday* (Beirut: Dar al-Kunuzal-Adabiyya, 1999), 5.

7. "Hassan al-Nassar: From Black Poems to a Disreputable Award," *Al-Rafidayn Weekly,* November 28, 2000.

8. Hassan al-Nassar, *Stand Up! Sit Down!!* (Beirut: Al-Muassa al Arabiyya li 'Dirasat wa 'l-Nashr), 21.

9. Miriam Cooke, *Women and the War Story* (Berkeley: University of California Press, 1997), 252. Quoting an Iraqi source, Cooke states that the number of Iraqi women in the Popular Army in 1982 was 4,000. One could also mention the presence of women in the Iraqi Air Force and other supporting military services.

10. As an exception, the works of Iraqi novelist Lutfiyya al-Dulaimi are significant and noteworthy.

11. Hassan al-Nassar, *And Said Some Women* (Traun, Austria: Dhifaf, 2001), 111.

12. Al-Nassar, *Stand Up! Sit Down!!* 113.

13. Nadhem, *Al-Nass wa al Hayat,* 35.

8

IMAGES AND STATUS
Visualizing Iraqi Women

NADA SHABOUT

Images of the destruction of Iraq's culture and society continue to arrive via television and the Internet. They announce a fatal crisis, particularly in view of the new rhetoric of occupation, sectarianism, insecurity, and instability. Yet various scenarios all advocating a new, improved, liberated, and democratized Iraq have been continuously disseminated as a sign of a successful mission by Western media and as preached and perhaps believed by the U.S. government.

In place of authentic Iraqi texts and voices, the media bombard us with images of the "new Iraq." At this critical juncture in history, as 2007 reveals an Iraq facing political disarray and civil war, we would do well to heed W. J. T. Mitchell's warning of the fallibility of pictures.[1] Perhaps an appropriate question to ask would be, What kind of [visual] objects does the new empire produce, depend on, and desire? Given the West's historical obsession with gender issues in Middle Eastern societies, it is no surprise that Iraqi women and their "image" have taken center stage in contemporary rhetorical battles. Seen by all as signifiers of cultural progress, Muslim women and their changing roles are often challenged and contested by their countries of origin and the West alike. They are "women of cover." The manner in which they appear and dress in public is seen by the West as problematic and a sure sign of oppression.[2] Their representation in Western media has been conditioned from the beginning by preconceived political ideologies and is disputed and resented by the women themselves.

The case becomes further complicated when considering women artists and their roles in forming culture. While little is known about contemporary Middle Eastern art in general, even less is known about the importance of women in the region's visual arts. The roles these women play in the field of visual arts are conspicuously absent from Middle Eastern studies and from gender studies as well. This chapter analyzes and compares various representations of Iraqi women resulting from rhetorical objectives aimed at shaping the "ideal Iraqi woman." It also discusses the changing roles and shifting status of Iraqi women artists, especially as they challenge these stereotypes.

GENDER IDENTITY IN IRAQ

Traditional nations, Arab ones included, value women as "biological producers of culture," as well as symbols of the continuity of traditional ideals.[3] Nevertheless, in Iraq's modern history women have been able to achieve much in terms of rights and authority. There are several well-known individual cases, the most famous being Naziha al-Delaimy, a physician, who in 1959 became Iraq's (and the Arab world's) first female minister (minister of municipalities). She was an inspiration to Iraqi women to organize the struggle for women's rights. Indeed, the lives of ordinary Iraqi women demonstrate countless examples of determination, assertiveness, and success.

During the construction of Iraq as a modern nation, women were perceived as an important contributive force. The first half of the twentieth century marked a surge in women's education, followed by a marked interest and fuller participation in political life.[4] Mobilization against Western imperialism, the fervor of Arab nationalism, and the rumblings of revolution were responsible for the creation of a number of women's organizations. Some of these organizations were affiliated with various political parties, such as the Iraqi Communist Party's Rabitat al-Mara al-Iraqiyah (League for the Defense of Iraqi Women's Rights) in 1959 and the Arab Socialist Ba'ath Party's General Federation of Iraqi Women in 1968.[5]

The strategic empowerment of Iraqi women under state-sponsored feminism continued and at times intensified under the Socialist Ba'ath Party. The latter exercised its power through rhetoric and policies that focused on encouraging women's participation in government, industry, and society in general.[6] One need look no further than the words of Saddam Hussein to recall this position: "The complete emancipation of women from ties which held them back in the past, during the ages of despotism and ignorance, is a basic aim of the party and the revolution."[7]

The Iraq-Iran war, however, caused the Ba'ath party position to shift. Instead of being acknowledged as powerful contributors to nation building, Iraqi women were slowly relegated to being "mothers of future soldiers" and eventually "mothers of martyrs." Women were no longer regarded as necessary civic participants. Instead, their only value lay in performing a biological God-given duty; i.e., reproduction. Thus the 1970s rhetoric espousing the equality of women and men, especially the significance of building a nation-state together, changed in the 1980s to that of a nation of militarized men defending weak, vulnerable Iraqi women. The 1990s, which witnessed the most comprehensive sanctions ever imposed on a country, called forth a new image of Iraq as a malnourished woman, weak and beaten. As expected, the wars were "fought by men in Iraq and suffered by women."[8] Moreover, the Gulf Wars ushered in "Islam" as a state ideology, thus imposing additional limitations on women in the name of religion, morality, and tradition.

Many of the new restrictions on women's rights became accepted norms for the generation that followed and a departure point for a number of political parties in the aftermath of the 2003 U.S.-led invasion and occupation of Iraq. The fragmented policies of the post-2003 Iraqi government have supported a favored colonial theme, positioning women as markers of social change and simultaneously exploiting them as symbols of defiance against U.S. occupation.

CONTEMPORARY IMAGES OF IRAQI WOMEN

Since the fall of the Ba'ath regime in April 2003, Iraqi women have been caught between two extreme and sometimes opposing rhetorical arguments. At one end is a practical discourse based on the deplorable lack of security and stability in the country. To keep women safe requires a higher level of restriction on women's freedom—be it freedom of speech, dress, or movement. This position is perhaps rooted in the Iraqi Shia coalition's desire for a substantive Sharia role in civil law. On the other side is an ideal rhetoric, with lofty promises of freedom and equality promoted and intensified by the increasing number of Iraqi women's organizations. These organizations advocate a stronger political role for women and a leading part in the country's reconstruction.

Riverbend, the infamous Iraqi female blogger, was able to present a more honest account of life in Iraq than any of the staged media reports. Here is an excerpt from her *Baghdad Burning, Girl Blog from Iraq*, dated August 23, 2003:

> Females can no longer leave their homes alone. Each time I go out, either a father, uncle, or cousin has to accompany me. It feels like we've gone back 50 years since the beginning of the occupation. A woman or girl, out alone, is at risk. An outing has to be arranged at least an hour beforehand. . . . I am female and Muslim. Before the occupation, I more or less dressed the way

I wanted to. I lived in jeans and cotton pants and comfortable shirts. Now, I don't dare leave the house in pants. A long skirt and loose shirt (preferably with long sleeves) has become necessary. A girl wearing jeans risks being attacked, abducted, or insulted by fundamentalists who have been . . . liberated! . . . Before the war, around 50% of the college students were females, and over 50% of the working force was composed of women. Not so any more. We are seeing an increase of fundamentalism in Iraq which is terrifying. For example, before the war, I would estimate (roughly) that about 55% of females in Baghdad wore a hijab—or headscarf. Hijabs do not signify fundamentalism. That is far from the case—although I myself don't wear one, I have family and friends who do. The point is that, before, it didn't really matter. It was "my" business whether I wore one or not—not the business of some fundamentalist on the street.[9]

Despite the free elections in January 2005, the Human Rights Organization reported that "the lawlessness and increased killings, abductions and rapes that followed the overthrow of the government of Saddam Hussein have restricted women's freedom of movement and their ability to go to school or to work."[10] Images of Iraqi women today are engulfed in the rhetoric of oppression, weakness, and lost rights. The U.S.-based Iraqi artist Leila Kubba contrasts the women she remembers from pre-invasion Iraq with the ones she encountered on her visit to Iraq in 2004. Kubba laments that these "bearers of the consequences of war," further burdened by "wearing *abayas*," now haunt and invade her paintings.[11]

It is most interesting to witness the metamorphosis of Orientalism as applied to images of today's "Oriental" women. Women of the Middle East, especially in the aftermath of Said's *Orientalism*,[12] have stopped being the sexual objects of desire and lust. In the newly constructed narrative of Iraq's culture, they have been transformed into unfortunate objects of pity. As in Afghanistan, there has been an immediate mobilization to "save and liberate Iraqi women."[13] Under the Western/American gaze, Iraqi women remain subjugated, and the specific intention is to liberate them to the status of American women. In other words, the new colonial rhetoric of the "democratizing project" that replaced that of the old colonial "civilizing project" has been extended to Iraqi women, perpetuating the dominant binary oppositions favored by the West. Instrumental in this project is the role played by expatriate Iraqi women. The Iraqi novelist and activist Haifa Zangana includes them in her designation "new colonial women." They are the women who accompanied or followed the U.S.-led forces into Iraq after long years of discontinuity. Many had good intentions, but their vision of Iraqi women is processed through American filters that largely misinterpret Iraq's social dynamics and women's roles in their society.

Photos of tortured Iraqi women at Abu Ghraib only validate the scenario of the oppressed Iraqi woman. Most narratives advanced by Western sympathizers overemphasize the victimized women's subsequent fate within their families (i.e., the horrific tradition of honor killing and Iraq's social definition of rape), while downplaying the act of torture itself and neglecting the dynamics that facilitated the violation in the first place.[14]

The "language" of photos appearing in the Western media around the time of the Iraqi constitutional debate—a debate that advocated women's participation and rights—necessarily reinforces the two conflicting rhetorical positions mentioned above.[15] An immediate and apparent contradiction between street and political rhetoric becomes obvious. All photos seem to have a similar composition: an Iraqi woman is shown on the street with a poster in the background of a powerful young secular woman. The young woman in the poster holds the promise of equal rights and gender liberation, in contrast to the real-life Iraqi woman (or women), dressed in the traditional *abaya*. The real-life figure(s) exhibit signs of age, fatigue, and worry and walks by with a bag of groceries or squats on the curb in front of the poster.[16] Several postings by U.S. bloggers questioned this visible disparity. One wonders if the aim of these posters and their appearance on the Internet spoke more to Western desires than Iraqi actualities. Were they simply the result of a Western public relations effort? Or were they perhaps an optimistic promise to Iraqi women that the "good old days" will return?

IRAQI WOMEN AND THE VISUAL ARTS:
A BRIEF OVERVIEW

The fall of the Baʿath regime in April 2003 devastated most Iraqi institutions and had an impact on the lives of all Iraqis. It is no exaggeration to suggest that Iraqi culture has suffered alteration to the point of complete destruction.[17] Cultural institutions, including museums and those who patronize such institutions, are now nonexistent. Consequently, creativity has been put on hold.

But where would Iraqi women artists fit within the discourse of changing social dynamics? Along with other aspects of culture, visual representations will most certainly be a strong candidate for reassessment within a stronger religious current. In a number of Iraq's neighboring nations, religious fundamentalism has had an impact on the development of the visual arts through the use of censorship and the endorsement of commercial abstraction and *horoufiah* works favored by the new art market of the Gulf region.[18] Yet if women are banned from participating in the so-called Iraqi reconstruction process, what artistic roles can possibly evolve for Iraqi women artists?

Visual expression has always been a leading force in the history of political and social change. The visual arts were undeniably instrumental in forging new Iraqi cultural icons during the 1950s search for visual identity.[19] A number of Iraqi women artists stand as pioneers; certainly their contributions and influence deserve further evaluation and elaboration. Madiha Omar (1908–2005) and Suad al-Attar (b. 1942) were two such women artists. In the 1940s Madiha Omar's work was the precursor to the popular trend of modern visual manipulations of the Arabic letter. Born in Syria in 1908 and orphaned at the age of four, she later moved to Baghdad to join her newly wedded sister. She became a naturalized Iraqi citizen in 1930 and was the first female to receive a European education funded by an Iraqi government scholarship. In Europe, she trained as a teacher but studied art on the side. After marrying an Iraqi diplomat in 1939, she moved with him to Washington, D.C., where she studied art at George Washington University and the Corcoran Art School. It was in the United States that she first embarked on her experimentations with the Arabic letter. Most of Omar's work remains undocumented, and, tragically, two hundred pieces of her work were destroyed, along with her house, in the U.S. bombing during the Gulf War.[20]

Suad al-Attar is one of Iraq's most renowned artists. Painting from an early age, her work was introduced to Baghdad society and artists through exhibitions at her high school. Supported and encouraged by Iraq's avant-garde Jawad Salim, she was accepted by and participated in many of the exhibitions that coined Iraq's modern art iconography. She was one of the few women artists involved in many of the functions organized by the Baghdad Modern Art Group. Her work introduced an introspective dimension to visual folkloric investigations explored by her male colleagues.[21] Much of her work, which she left behind in her Baghdad house when she relocated to London, has been looted.

Iraqi modern art suffered a blow in June 1993 with the death of the Iraqi artist Laila al-Attar, director of the former Saddam Center for the Arts (the Iraqi Museum of Modern Art). She and her husband were killed in the U.S. bombing of Baghdad; their daughter was blinded in the attack.

Laila's work was renowned not only in Iraq but also throughout the entire Arab world. She has also been acknowledged for her substantial contributions to the advancement of women's rights. A daring and adventurous

FIGURE 8.1

Suad al-Attar, 1988. Oil on canvas. From the collection of the Iraqi Museum of Modern Art. Image from database collected by author

visual artist, Laila wrote the following about her work: "I am trying to bring into the society the role of women, the dignity of their existence, and their humanity by means of lines blended with waves of color, sincere feelings, and true wishes."[22] The styles of these two gifted sisters (Suad and Laila) present modern articulations and syntheses of Mesopotamian and Islamic aesthetics, expressed in two distinct and personal styles. Their work explores the inner feminine world in expressive surrealistic styles that mix fantasy and myth with reality.

A large number of Iraqi women artists were represented in the collection of the Iraqi Museum of Modern Art. Nevertheless, as is the case with other realms of Iraqi life and culture, there are conflicting narratives about "art under Saddam." On the one hand, most Iraqi artists contend that they had complete freedom to create what they desired.[23] On the other hand, one encounters contradictory statements on the Internet, such as the following by Malak Jamil: "Few women had the opportunity to participate in art exhibitions and cultural activities during the last regime. It is high time that women contributed to the scene along with the men; after all, we have many female artists in Iraq."[24]

FIGURE 8.2
Suad al-Attar, London, 2007. Photo courtesy of author

VISUAL ARTIST HANAA' MALALLAH:
REFUSING GENDER LABELS

Hanaa' Malallah is one of the few Iraqi women artists who chose to remain in Baghdad, continuing her professional activity and staying committed to her artistic vocation during long years of sanctions and war. Hanaa' was fully trained at Iraqi art institutions, attaining artistic maturity in the 1990s. She received her undergraduate degrees in graphic arts and painting from the Baghdad Academy of Fine Arts in 1978 and 1988. She was awarded a doctorate in the philosophy of painting in February 2005 from the College of Fine Arts of Baghdad University. She held her first one-woman show in Baghdad in 1987. Since that time she has been widely exhibited in Iraq and the Arab world, as well as in key European cities.

Hanaa' is classified as part of the eighties generation of Iraqi artists. What distinguishes this generation from the preceding ones is their imposed physical and intellectual isolation, courtesy of three decades of war. Hanaa', however, credits this isolation to having led her generation's return to their ancient Mesopotamian heritage. She insists that this return was not the consequence of "nostalgia" but rather "a conscious return to the roots made more palpable existentially and creatively by the precarious realities that have continued to bear on every aspect of their lives."[25] She evaluates this return as the generation's effort to reconcile the contradictions they faced in a glorious past and a ruinous present.

Hanaa' refuses to be evaluated on the basis of her gender. As a devotee to the "death of the author" theory, she is vehemently opposed to gendering art. She sees herself as a member of the Iraqi art force, whose work must be evaluated on its own merit.[26] Yet she is well aware that women artists need a stronger presence in Iraq's art history. For the lack of a better term, Hanaa' is considered an abstract artist, an identification that she adamantly contests. Hanaa' did not pursue abstraction as an artistic style. Her representations embody epistemological understanding of the things represented and not their image. Versed in semiological analysis, she follows in the conceptual and contemplative footsteps of the late Shakir Hassan Al Said, one of Iraq's most influential and prolific artists, theoreticians, and art historians, as well as a cofounder of the Baghdad Modern Art Group.

To Hanaa', visual expression is necessary to counter what she perceives as "memories' erasure."[27] Nevertheless, she constantly pushes beyond the boundaries of painting. Her interest in the visual is propelled by a strong intellectual curiosity and discontent with the visible and by a need to tran-

FIGURE 8.3

*Hanaa' Malallah and Dia Azzawi at "Sophisticated Ways: Destruction of an Ancient City,"
June 6–September 6, 2007, Aya Gallery, London. Photo courtesy of author*

FIGURE 8.4
Hanaa' Malallah, Map of Baghdad, *2007. Photo courtesy of author*

scend and investigate past and future connections. Some of her earlier work researched the visual possibilities inherent in Sufi talismanic creations and numerical associations and incantations. Her work, however, displayed equal concern with tactile and graphic qualities.

In a March 2005 joint exhibition at Al-Athar Art Gallery in Baghdad, Hanaa' continued her deconstructive experiments. She dedicated her work to what she viewed as "a series of stylistic deviations," a process by which she obliterates her role as a painter, or the person responsible for the creation of the work. She does this by eliminating the borders of the painting and transcending to the realm of "nonpainting," where she becomes a mere element in the process. Her objectives include physically transforming the surface of the work from a traditional fixed format to an adjustable and exchangeable object—allowing the viewer to forsake the traditional "viewing" experience by becoming an active participant in shaping the new form, through handling it, folding it, or moving it.

Another of her experiments investigated the episteme of the ornamentation on the prayer rug. In these works, she continued the investigations she initiated in her doctoral dissertation, centered on a search for the logical and mathematical structure of Mesopotamian art. Hanaa''s prayer rug is made of canvas and paper and folded into a thin flat codex. Its rich geometric designs are transformed into simplified and abstracted ancient Mesopotamian symbols. The weave of rich colors characteristic of prayer rugs is replaced by the solidity of black, a color present in all of her work. For many Iraqi artists, the color black has become synonymous with Iraq itself (*ardh al-Sawad,* the black earth). Aside from the association of black with grief and martyrdom and its cultural presence in *abayas* and religious symbolism, this hue became Hanaa''s preference by the same process of negation that delivered her to the nonobject of the intangible, or spiritual, dimension.

While Hanaa' has always preferred working alone in her studio and for long hours, she was forced into this seclusion after 2003 because of concerns for personal safety. As a result, her art was affected by her daily realities. While she continued to explore forms and their transformations, images that immediately surrounded her replaced those of historical or contemplative realities. The burning of Baghdad affected her immensely, to the extent that she began to research and interpret visually the many times Baghdad had been burned throughout history. She documented twenty-two historical incidents.[28] Yet the most horrific of all her Baghdad experiences has been the 2003 looting and destruction of the Iraqi National Museum. To Hanaa', the museum was a focal point in Iraq's visual education, especially during the years of isolation. Since 2003 Hanaa' has dedicated a series of works to this topic, in an effort to process an incomprehensible act that she perceives as a direct attack on Iraq's national identity. The looting of the Iraqi museum under the watchful eyes of the U.S. military eliminated any notions she might have entertained of a civilized West.

As a lecturer in graphic art at the Institute of Fine Arts, Hanaa' opted not to accept a 2005 offer to become a visiting professor at the College of Fine Arts at the University of Jordan. The new position would have provided peace of mind and mobility. However, she chose to remain in Iraq, facing restrictions on her movement and on her efforts to preserve Iraq's modern heritage. Hanaa' was involved in a short-lived organization concerned with "Iraqi artists' memory," an attempt at documentation and restoration following the nearly complete destruction of the Iraqi Museum of Modern Art, its content and archives.[29] Yet this effort was doomed from the beginning due to the absence of security.

Eventually Hanaa' applied for a visa to attend the opening of a contemporary art exhibition that included her work and which was organized by the University of North Texas. Hanaa' had to endure difficulties and threats to her safety in order to make the several trips needed to the U.S. Embassy in Amman, Jordan, since the embassy in Baghdad processed only government-related affairs. While thrilled that she no longer needed a *muhrum* (a man who is not forbidden to her) to accompany her outside of Iraq, she soon realized how dangerous it was for a woman to travel alone.[30]

Today, Hanaa' fears for her life should she return to Baghdad. At the institute, only a few classes meet, and there are certainly no new opportunities for creativity. In London, Hanaa' is embarking on a new series of works centered on the Iraqi flag. Interestingly, while in Iraq, Hanaa''s references to Iraqi heritage had been through aesthetic investigations into the evolution of symbolism. Now outside of Iraq, she continues with aesthetics experimentation, this time, however, through direct use of national imagery.

CONCLUSION

Given the general chaos in Iraq and the unpredictability of its future, Iraqi artists have thus far been unable to secure a place for themselves. Moreover, many have been forced to leave the country because of threats against their lives and the lives of their families. The systematic destruction of Iraqi intellectual life has forced many artists, male and female, to flee. Those who have no choice but to remain are completely without support, as no institutional structure currently exists for either the performing or the visual arts.

The unity enjoyed by Iraqi artists in the 1980s, based on their shared isolation and repression, has been completely shattered. Following the collapse of Saddam's regime, there seemed to be a moment of hope, but that optimism has long since evaporated under the ongoing violence and growing religious fundamentalism. "Artists are shying away from nudes and other subjects that might offend Islamic sensibilities," Al-Sabti says.[31] A new trend towards religious painting is developing instead.

Women artists are especially feeling the brunt of the situation. Increasingly concerned about their physical well-being and personal safety, they have been forced to abandon their artistic endeavors and "remain under the radar." Even if this situation is only temporary, the ramifications will have long-term effects on the future of contemporary Iraqi art. Moreover, the images of Iraqi

FIGURE 8.5
Khalid al-Rahal, The Mother *(1950s) after restoration. Baghdad, Iraq.*
Photo courtesy of author.

women, images that were once carved in stone around the city of Baghdad in the forms of Kahramana and Shehrezad—strong and sensual creations by Iraq's most renowned sculptors—have long been replaced. Today, in the name of democracy, the projected image of the Iraqi woman as weak and needy is being codified and enforced.[32]

NOTES

1. W. J. T. Mitchell, *What Do Pictures Want? The Lives and Loves of Images* (Chicago: University of Chicago Press, 2006).

2. President George W. Bush, "Bush Gives Update on War against Terrorism," CNN .com/USA (October 11, 2001). http://archives.cnn.com/2001/US/10/11/gen.bush .transcript/ (accessed April 20, 2007).

3. I borrow this definition from Nadje al-Ali.

4. It is reported that the first Women's Grammar and High School in Iraq was established in 1899. See Jacqueline S. Ismael and Shereen T. Ismael, "Gender and State in Iraq,"

in *Gender and Citizenship in the Middle East,* ed. Suad Joseph (Syracuse, NY: Syracuse University Press, 2000), 186.

5. For detailed accounts of women's perceptions and roles in the Iraqi political scene, see Nadje al-Ali, *Iraqi Women: Untold Stories from 1948 to the Present* (London: Zed Books, 2007), 56–108.

6. Ismael and Ismael, "Gender and State in Iraq," 207.

7. Saddam Hussein, *The Revolution and Women in Iraq,* trans. Khalid Kishtany (Baghdad: Translation and Foreign Languages Publishing House, 1981); quoted in Al-Ali, *Iraqi Women,* 131. Article 12 of the general principles of the Ba'ath Party states: "Arab women are entitled to all the advantages awarded them through civil rights. The Party will help them to fight for full access to these rights."

8. Ismael and Ismael, "Gender and State in Iraq," 202.

9. Riverbend, *Baghdad Burning: Girl Blog from Iraq,* "Saturday August 23, 2003: We've Only Just Begun . . . ," 16.

10. Jeremy Lovell, "Amnesty: Iraqi Women No Better Off Post-Saddam," February 22, 2005. www.commondreams.org/headlines05/0222-08.htm (accessed April 21, 2007).

11. Courtney C. Radsch, "Artist Looks at Her Native Iraq behind Women's Veils," *New York Times,* March 21, 2005. http://proquest.uni.com/pqdweb?did=810622051&sid=1&Fmt=3&clientld=87&RQT=309&VName=PDQ (accessed April 20, 2007).

12. See Edward Said, *Orientalism* (New York: Vintage Books, 1994). Prior to publication of Said's book, the term "Orientalism" was generally employed to signify either scholastic studies of the "Orient" or a school of painting consisting of mostly European artists who visited the Middle East and North Africa. Said argued that in both cases the term signified the West's preconceived notions of what the "inferior Orient" should look like, creating a binary opposite that continuously asserted the "self" (the West) against the "other" (the Muslim sphere of the globe).

13. Lila Abu-Lughod, "Do Muslim Women Really Need Saving?" *American Anthropologist* 104, no. 3 (2002): 783–790.

14. See Mary Ann Tetreault, "The Sexual Politics of Abu Ghraib: Hegemony, Spectacle, and the Global War on Terror." *NWSA Journal* 18, no. 3 (Fall XXXX): 33–50; Lila Rajiva, "Iraqi Women and Torture, Part IV Gendered Propaganda, the Propaganda of Gender," www.dissidentvoice.org (August 9, 2004). www.dissidentvoice.org/Aug04/Rajiva0809.htm (accessed April 20, 2007).

15. See photo at "Iraq Constitution-Making: What Happens Now?" (August 23, 2005), Iraq Working Group. www.usip.org/events/2005/0823_constitution.html (accessed April 20, 2007).

16. *Abaya* was not always viewed as a sign of oppression. It was the traditional overgarment worn by Iraqi women. During the mid-twentieth century, most young women abandoned it in favor of completely Western attire, but older women, especially traditional women, continued to wear it in public.

17. See Nada Shabout, "The Iraqi Museum of Modern Art: Ethical Implications," *Collections: A Journal for Museum and Archives Professionals from the Practical to the Philo-*

sophical 2, no. 4 (May 2006); and Nada Shabout, "Preservation of Iraqi Modern Heritage in the Aftermath of the U.S. Invasion of 2003," in *An Anthology on Ethics in the Art World,* ed. Gail Levin and Elaine A. King (New York: Allworth Press).

18. Initially *horoufia,* literary letterism, was the name given by journalists to Arab modern art that included and manipulated the Arabic letter or text.

19. See Nada Shabout, *Modern Arab Art: Formation of Arab Aesthetics* (Gainesville: University Press of Florida, 2007).

20. Wafaa Salman, "The Life and Art of Madiha Omar," *Al-Wafaa News,* no. 20 (Fall 1994): 3–7.

21. Interview by author at her exhibition at the Leighton House Gallery, London, May 20, 2006.

22. As quoted in *Iraq* (Baghdad: Ministry of Culture, 1995).

23. As reported by all Iraqi artists with whom I have been working. Also see Mona Mahmoud, "Postwar Artists, Art World Will Illustrate New Time and Place," *USA Today.* www.usatoday.com/news/world/iraq/2005-07-21-artists-iraq_x.htm (accessed April 20, 2007).

24. PeaceWomen: Women's International League for Peace and Freedom, Suffering for Their Art, April 1, 2005. www.peacewomen.org/news/Iraq/April05/suffering.html (accessed April 21, 2007). Nevertheless, such claims need to be investigated in a political context of unconscious fear and denial.

25. Hanaa' Malallah, "Consciousness of Isolation," trans. Alia al-Dalli and Lily al-Tai, in *Strokes of Genius: Contemporary Iraqi Art,* ed. Maysaloun Faraj (London: Saqi Books, 2001), 64.

26. Telephone interview by author, July 2005.

27. Malallah, "Consciousness of Isolation," 66.

28. Telephone interview by author, July 2005.

29. The group's membership includes Iraq's previous minister of culture, Mufid al-Jazairi; the former deputy minister of culture, Maysoon al-Damluji; and the renowned Iraqi poet, Latifa al-Delaimy, among many other noted Iraqi intellectuals.

30. A *muhrum* is a chaperone, generally a male family member, whom the woman cannot marry—usually fathers, uncles, brothers, and nephews. In certain cases, female *muhrums* are allowed as well.

31. Mahmoud, "Postwar Artists, Art World Will Illustrate New Time and Place."

32. The city of Baghdad is/was host to a number of public monuments by renowned Iraqi sculptors that represent women from Iraq's history.

9

IN SEARCH OF IDENTITY

Hijab *Recollections from West Beirut*

NADA S. FULEIHAN

In autumn 1983, a young woman at the American University of Beirut entered the cafeteria wearing a *hijab*.[1] Heads turned, and whispers were audible throughout the room. The *hijab* itself was not unusual in West Beirut, where traditional and Western lifestyles had peacefully coexisted throughout the civil war. What made the *hijab* remarkable was that the student had not been *muhajjaba*[2] up to that point. That is, she had never previously committed to the *hijab* as a sign of Islamic identity. Over the next several years, numerous Muslim Lebanese women would be joining the Islamic movement. Increasingly, the collective transformation to *hijab* would make family, friends, and associates unsure as to how to respond to the young women making this very personal choice.

Like the rest of my peers, I was uneasy about this transformation. The Islamic movement was gaining momentum in Lebanon; many secular and non-Muslim female students were concerned about the implications of the *hijab* phenomenon. What might this movement mean for Lebanese women in general? I could not deny that the *hijab* was silently giving voice to my own suppressed feelings of anger and loss, feelings I had been harboring since Israel's invasion of South Lebanon in summer 1982. The invasion had culminated in the subsequent occupation of West Beirut and in the Palestinian refugee camp massacres at Sabra and Shatila. Despite my strong opposition to all forms of coercion, including enforced dress codes, I saw the *hijab* in a different light: an expression of Lebanese self-assertion and defiance and a sign of grief for the human catastrophe buried along with thousands of corpses that summer.

In this chapter I explore my own memories, as well as those of my peers, to understand the impact of the *hijab* in Beirut during the early eighties. My goal is to describe the perceptions and reactions to the *hijab* based on my own experience as a college student in West Beirut and the experiences of friends and associates living and studying there during most of the civil war. I interviewed eight women—all students at the American University of Beirut in the early 1980s—who volunteered to share their recollections. The interviews, completed by telephone or e-mail, consisted of unstructured, open-ended conversations about their memories of the *hijab* and how its emergence affected their past and present sense of personal identity. The interviewees were Christian, Muslim, and Druze. Confidentiality was prerequisite to candid interviews; therefore, my intention is to describe their experiences with accuracy, yet without compromising their anonymity.

In these recollections, I discovered a proportional correlation between the level of awareness of the civil war in general and our sense of personal identity. The Israeli war of 1982 dramatically changed our awareness of the Lebanese conflict and how each of us viewed the *hijab* and the Islamic revival that was taking place. At that time we perceived the *hijab* as a means of both expression and suppression for women; in no way did the *hijab* serve as an identifying factor, in terms of distinguishing Sunni from Shi'a. Clearly, our perceptions of *hijab* were very different prior to the war. As would be expected, these perceptions evolved and changed during and after the Israeli invasion.

PERCEPTIONS OF THE CIVIL WAR BEFORE 1982: AN EXTERNAL CONFLICT

I had resided in West Beirut since 1975, the year signaling the onset of the civil war. I was conscious of the diversity represented by the two main sections of the city: West Beirut, with its multiconfessional population, and East Beirut, an increasingly Christian and less pluralistic enclave. I was from a Christian background, felt proud of the diversity of West Beirut, and strongly identified with it. Nevertheless, my awareness of the religious and cultural makeup of the city did not go far in grasping the complexities of the conflict unfolding around me.

West Beirut comprised small, fragmented enclaves, each with its own set of cultural and religious affairs. Daily life was confined to very small circles between home, work, or school, and the level of awareness about what was taking place in other neighborhoods was limited. I lived in the Ras Beirut enclave, which remained relatively safe throughout the war. Like the women I interviewed, I lived in a sheltered bubble focusing on school and teenage matters. It was undoubtedly a coping mechanism and a form of survival, but it disconnected us from the reality of others around us, as well as from the conflict itself. The war, although present in every aspect of my life, was not my war; rather, it was the war of militias. Political and military details remained peripheral unless they had a direct impact on my safety or that of my family.

"I was too young and not fully aware of what was going on."[3] This was a leitmotiv that came up in almost every conversation with the women sharing their memories. For all of us, the war was a series of armed confrontations, shelling, and assassinations that we lived through without much analysis or reflection. As teenagers and young adults, we were detached; many remember this detachment as a coping mechanism, a way to preserve sanity in the midst of utter chaos.[4] In hindsight, now that youth and inexperience are behind us, we more clearly recognize the multiple layers and intricacies of the war.

THE 1982 ISRAELI INVASION: NEW IDENTITY

The Israeli invasion of 1982 changed everything. Suddenly, the war was no longer an external conflict but a personal one. A new sense of belonging and identity emerged among those who endured the bombings and the siege. This identity was based on two factors: the breakdown of the social enclaves around which people had organized their lives in West Beirut and a sense of solidarity born from the extreme fear and despair caused by the bombardments.

The Israeli sweep toward Beirut pushed thousands of families fleeing the inferno of the south into the city and brought them directly into West Beirut's schools, commercial centers, and vacant apartments. Their living conditions were deplorable, and it was a wake-up call for many of us who until that time had remained sheltered. Ussama Makdisi writes about the "loosened social boundaries" that reshuffled people's compartmentalized lives throughout the civil war.[5] The invasion and siege of 1982 created the opportunity for people from different regions and enclaves to meet each other, and united them as they faced the same desperate, life-threatening circumstances.

The scale of fatalities, casualties, and destruction that took place generated deep fear and resentment of one common enemy; together we suffered outrage at the injustice and inhumanity of the situation. This outrage was exacerbated by the perceived indifference on the other side of Beirut, where many, including myself, sought temporary shelter at one time or another. The contrast between the normality of life on one side of Beirut, where Israeli soldiers moved freely in the streets, with the total annihilation that was taking place on the other side was chilling.[6]

Danger pulls people together despite their differences, argues Maria Holt in her essay "Lebanese Shiʿa Women and Islamism."[7] During the invasion and siege of West Beirut, the class, religious, and cultural nuances that differentiated the population seemed to disappear, as people shared equally in the same fate. Many of the peers I interviewed recalled, almost with nostalgia, a feeling of belonging and solidarity with all Lebanese. However, this proved a fleeting moment.

AFTER THE WAR: LOSS AND SEPARATE IDENTITIES

One woman remembered commenting to a family member at the beginning of 1983, "It's not normal that life goes on as usual after what happened."[8] The rapid normalization of life in Beirut following the horrific trauma that people experienced generated a sense of loss and void that, for many, precluded their full participation in the city's new optimism. In his book *Pity the Nation,* Robert Fisk writes, "The results of the Israeli Invasion were still evident for anyone who cared to look, and it was still possible, amid the new economic growth and noisy optimism of Beirut, to come face to face with something infinitely terrible."[9] As the two sides of the city merged after many years of isolation, the definitions of identity changed almost overnight, without the emergence of a single, strong Lebanese identity. Instead, each group reached into the deeper levels of their convictions, and as Miriam Cooke points out, "became aware of itself more than ever as an autonomous entity."[10]

The 1982 war had wiped out existing political and social groupings, replacing them with a polarized system of extreme and narrow identities. For the few years that followed, Lebanon endured a fast-forward mode of armed confrontations and power struggles. Political alliances kept shifting without any perceived goal other than to contest each other for power. In that environment emerged the new, young image of *hijab* on the streets of Beirut. With all the layers of symbolism associated with it, the newly visible *hijab* made many students reevaluate how they defined and identified themselves. In *Beirut Fragments,* Jean Makdisi asked the following question: "if the chador[11] is taken to be symbolic of a woman's submission, can it not be also be symbolic of political rebellion and protest?"[12]

THE *HIJAB:* DUAL PERCEPTIONS

In the aftermath of the 1982 Israeli invasion, I viewed the *hijab* as a symbol of resistance, protest, and grief. I saw it as a sign of solidarity, honoring the tragedy we had lived through and reminding us of the continuing Israeli occupation in southern Lebanon. Although the *hijab* reflected a new Islamic revival, which in later years would evolve into an institutionalized political and social entity, I did not, in the beginning, connect the *muhajjabat's*[13] commitment to a political agenda but rather viewed it as a courageous statement of personal and religious identity. I respected the choice to wear the *hijab* but at the same time was uncomfortable with the idea that one's identity and allegiance could be expressed in this way. In my opinion, the *hijab* was a paradox: it empowered women to take action but restricted them to the patriarchal interpretations of Islam.

Fatima Mernissi explains that identity gives meaning to life, a feeling that one can make a difference in one's environment no matter how small it is.[14] "The fundamentalist wave is a statement about identity," she asserts.[15] Without being aware of the different contexts and meanings of the *hijab* at that time, I appreciated intuitively the statement and searched for an expression of my own identity. In reality, my reaction was not only to the *hijab* itself but also against those who rejected it as "un-Lebanese," individuals who tagged it with old racist and colonial stereotypes as backward, rural, and a sign of ignorance and submission.

These stereotypes clearly did not fit the women I encountered in the streets of Beirut and on the university campus, women who were actively involved in social and student affairs. In her description of the new *muhajjabat* in Lebanon, Holt emphasizes their determination:

> These women are well educated, articulate, and decisive. They have witnessed the horrors of war, the utter dislocation of their society, and have come to the conclusion that religion is the only way to restore a sense of moral rightness to their lives. This accounts for the purity and fervor of their vision.[16]

Although her study focused on Shi'a women in Lebanon, this distinction between Shi'a and Sunni did not influence my personal perception of the *hijab* as an activist response to the critical events of the early eighties. In comparison to the *muhajjabat's* social engagement, I seemed to be silent and subdued. Their commitment made me question my role and responsibility to the community, although I lacked clarity (as did most of the women I interviewed) as to exactly which community I belonged.

I projected onto the *hijab* my own frustrations and feelings; yes, it was a way to give voice to our common experience of the 1982 war, but its Islamic aspect clearly divided us. These were devout Muslim women, and I was Christian. Truthfully, I was disconnected and out of touch with the realities faced by women adopting the *hijab*. Looking back, it is with chagrin that I acknowledge this; I understood neither their personal, spiritual, or social motivations nor the Islamic political movement promoting their decision. Certainly I admired their courage, their willingness to take action and stand up for their personal beliefs, even at the risk of antagonizing or alienating their less religious families. However, theirs was a choice tailored only to an Islamic fit. Furthermore, this choice contradicted my principles of women's rights, which I believed could not be safeguarded by religion.

The story of Hajjeh Zahra in Lara Deeb's *Gender and Public Piety in Shi'i Lebanon* illustrates the search for personal identity that many young women experienced following the 1982 war.[17] Zahra's call to wear the *hijab* came after a major "catalyzing" experience.[18] A student at the American University of Beirut, she volunteered by doing humanitarian work during both the 1978 and 1982 Israeli invasions and participated in the cleanup after the massacres at the Sabra and Shatila refugee camps in 1982. Deeb writes:

> [The] strain prompted her [Hajjeh Zahra] to focus solely on her studies and work. It was during this time that she joined the newly organizing Islamic movement on campus. She became religiously committed and chose to wear the hijab, a decision which set her apart from her less religious family.[19]

Many individuals were involved in rescue efforts; others experienced horrific events firsthand. Women like Hajjeh Zahra turned to religion for answers. For those outside the Islamic movement in the early 1980s, the traumatic experience of the Israeli invasion produced the same search for meaning. Instead of turning to organized religion, however, they chose to complete their studies and pursue their life's work.

PEER RECOLLECTIONS

All the women who shared their recollections perceived the *hijab* as oppressive to the women who adopted it, although some remember trying to rationalize and understand the decision. Most of them rejected it as religious fanaticism or the result of coercion. One of the women, a Muslim herself, emphasized that Islam does not require a woman to cover her face or body. It was her belief that, in a general atmosphere of religious fervor, there must have been a form of indirect coercion, a pressure to adopt a dress code in return for approval from the community.

Another woman disapproved of the *hijab* but saw it as a natural progression given the political void created by the 1982 war. She suggested that the Iranian revolution had perhaps served as a model, an inspiration for many young women to adopt the *hijab*.

Another respondent remembered feeling extremely resentful of the *hijab,* yet recalled making a conscious effort to rationalize it. In short, she had held a dualistic view:

> I defended it when it was attacked and attacked it when it was defended.
> I remember even then arguing with a relative and saying, "They're free, if this is how they feel, if this is their only recourse, then they should be able to express it." Of course, then I was naive.[20]

Overall, she considered the veil a symbol of patriarchal dominance over women — especially when a friend of hers adopted the *hijab* after getting married.

Interestingly, it should also be noted that when the *hijab* was worn with flair — that is, when it was personalized, colorful, and creatively draped — friends and family were more likely to tolerate the decision. By contrast, when the *hijab* was severe, drab, and paired with a long coat,[21] the wearer was not as favorably perceived.

As students living in West Beirut in the early eighties, our perspectives reflected our backgrounds: middle class, secular or moderately religious, and educated with a liberal Western bias. While a significant number of those young women adopting the *hijab* were themselves middle-class students, many others (who recognized the validity of their choice) simply could not accept it as an option.

Furthermore, although we had assimilated Islamic culture simply by living in predominantly Muslim West Beirut, we were still outsiders. Disconnected from the realities of a significant part of the Lebanese population, our integration was superficial at best. Clearly, only Muslim women were apt to consider the *hijab* and did so in tandem with their growing concerns about religious expression. We certainly did not understand, nor were we aware of, the political implications behind the *hijab,* which were present from the beginning of the Islamic movement. Although a spiritual commitment, the *hijab* also carried a political symbol of resistance against the Israeli invasion and occupation of South Lebanon and a rejection of the policies of the Christian Westernized right wing.

The *hijab* became linked to Lebanese resistance and national identity — but only among those who wore it or belonged to the Islamic movement.

For many of us who shared patriotic sentiments but were opposed to the movement's methods and channels of expression, the *hijab* became exclusive and polarizing. As the political gap between Islamic fundamentalism and the pro-Western right wing widened, many secular women felt increasingly ambivalent about the *hijab*. While giving partial voice to their nationalistic sentiments, it fell markedly short of being an appropriate symbol for unifying Lebanon's diverse populations.

CONCLUSION

As political alliances shifted, the early eighties in Lebanon became a time of extreme unrest. The long-term division of Beirut into east and west sectors had created multiple identities. These identities became deeply polarized after the 1982 Israeli invasion, leaving many in the middle.

As teenagers and young adults, the women I interviewed were still searching for their own personal identities and testing the waters of independence. For them, the *hijab* emerged as a controversial model. Although the *muhaj-jabat* (veiled women) were not passive women, their decision to wear *hijab* was largely perceived as a form of patriarchal coercion and religious fanaticism. When I asked one friend about her view of the *hijab,* she responded, "I totally rejected it then as [a form of] fanaticism, but I have changed. I know a lot more about it now, and although I still do not agree with the necessity to veil, it does not bother me as much."[22] Another friend referred to feeling conflicted about the *hijab* then and now (after the 2006 Israeli war). She explains, "It is an ongoing battle in my mind between . . . rational and emotional perceptions."[23]

Although some women outside the Islamic movement recognized the *hijab* as a symbol of protest and resistance, they still felt alienated by its religious connotations. While many among us searched for a national Lebanese identity, the *hijab* ultimately provided a sense of identity only for those women who wore it.

The recollections presented in this chapter suggest that there has been no real meaningful integration of the various cultural and religious groups in Lebanon. Political alliances have proven anathema to mending Lebanon's fragmented society. What Lebanon needs are sincere efforts by sectarian groups to reconcile and integrate on a personal rather than political level. To avoid the seemingly endless pattern of sectarian conflict, it is vital that opposing groups (including the teenagers and young adults of these diverse populations) engage in meaningful dialogue about each other and about their recent history.

The *hijab* and the Islamic way of life have become defining factors among Shiʿa women in Lebanon. Yet they still perceive themselves as part of the Lebanese fabric, as Holt argues, and are attached to their Lebanese identity.[24] By socializing, exchanging ideas, and creating safe discursive environments, perhaps Lebanese women from diverse backgrounds could begin to honor rather than fear each other, promote mutual understanding, and contribute efforts toward a meaningful experience of national identity.

NOTES

1. Islamic headscarf, veil.

2. A woman who commits to wearing the *hijab*.

3. Telephone and e-mail interviews, January, February, and March 2007.

4. Catherine Bashshur, an American educator living in West Beirut during the war, describes in an interview the protective intentions that made parents push their children to detach from the war and focus on their education. Mary Bentley Abu Saba, "Profiles of Foreign Women in Lebanon," in *Women and War in Lebanon,* ed. Lamia Rustum Shehadeh (Gainesville: University Press of Florida, 1999), 247.

5. Ussama Makdisi, "Reconstructing the Nation-State: The Modernity of Secularism in Lebanon," *Middle East Report* (Summer 1996).

Makdisi refers to Hashim Sarkis's chapter, "Territorial Claims: Architecture and Post-War Attitudes Toward the Built Environment," in *Recovering Beirut: Urban Design and Post-War Reconstruction,* ed. Samir Khalaf and Philip S. Khoury (Leiden: Brill, 1993), 100–127. Hashim Sarkis discusses the "territorialization" of identities during the war by pointing out that the violence provided new "spatial opportunities" to redefine identities that emerged after and because of the onset of physical destruction (118–119).

6. For more recollections of a similar experience see Abu Saba, "Profiles of Foreign Women in Lebanon," 238.

7. Maria Holt, "Lebanese Shiʿa Women and Islamism," in *Women and War in Lebanon,* ed. Lamia Rustum Shehadeh (Gainesville: University Press of Florida, 1999), 168.

8. Telephone and e-mail interviews.

9. Robert Fisk, *Pity the Nation: The Abduction of Lebanon* (New York: Thunder's Mouth Press/Nation Books, 2002), 465.

10. Miriam Cooke, *War's Other Voices: Women Writers on the Lebanese Civil War* (Syracuse, NY: Syracuse University Press, 1996), 22.

11. A *chador* is a long veil that covers all of a woman's body except her face.

12. Jean Makdisi, *Beirut Fragments* (New York: Persea Books, 1990), 145.

13. The women who wear the headdress.

14. Fatima Mernissi, *Beyond the Veil: Male-Female Dynamics in Modern Muslim Society* (Bloomington: Indiana University Press, 1987), 9.

15. Ibid.

16. Holt, "Lebanese Shiʿa Women and Islamism," 188.

17. Lara Deeb, *An Enchanted Modern: Gender and Public Piety in Shiʿi Lebanon,* Princeton Studies in Muslim Politics (Princeton: Princeton University Press, 2006), 187–191.

18. Ibid., 188. See also the personal accounts of two *muhajjabat* in Maher Abi Samra's *The Women of Hezbollah* (Icarus Films, 2000).

19. Deeb, *An Enchanted Modern,* 189.

20. Telephone and e-mail interviews.

21. Ibid.

22. Ibid.

23. Ibid.

24. Holt, "Lebanese Shiʿa Women and Islamism," 192.

10

LEADERSHIP OF LEBANESE WOMEN
IN THE CEDAR REVOLUTION

RITA STEPHAN

The night after Lebanese Prime Minister Rafiq Hariri was assassinated, a small group of men and women gathered in downtown Beirut to light candles and pray. From a dozen individuals grew the "Lebanon Spring Revolution," the aim of which was to liberate Lebanon from fifteen years of foreign influence. Candles and prayers evolved into a series of protests and demonstrations that ultimately led to significant political and social changes in Lebanon. The Lebanon Spring Revolution, or the "Cedar Revolution," as President George W. Bush called it,[1] became a movement that fulfilled many people's dreams for independence and sovereignty.[2] Only on rare occasion in the modern history of the Middle East have citizens organized collectively to express their opinions in such a manner, risking arrest and death. Rare too are those occasions on which women have assumed leadership roles and swelled the ranks of political protest.

In this chapter I argue that as Lebanese women filled the streets to demonstrate in March 2005, they transformed the image of Muslim and Christian Lebanese women. The new image of women as politically active citizens made it possible for them to engage in politics at a much greater level of visibility than ever before. By openly mingling with men protesting in the streets, by contributing to key aspects of the movement in terms of planning, and by organizing their own demonstrations, these women in essence added a "feminine" element to the resistance.

This chapter addresses the following questions: Who were the women participating in these demonstrations? What were their reasons for joining the movement? What were the strategies and approaches they applied in the various protests? Through their own words, I explore their motivations and self-perceptions. My data are based on stories and interviews from four major Lebanese newspapers published in French, English, and Arabic after February 15, 2005. In addition, I draw from electronic sources and major international news organizations. Finally, my research includes in-depth interviews with key participants such as Nora Jumblat, wife of a prominent Druze leader, of the March 14 Revolution; and Rima Fakhry, a high-ranking female official in Hezbollah, of the March 8 demonstration. My research was conducted mostly between summer 2006 and spring 2007, a period marked by blurred boundaries and complex alliances. In 2006 the lines that now divide Lebanon — specifically, the political tension between the March 14 and March 8 groups — had yet to be clearly defined.

THE LEBANON SPRING REVOLUTION:
A BRIEF HISTORY

On February 14, 2005, a massive car bomb exploded in Beirut, taking the life of former Prime Minister Rafiq Hariri and several other people. This tragedy left the entire country in shock and in a general state of insecurity and political instability. Citizens immediately gathered at the assassination site next to the St. George Hotel, a site that became known as "ground zero." The scene, as described by Nora Jumblat, became the epicenter of ensuing protests:

> On Tuesday night, the 15th of February, [my driver and I] went down [to Martyrs Square, the site of Rafiq Hariri's assassination] and I saw a few people standing there with candles, just about ten to fifteen people and I went down. They said, you want to put a candle here, and I said, yeah of course. I said, who are you? And they said, you want to sign this petition? And the petition said they're asking for an international investigation of the Hariri [assassination]. And I said, who are you? They said, we're nobody, we're just citizens and we think. Can you help us? . . . They were ten or fifteen, and there was nobody, nobody, in town; it was a ghost town. So I said, yes of course, how can I help you? They said, if you can bring the press and we can do something around it.[3]

At first people gathered to pray for the souls of the victims and to light candles. They also came to search for the missing, whom the government had failed to find. A petition was circulated demanding an honest investigation to uncover the identity and motives of the assassins. The petition demanded that these individuals be brought to justice. "On impulse they asked passersby to sign a petition calling on the pro-Syrian Lebanese government to resign; after four days, they were wrestling with a scroll of signatures some 400 meters long."[4] Asma-Maria Andraos, who, along with several dozen friends, initiated the petition, states that no one had an overarching political plan in mind. Rather, they simply viewed the petition as a way to express anger over the crime and the deteriorating conditions in the country.

Nevertheless, those spontaneous expressions of agony became a burgeoning protest movement. As it grew, the core group that had sprung up spontaneously, connected by their anger and grief, took responsibility for organizing and maintaining the movement. Simply put, there was no way back. Again, Nora Jumblat, who supported the grassroots protests from the beginning, describes what happened:

> And CNN was there and Brent Sadler and they spoke to me and they spoke to others and they said would it fizzle out? This was the second time we were [marching]. We went to the Parliament, and then went [to Martyrs Square]. We were [all from different parts of Lebanon], women, [and] all kinds of people, just about a hundred or two hundred people. And I said no I don't think it would fizzle out. Of course I thought, on the contrary, that it would fizzle out. But at the time you had to give this impression to the outside press and there were no deputies, no members of Parliament, there was nobody of the sort.[5]

Jumblat's reference to deputies and members of the Parliament (MPs) highlights the lack of official sponsorship of any activities in the early stages of protest. However, in less than a week the protest had drawn people from all walks of life, eventually gaining the sponsorship of professional syndicates, political parties, government officials, artists, and intellectuals.

Thousands of people gathered every night, and the government grew weary of them. On February 28, 2005, the minister of interior claimed the demonstrations were unlawful, and a military judge imposed a ban on assembly starting at 5:00 A.M.[6] This declaration set the stage for the largest collective show of civil disobedience in Lebanese history, as thousands of people from all over the country crowded into the streets. By 6:00 P.M. that same day, due to pressure exerted by the crowd, the pro-Syrian prime minister resigned. Five days later, Syrian President Assad announced plans to withdraw his forces from Lebanon.

The Syrian-backed government, along with the Hezbollah leadership,[7] organized a counterdemonstration of 800,000 protesters on March 8 at the Riyad al-Solh Square. The purpose of this countermovement was to express support for and loyalty to Syria and to reject Western interests in the region.

However, on March 14, 2005, 1.2 million Lebanese filled the streets of Beirut and its suburbs, setting a record for Lebanon's largest demonstration ever. Syrian troops left Lebanese soil on April 27, 2005, and less than a month later the anti-Syrian alliance led by Saad Hariri—son of Rafiq Hariri—won control of the Parliament. It is noteworthy that in each of the protests, female presence was noticeably significant. Below I discuss images of women participants in key demonstrations.

THE OVERNIGHT SIT-IN: FEBRUARY 28, 2005

To those individuals who had been protesting for two weeks, the day seemed very much like the one before. However, the government decided otherwise. On this day the minister of interior issued a referendum banning all demonstrations and invoked the military to take action. I vividly remember flipping through all the Arabic satellite channels at home in Austin, Texas (including Al-Jazeera, al-Arabia, LBC, and Future, in addition to Western channels), and asking myself, What will be the fate of all those men and women? I remembered the 1980s in Syria, Iraq, and China when similar protests involving innocent citizens ended in violence. Images of young, idealistic Chinese students in Tiananmen Square (1989) remained especially vivid in my mind. Yet my anxieties proved unfounded; the demonstrators in Beirut emerged unshaken, victorious. Over a year later, when I asked Nora Jumblat if she had been afraid the government would react violently to the sit-in, she replied, "No, I was not scared. . . . I did not stop to think."[8]

Collectively, the youth—joined by parents, deputies, and party leaders—arrived at ten o'clock the night of the 27th and slept in the streets.[9] Entire families spent the night at Martyrs Square. Edgar, a father of three, insisted, "I want my children to live in an independent and sovereign country."[10] The soldiers were given orders to block the roads and prohibit newcomers from joining the Martyrs Square protest. But demonstrators insisted on handing the soldiers white roses and asserting their desire to have no foreign army on their soil.[11] In Jumblat's words, "We've been here 24 hours. People have been able to reach the square thanks to the army. The army had very different orders, but they have allowed the people to come here and to meet and you can see the result."[12] The crowd began the countdown at dawn, and when the clock struck 5:00 A.M., they all cheered victoriously. By 6:30 P.M., the protest had grown even stronger, forcing Prime Minister Omar Karami to resign.[13]

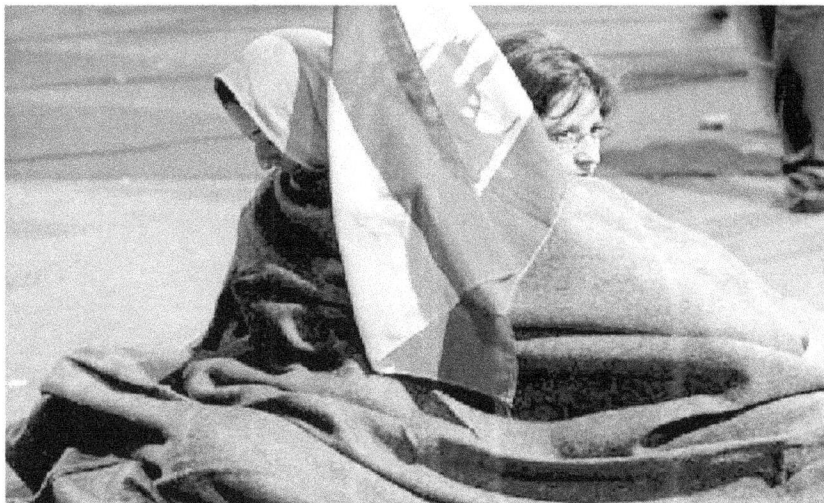

FIGURE 10.1

The sit-in brought these two girls under one flag. Al-Mustaqbal, *March 3, 2005*

THE MARCH 8, 2005, PROTEST

Several Pro-Syrian political groups, including the Shiʻite Hezbollah party, called for a "massive popular gathering" to assert Lebanon's intimate bond with Syria and to draw attention to the Israeli and American interference in Lebanese politics. The estimated 800,000 protesters had an important message to convey to their fellow Lebanese and to the world. ʻAnisa al-Amin Merei, a progressive Shiʻa from southern Lebanon, provided a unique perspective on the gathering:

> I watched the Riyad Solh scene and I saw the gathered crowd, their strong fists holding onto the Lebanese flag. As I listened to the speech of the Sayed [Hasan Nassarallah], my eyes became full with tears. . . . I sympathize with these people who carry with them a long history of Israeli repression and Lebanese rejection. In their gathering one feels censure and apprehension. They blame the constitution that treats them as refugees and all Lebanese who did not care about the southerners [during the Israeli occupation] as they slept in a different place every night. . . . People who demonstrated in Riyad Solh Square did not want to repeat their past experience. They have known the reality of death, the death of their fathers and sons, the death of places, and the total wiping out of memory that leaped through

FIGURE 10.2
Hezbollah Women's Demonstration. Al-Mustaqbal, *March 12, 2005*

history. They feared and reproached the mood of dismissal and displacement which is again moving to the stage of exploitation and invasion. The southerner fled to the front lines crying: "I am here. I am from here, from this downtown too. I am not only the guard of the southern frontiers, although I have guarded and continue to guard the nation's borders."[14]

Needless to say, the opposing camp was not happy with this demonstration. They belittled it and demeaned its passion. Some made claims that the rally was comprised mostly of Syrian intelligence agents and poor Shi'ites from the south, so that they were not 100 percent Lebanese. Others claimed, "They didn't come by their free will."[15]

A HISTORIC EVENT: MARCH 14, 2005

To commemorate the one-month anniversary of the assassination of Prime Minister Hariri, over one million Lebanese men, women, and children rallied in central Beirut chanting, "Freedom, Sovereignty, Independence." They came from every Lebanese region and from all faiths, partly in response to the March 8 rally. Their message was twofold: the majority want Syrian troops out of Lebanon, and pressure must be continually exerted on the establishment to step away from the politically dishonorable situation in Lebanon. It was the largest demonstration in Lebanon's history. Not only did this protest receive approval from a number of international political leaders, but it also received significant media coverage, ensuring that it was viewed around the world. Multiple political parties were involved in organizing the demonstration, and Hariri's Future Movement (political party, television station, and newspaper) took an active role in orchestrating the various events that day.

The demonstrators demanded an international investigation of the circumstances surrounding Hariri's murder, the arrest of the chief security officers in the Lebanese government, and the total withdrawal of Syrian forces from Lebanese soil. Women were heavily represented, both as leaders and as participants. Bahiya Hariri, a member of Parliament from Sidon and sister of the slain former prime minister, addressed the crowd: "Your family and all the Lebanese will keep your history alive. We came to vow before you that we will not let anyone hurt our Lebanon, the Lebanon you wanted, and we will proceed with the path you drew for us."[16] In the crowd was Maya, a thirty-eight-year-old Shi'ite Muslim archaeologist, who considered the demonstration a good first step: "There may be many more [steps] to take. Maybe these won't be taken in the streets like today, but we must continue."[17]

MOTHER'S DAY: MARCH 21, 2005

During all the events following Hariri's assassination, women's organizations were united in expressing their anger and demanding the establishment of an investigative commission. When Mother's Day arrived, a young woman, Leila Saad, issued a call to all Lebanese mothers to pray at 12:55 P.M. (the time the assassination took place) wherever they were:

> "Lebanon needs our prayers," she proclaimed, "Lebanon is like a sick child in desperate need of care. We must act like we do when our children get sick. We must come together and pray intensely for the health of our country."[18]

Various women's associations and civil society organizations echoed Saad's call in a show of solidarity.[19] Hundreds of mothers, sisters, wives, and daughters arrived from regions throughout Lebanon, some dressed in black and others in white, carrying candles and demanding the truth.

"This is a sad day for all mothers in Lebanon," said a woman who came from the city of Akkar in northern Lebanon. "We did not have the desire to celebrate our holiday while all of Lebanon is mourning. The best Mother's Day gift we could receive is to know the truth about the circumstances of the attack. This is the only thing that would bring true pleasure to our hearts. We all wish to uncover the truth quickly in order to be able to celebrate our holiday next year in peace."[20]

THE QUAKE OF LOVE: MARCH 28, 2005

On March 19, 23, and 27, a number of bombs exploded in Beirut's Christian suburbs, killing five and injuring twenty. People knew that these explosions were set off to terrify and divide them. Women's associations called on all women to overcome their fears, assemble in the streets, and carry the following messages: "No to Fear and Yes to National Unity," "Enough Terrorism, Our People Are Fearless," and "Stop State Terrorism." They called this protest movement "the quake of love."[21] Thousands of women, dressed in white, responded to the call and filled Martyrs Square. While some associations provided buses to transport their members, most participants organized themselves in small groups of friends and colleagues. They were all motivated by the same desire: to show that women also have a powerful message. They chanted:

"Every mother, every child, and every heartbeat asks the same question: Where is the Truth?"
"We want love, we want peace, and we want truth and freedom."[22]

This demonstration brought together a cross section of social classes: wives of dignitaries, female parliamentary members, little girls dressed in white, old veiled women whose backs were bent with age, progressive modern young professionals, and housewives who refused to play a secondary role in the struggle for independence. MP Nayla Moawad addressed the crowds: "We have come to say enough to the attacks and the explosions. They do not scare us. We demand the truth, free elections, and a free and independent international commission of investigation. Each new explosion adds a page to their file which is already full of security violations. This file will be examined by the international investigation commission."[23]

UNITED WE RUN: APRIL 11, 2005

A committee headed by MP Bahiya Hariri and Nora Jumblat organized Lebanon's National Unity Festival in downtown Beirut. This spectacular marathon was packed with families from all regions of Lebanon who came to show their support.[24] One young participant named Mirna, age twenty-two, viewed her participation in the marathon as a duty "which every true patriot should feel." She said, "As I ran, I truly felt that I'm doing this for Lebanon. We should show everyone that we are united regardless of what happens."[25] Similarly, a six-year-old named Jennifer, also at the marathon, was happy to be doing something positive for Lebanon. Her father insisted, "I want my daughter to grow up loving everything, and appreciating life and freedom, and [to] be open to others' opinions rather than [having to] teach her to stand against other Lebanese citizens whenever they disagree on something."[26]

TWO WOMEN MAKING A DIFFERENCE

Tracing the biographical trajectories of specific leaders and members of political protests often illuminates the real social tensions and aspirations embodied in the movement itself. I have chosen two women who illustrate the diversity of individuals leading the protests over Hariri's murder. One of the leaders of the Spring Revolution was a familiar face to the Lebanese public, Nora Jumblat, mentioned previously. The other prominent individual is Asma-Maria Andraos, featured in *Time* magazine as one of the thirty-seven heroes of 2005 "changing the world for the better."[27]

Jumblat's name has been associated indissolubly with this revolution from beginning to end. A Syrian-born Sunni and graduate in art history from L'École des Beaux Arts in Paris, she married one of Lebanon's political idols and its most prominent Druze leader, Walid Jumblat. Mrs. Jumblat has been a renowned public figure since 1984.

The day after Hariri's funeral, she was recruited by the protesters at ground zero. For almost three months, she managed many of the protest's logistics and organized various aspects of the revolution. For example, she designed the white and red foulards worn by all politicians and leaders. She personally purchased the material and sewed it with a team of assistants. Later she commissioned an atelier to produce these foulards professionally for the movement. She coordinated food distribution to those participating at the sit-in in downtown Beirut. When the first demonstration headed to the streets, she made sure that banners, Lebanese flags, and signs were distributed from

FIGURE 10.3
Mrs. Nora Jumblat handing soldiers red roses. Al-Mustaqbal, *February 22, 2005*

her office. Mrs. Jumblat coordinated with the *Annahar* newspaper to hide all the protest materials in its trucks: "They came in here and all the students came . . . and all the parties . . . to take all the banners and everything. That was the beginning of everything. Of course different parties started doing their own things [later]."[28] After she coordinated a couple of the demonstrations from her office, the army and the pro-Syrian government discovered Mrs. Jumblat's activities. At that point, she and other organizers moved the distribution center to a new location.

Nora Jumblat became the natural mediator between demonstrators in the street and members of the elite class. As social movement scholars have noted, ordinary citizens engaging in social movements normally lack direct access to power and resources. Thus including sympathetic members of the elite as allies increases a movement's chance for access and success; this holds true even if those individuals' political influence is minimal at the moment the social movement is formed.[29]

In contrast to demonstrations organized by social activists or political parties, this was a movement spontaneously organized by ordinary citizens. Asma-Maria Andraos, a thirty-four-year-old Christian woman, found herself in the role of organizer and activist overnight. She made the dream of revolution a reality. She had never been an activist but felt unable to continue her life detached and unengaged. In her own words, "I went from someone who was disinterested in Lebanon's politics, sort of sleepwalking and living in a bubble; then I was awakened."[30]

As a public relations consultant and event planner, Andraos had been working to promote Lebanese businesses. In 1999 she and Michael Nakfoor started their firm, Stree, to develop specialized event marketing, public relations, and live communications.[31] In order to escape the hardship of the 1980s civil war, Andraos's parents had sent their young daughter abroad to study and live. After the war, she returned to build her future, as well as that of Lebanon. The day after Hariri's funeral, she and her friends began a sit-in at ground zero to express their anger. They drew up a petition calling on the pro-Syrian Lebanese government to resign. Four days later, they had four hundred meters of signatures and a movement to sustain. Andraos saw the protest as "the moment in Lebanon's history to change everything, to gain its true independence, and we had to sustain it till our demands were met."[32]

Indeed Andraos's transformation into a political agent was entirely spontaneous, resulting from her unpremeditated participation in the protest demonstration. Along with other emerging activists, she formed Civil Society 05, an umbrella group under which existing nongovernmental organizations could form a nonpartisan movement.[33] The group arranged supplies of food, tents, and other necessities for protest participants. On achieving their immediate goals for independence, Andraos and her colleagues created the 05 Amam, literally, "to the front," which was intended to function as a forum for nonpolitical organizations to cooperatively create a reform plan and present it to the new Lebanese government.[34]

A PORTFOLIO OF WOMEN PROTESTERS

Middle Eastern women have often been depicted as passive political actors.[35] However, a number of scholars have pointed out how changes in a nation's social and political landscape affect women's rights and participation.[36] Others have noted women's increasing awareness of their rights as citizens.[37] The Lebanese resistance movement was infused with this new type of consciousness. 'Anisa al-Amin Merei's testimony below illustrates the surfacing of a strong national identity that brought young, old, veiled, secular, Christians, Muslims, foreigners, natives, and men and women together as allies in the Lebanon Spring Revolution:

> I have fought my Shi'ite identity to gain . . . my Lebanese identity and citizenship. . . . My southerner and Shi'ite self is at peace with this Leban-

ese Arab woman who is me. With all my Shiʿite-ism and southernness and modernity and professionalism as a psychologist, I strive to liberate my soul from all her inhibitions.[38]

Merei claims that in this revolution, women's sense of their national identity superseded their religious, kinship, and regional allegiances. This same sentiment rang true for Nada, a forty-year-old architect, who stated:

> These are the true democratic days. It is incredible because this has never happened in the Arab world. It is up to us to decide how we shall live. It is no longer acceptable for each to remain in his position. . . . It is time that we take charge of our own lives.[39]

For the most part, the courageous women participating in the protests were ordinary citizens. A good example is Otor, a middle-aged woman who joined the February 28 sit-in even though she was undergoing cancer treatment. She explained, "It is my duty to be here [demonstrating], even though this is against the wishes of my doctor. I am unable to stay at home because now we have to mobilize."[40] Other women broke social norms and traditional restrictions. One such woman, Samia, sixty-seven years old, left her husband behind on February 28 to spend the night away from home for the first time in her life.[41] Other protesters, such as eighteen-year-old Enas, defied her parents to join the demonstration at the square. Enas explained, "My parents are not happy with me being here; they are worried that Syrian and Lebanese secret intelligence will take down our names and pictures to harass us later on."[42] Fortunately, Enas and others whose identities were publicized in these protests did not suffer arrest or harassment, because on March 14 a new coalition won the election and took control of the government.

There were also women like Lena, age thirty-five, eight months pregnant when she joined the March 14 demonstration. Her dream was that political change would be the path to a bright future for her unborn child: "My child is going to be born into a free country. He is going to be the child of independence."[43] Women felt that they were making a significant contribution to liberating their country and that they were answering the call of duty as Lebanese nationals.

Women also participated because they felt an obligation to voice their loyalty to Syria and assert their significance in Lebanese politics. In my interview with Rima Fakhry, the only female senior officer in Hezbollah, she justified the appeal of the March 8 rally.

Stephan: What was your role and position from what happened on March 8?

Fakhry: We were in the midst of all this turmoil.

Stephan: Did you go down to the street?

Fakhry: Is it possible to send the people to the streets and stay at home one-self? I went down with my children, too. . . . There was a general popular feeling of obligation to go. . . . There were many people in the Solh Square who did not belong to any political party. I went to demonstrate because I was carrying a heavy burden in my heart. Many important changes were happening on the ground, and I needed to be present.[44]

MOTIVATIONS FOR PARTICIPATION

In response to the national crisis, Lebanese men and women learned first-hand that power lies in unity. Their resolve and desire for social and political reforms are reflected in the declarations of Myriam and Danielle, twenty-four-year-old students:

We are all together here to say that we have had it.

We came here to express our opinion and no one can intimidate us any-more. We have had enough of being ruled by incompetent people. We deserve to be represented by a new political class that stands for us.[45]

Even Fatma, a veiled Sunni woman, identified with the liberation cause and strategies: "We are coming to liberate our country. We are coming to de-mand the truth."[46] She shared this solidarity with Suzy, a liberal arts student, who never considered the thought of retreating:

Now? And after the resignation of the government? . . . We are spread throughout the country, and our morale is very high. No one thought that the government would fall so quickly. This is the beginning of an inevitable march towards victory.[47]

As the movement grew, the feeling of solidarity in the project to liberate Lebanon from foreign interference also grew, unleashing a long-held, deep sense of national identity. However, others joined the demonstrations be-cause—in a real material sense—life had been temporarily interrupted. Lina, the owner of a shoe store near downtown, was unable to make a living. She explained, "I would come, open the shop, and close it without anyone visiting it. So I just ended up joining the protesters in Martyrs Square as there isn't much to do anyway."[48] Similarly, a high school student named Olle joined the February 28 demonstration because her school was closed and she did not want to "sit at home and feel useless."[49]

Tayma, a university student, wanted to see her father, who had lived through the civil war and saw many of his dreams shattered, regain a modicum of hope. She expressed joy in being able to contribute to the advancement of her country towards democracy and sovereignty: "We never knew an independent Lebanon," as it was before the fifteen years of civil war. She continued, "We are too young. But this is our right which we shall pursue."[50] Ordinary Lebanese citizens and the elite joined hands after the assassination of Prime Minister Rafiq Hariri, creating unexpected alliances. Together they brought a new political order to Lebanon, and within that collective project, traditional definitions of female social and political roles were dissolved.

GENDER AND RESOURCE MOBILIZATION STRATEGIES

Social movement theorists emphasize the role of culture as the sphere of embedded relationships. Culture presents itself as a tool kit that helps movements construct meaning that relates to "the processes by which culture is adapted, framed, and reframed through public discourse, persuasive communication, consciousness raising, political symbols, and icons."[51] The Cedar Revolution was embedded in Lebanese gender relations as well as in cultural mores and symbols. Although women actively took part in the Cedar Revolution, their quest for equality and rights changed very little as a result. Indeed, since the revolution of 2005, it has been politics as usual in Lebanon.

One must consider that women's participation in the Cedar Revoution was influenced by class conflict, kinship structure (including gender roles and stereotypes), and culturally relevant attributes. Historically, women's activism emerged in the nineteenth century in the United States, Europe, and Lebanon and the rest of the Middle East as a result of an elite class of women engaging in public advocacy. These women were usually born into families committed to reform and social justice.[52]

Symbolic of class separation and distinction in the Lebanon Spring Revolution were the specific fashions worn by the middle-class women. Some commentators described this distinctive feature of the movement as the "Gucci Revolution,"[53] referring to those women who carried Louis Vuitton purses and Gucci backpacks while chanting anti-Syrian slogans.

In addition to the class factor, kinship structure played a significant role in the Cedar Revolution, as it has throughout Lebanese history. In the March 14 movement in particular, the women leading the way were primarily relatives of powerful (and often deceased) men. For example, at the forefront were Bahiya Hariri, Rafiq Hariri's sister, and Nora Jumblat, Walid Jumblat's wife. Also in a position of leadership was Nayla Moawad, Rene Moawad's widow. With very few exceptions, women's only path to power in Lebanon, as elsewhere in the world, has been through family affiliation. While some scholars and activists look askance at the rise of these women, their entry into politics is paving the way for a larger number of women to participate in the public sphere and perhaps eventually to acquire power. The feminist literature has been mostly silent about the political roles and contributions of political wives, with the exception of Jo Freeman's study on political women.[54]

In truth, Middle Eastern feminism cannot be understood unless we grasp two factors that determine its image and form: (1) the importance of kin groups in the Middle East and (2) the importance of Arab nationalism. Family and kinship groups are the fundamental social factors confronting all organizations, state or private, in the Middle East.[55] Therefore, the level of empowerment experienced by some contemporary women diverges in real life from the stereotypes often on display in the literature of Middle Eastern gender relations. The second factor is more complex and is widely expressed in the views of Third World feminists. A history of colonialism and the existence of long-term Western hegemony in the Middle East mark all political movements in the region. These political movements not only look inward, towards achieving change in a given community or state, but also look outward, to the West, inasmuch as the West provides both resources and limits. In addition, association with the West can decisively shape the image of a given group; for instance, an increase in the unpopularity of the West may lead to unpopularity of groups that are, fairly or unfairly, perceived as connected to the West.

Since the 1970s, when discussions of women's agency were initiated by traditional radical feminists like Shulamith Firestone[56] and Kate Millett,[57] male dominance, seen as an abiding feature of patriarchy, has been at the core of the problem of women's rights. Therefore, many radical feminists advocated various forms of female separatism that would empower women to become economically, civilly, and politically independent and free of any compromise with the ultimately irredeemable patriarchal system. The central feminist tradition in the West, though radical about separatism, was actually in conformity with a very Western, very patriarchal notion of the detached self. Feminists tend to agree with social movement and political theorists that the utility of the family for women's empowerment and increased participation in public life is irrelevant.

The Cedar Revolution did not challenge gender and class conflicts; rather, it may be recorded as a people's movement emerging from a solid foundation of cultural symbols and social networks specific to Lebanon. Sidney Tarrow speculates that the formation of social movements depends on the emergence of dense social networks, the production and transmission of culturally appropriate yet action-oriented symbols, and finally, sustained interaction with the authority they are protesting.[58]

I argue that Tarrow's model fits the unfolding of the Cedar Revolution. In it, strong social networks emerged not only among the revolution supporters but also among their opponents. The effects of this became evident in the giant March 14 demonstration as people leveraged their familial and social networks to recruit demonstrators in a short time. For instance, a woman named Oumayma brought her three children, husband, and mother-in-law,[59] while Mey, a thirty-year-old Arabic literature teacher, organized a large convoy of entire families from her hometown.[60] Dense networks traversing social, religious, and ethnic lines were also exemplified by Christian and Muslim men, women, and children praying in unison over Hariri's grave. In turn, these moving images drew tremendous support and sympathy from the international community, providing a virtual community of supporters.

Second, the symbols inherent in Tarrow's model emerged in the course of the protests, connecting individuals with the ideology and mission of the movement. The most significant symbols were slogans that protesters chanted demanding "Horriyeh, Siyadeh, Istiqlal" (Freedom, Sovereignty, Independence) and "Haqiqa, Horriyeh, Wahdeh Wataniyeh" (Truth, Freedom, National Unity). These slogans accompanied the "repertoire of contention" in all rallies, marches, and campaigns.[61] Color emerged as another symbol of the revolution. The white and red shawls that Jumblat and her assistants designed and produced became symbols for the resistance. Blue ribbons were also worn by political and community leaders and by citizens to symbolize their demand for the truth about Hariri's assassination.

Finally, protesters were in constant face-to-face interaction with the forces of authority, engaging army units in direct and indirect dialogue. Perhaps most stunning was the protesters' interaction with the soldiers themselves, who, by and large, remained cordial throughout the entire campaign. According to one young woman:

A group of young demonstrators, who were going through the center of Baabdate, hid their flags and foulards in the back of the car. They were

FIGURE 10.4
A crowd numbering 11,200 men and women displaying a huge Lebanese flag

surprised to be asked by a member of the internal security forces why they were late, and were told to raise their flags without any fear.[62]

Protesters drew back from antagonizing the soldiers. Instead, they praised their professionalism and demanded that they be the only legitimate army to defend Lebanon; that is, they rejected the presence of the Syrian army on Lebanese soil. Men, women, and children offered flowers to the soldiers, who ignored orders to obstruct the movement of the demonstrators on several occasions.

In addition to asserting protesters' collective identity, Melucci argues that new social movements have succeeded in applying tactics and activities that capitalize on cultural forms such as concerts, parades, and arts and that they have been able to reach the larger public by means of information technology.[63] Indeed, news accounts report how art and media technology were integrated into the Lebanon Spring Revolution. Thanks to information technology, the protesters formed coalitions and obtained popular support not only in Lebanon but also around the world. This global presence was reflected back to the movement by the new media—namely, internationally available cable TV and the Internet—allowing for instant response and participation.

Merei captures this aspect of the revolution in her description of the protesters as "men and women whose power were candles, flowers and SMS messages."[64] Artistic talents were especially applied on March 12 when protesters created a mural of the Lebanese flag on colored cardboard, which 11,200 men and women carried over their heads.[65] Realizing the importance of symbols of unity, thousands of protesters later formed a human chain that extended more than two kilometers from Martyrs Square, the location of Hariri's grave, to the place where he was assassinated.[66]

While the style of the Lebanese revolution corresponds with scholars' descriptions of social movements, it had distinct unique features as well. Samir Khalaf of the American University of Beirut posits that while the March 8 rally "was somber, stern, [and] almost monolithic in its composition and message," the March 14 demonstration was a "spirited spectacle."[67] Khalaf claims that "by acquiring a life of its own, the uprising was 'lebanonized' into a mélange of seemingly dissonant elements: it became a rock concert, a triumphal post–World Cup soccer rally, something of a carnival."[68]

Once again, I would suggest that the revolution was not only "lebanonized" but also feminized in many ways. First, consider the prevalence of flowers and candles used and distributed by the protesters. Flowers and candles are usually stereotyped as objects appealing mostly to women. Hence their abundant use in the protests indicates a distinctly feminine influence. Second, the body and its adornment served as an instrument of protest as well. In the crowds, one observed a "rich diversity of dress codes, including traditional horsemen with Arab headdresses, clerics in their distinctive robes and turbans, and young girls with bare midriffs and pierced navels. . . . Those who were not carrying flags had them smeared on their faces or tattooed and inscribed on visible parts of their bodies."[69] The feminization factor was eloquently depicted in Merei's description of the significant contributions women made to this revolution:

> They turned their country into a flag, an anthem, a candle and a flower. Does the country need more than love? This is an emerging language that the youth created and the women dedicated: mothers, friends, lovers and sisters. This language became a flag and a national anthem of a country that has been historically suppressed. They are guarding this nation for a beautiful tomorrow for their men by protecting them from war, submissiveness and helplessness.[70]

CONCLUSION

Together men and women demonstrated, protested, expressed their opinions, and demanded the right to decide their destinies in the Lebanon Spring Revolution. This is a unique phenomenon in the Middle East, which has been notoriously unreceptive to both democratization and women's political participation. In the past, women's participation was mostly "individualistic, timid, uninformed, complicated with social restrictions, and alienated from contemporary politics."[71] However, the Cedar Revolution was different because women participated without being manipulated by political parties or restricted by traditional gender roles.

Lebanese women and men have taken a remarkable step towards democracy and have become imbued with its spirit. Democracy, according to Sartori,[72] may only be realized when people become aware of their need for it. The spirit of democracy, which was indeed floating in the air of the revolution and in the hearts of the protesters, became readily apparent in the movement's activities, slogans, and so on. However, Mona Modad poses a relevant question:

> Will this wonderful phenomenon finally prove that Lebanon is ready to embrace democracy and accept women as equal citizens? Or, is it just an unprecedented phenomenon that shows the unfortunate situation in Lebanon? We no longer know which is more miserable and oppressed: a nation stripped of its sovereignty and freedom, or its women deprived of their political rights?[73]

Three years after liberation from Syrian occupation, Lebanon is still not ready to embrace full democracy or accept women as equal citizens. In fact, advocates for women's rights have not achieved any in-depth progress towards advancing women's political and civil rights in Lebanon.

In this chapter, I have attempted to illustrate how the Lebanese resistance movement gained new meaning when Lebanese men and women demonstrated together. The March 14 demonstration of one million protesters crystallized into a liberation movement that succeeded in fulfilling the dream of sovereignty—and peacefully expelled the Syrian army from Lebanese soil.

While the liberation movement succeeded, the countermovement of March 8 did not exactly lose. Men, women, and children filled the streets in both demonstrations. Each movement created its own symbols and engaged in its own actions signifying collective identity and unity. Both movements carried Lebanese flags to show their national solidarity and had women participants; both failed in the long run to deliver women full citizenship rights.

Lebanese women, often considered indifferent to political processes and outcomes, became liberators and resisters in March 2005. In order to frame the participation of women in this revolution, I have constructed the sociopolitical context in which the protests occurred. I have also demonstrated the

diverse backgrounds of the women who engaged in the movement and discussed their reasons and motivations for doing so. As women assumed leadership roles in the Lebanese freedom movement, they created a more tolerant,
less violent, and more feminized style of protest. The Cedar Revolution left
an indelible image of women as active and equal citizens in their society. Their
spontaneous, dynamic activism reveals an unmistakable sense of ownership.
When the need presented itself, Lebanese women demonstrated an unprecedented political maturity, bringing new meaning to the word "patriotism."

NOTES

The author wishes to thank Mounira Charrad for her comments and suggestions; and
Guita Hourani, Rudy Sassine, and Elie El-Mir from the Lebanese Emigration Research
Center at Notre Dame University in Lebanon for their assistance in obtaining the data.
This research was supported by the American Association of University Women and PEO
International. All translations are the author's, except when a translated document is
cited.

1. "[The] President noted . . . that there was a rose revolution in Georgia, an orange
revolution in Ukraine, a purple revolution in Iraq." "In Lebanon, we see growing momentum for a 'cedar revolution' that is unifying the citizens of that nation to the cause of true
democracy and freedom from foreign influence." Paula J. Dobriansky, Under Secretary
of State for Global Affairs, "Remarks on Release of Country Reports on Human Rights
Practices for 2004," February 28, 2005. www.state.gov/g/rls/rm/2005/42793.htm.

2. Some argue that although the Cedar Revolution started as a grassroots movement,
it was soon hijacked by the Hariri group and politically geared to advance their political
interests.

3. Interview with Nora Jumblat, Beirut, July 10, 2006.

4. Scott Macleod, "Days of Cedar," *Time,* November 2, 2005. www.time.com/time/
magazine/article/0,9171,1112768,00.html.

5. Jumblat interview, 2006.

6. Manal Sheea, "The Sky Is Their Cover and the Flag Is Their Weapon, along with
the White Flowers Which They Offered to the Soldiers, Demonstrators in the Freedom
Square Awaited a New Dawn: We Will Not Leave Unless the Syrians Apologize and the
State Shows Remorse for their Crime," *Annahar,* March 1, 2005.

7. *Hezbollah* literally means "the Party of God." Founded during the fifteen-year
Lebanese civil war (1975–1990), Hezbollah continues to be known for armed resistance to
Israel.

8. Jumblat interview, 2006.

9. Sheea, "The Sky Is Their Cover."

10. "Seuls, en famille ou entre amis pour passer la nuit," *L'Orient-Le Jour,* March 1,
2005.

11. Roula Abdallah, "Fifteen Thousand White Roses Offered by the Beirut Social Development Organization," *Al-Mustaqbal,* March 1, 2005.

12. Adnan El-Ghoul, "Lebanese Bread through Army Cordon with Roses," *Daily Star,* March 1, 2005.

13. "The Government Falls under Popular Pressure and the Hammer of the Resistance," *Al-Mustaqbal,* March 1, 2005.

14. 'Anisa al-Amin Merei, "A Shiite Progressive Woman," *Annahar,* March 30, 2005.

15. Scott Wilson, "Rallies Highlight Rifts in Lebanon: Lebanese Opposition Answers Hezbollah with a Huge Anti-Syrian Demonstration," *Washington Post Foreign Service,* March 15, 2005, A16.

16. Ibid.

17. Ibid.

18. "Des mamans du Liban se recueillent sur la sépulture, place des Martyrs," *L'Orient-Le Jour,* March 22, 2005.

19. Scarlett Haddad, "Les Femmes dans la rue pour défier les poseurs de bombes," *L'Orient-Le Jour,* March 22, 2005.

20. "Des mamans du Liban se recueillent sur la sépulture, place des Martyrs."

21. Manal Sheea, "Thousands of Women Delivered One Message: Our Unity Is Greater than All Their Explosions," *Annahar,* March 29, 2005.

22. Ibid.

23. S.H., "Manifestation—Lorsque les femmes veulent faire entendre leur voix, place des Martyrs: Par milliers, elles ont réclamé la vérité de défié la peur et l'Angoisse," *L'Orient-Le Jour,* March 29, 2005.

24. Michael Dempsey and Hania Taan, "Lebanon Kicks off National Unity Festival: Thousands Take to Streets to Participate in Celebrations," *Daily Star,* April 11, 2005.

25. Leila Hatoum, "Tens of Thousands Mark Civil War's Beginning with 'Unity Run': Young, Old, Christian and Muslim Run for Lebanon," *Daily Star,* April 11, 2005.

26. Ibid.

27. Rym Ghazal, "Asma Andraos Honored as 'Hero of Change,'" *Daily Star,* October 14, 2005.

28. Jumblat interview, 2006.

29. Dieter Rucht, "Campaigns, Skirmishes, and Battles: Anti-Nuclear Movements in the USA, France, and Western Germany," *Industrial Crisis Quarterly,* no. 4 (1996): 193–222.

30. Macleod, "Days of Cedar."

31. *Stree.* www.stree.biz/about_stree.html.

32. Ghazal, "Asma Andraos Honored as 'Hero of Change.'"

33. Macleod, "Days of Cedar."

34. Ghazal, "Asma Andraos Honored as 'Hero of Change.'"

35. See J. M. Peteet, *Gender in Crisis: Women and the Palestinian Resistance Movement* (New York: Columbia University Press, 1991).

36. See Mounira Charrad, *States and Women's Rights: The Making of Postcolonial Tunisia, Algeria, and Morocco* (Berkeley: University of California Press, 2001).

37. See Ellen Fleischmann, *The Nation and Its "New" Women: the Palestinian Women's Movement, 1920–1948* (Berkeley: University of California Press, 2003); and A. Kawar, *Daughters of Palestine: Leading Women of the Palestinian National Movement* (Albany: State University of New York Press, 1996).

38. Merei, "A Shiite Progressive Woman."

39. "La 'Révolution du Cèdre': Un avant-goût de liberté," *L'Orient-Le Jour,* March 3, 2005.

40. "Seuls, en famille ou entre amis pour passer la nuit."

41. Ibid.

42. Rym Ghazal, "Anti-Syrian Protests Continue Despite Announced Redeployment: Campers Determined to Stay Until the Complete Withdrawal of Troops," *Daily Star,* March 8, 2005.

43. Jessy Chahine, "'We Are Coming to Free Our Country and Demand the Truth,'" *Daily Star,* March 14, 2005.

44. Rima Fakhry, interview by author, Beirut, July 2006.

45. Linda Dahdah and Habib Battah, "People Power Forces Cabinet of Karami Government: 'No One Can Intimidate us Anymore,'" *Daily Star,* March 1, 2005.

46. Brent Sadler, "Hariri Sister Calls for Justice," *CNN,* March 14, 2005.

47. Scarlett Haddad, "Place des Martyrs, l'espoir retrouvé des jeunes: Nous ne quitterons qu'après le départ des Syriens," *L'Orient-Le Jour,* March 2, 2005.

48. Jessy Chahine and Rym Ghazal, "'People Power' Keeps up the Pressure: Protesters Determined to Stay Put," *Daily Star,* March 2, 2005.

49. Ibid.

50. Haddad, "Place des Martyrs."

51. Hank Johnston and Bert Klandermans, *Social Movements and Culture* (Minneapolis: University of Minnesota Press, 1995), 5.

52. Leila J. Rupp and Verta A. Taylor, *Survival in the Doldrums: The American Women's Rights Movement, 1945 to the 1960s* (New York: Oxford University Press, 1987).

53. Willisms. www.willisms.com/archives/2005/03/more_on_the_bab_1.html.

54. Jo Freeman, *A Room at a Time: How Women Entered Party Politics* (Lanham, MD: Rowman & Littlefield, 2000).

55. Charrad, *States and Women's Rights.*

56. Shulamith Firestone, *The Dialectic of Sex: The Case for Feminist Revolution* (New York: Morrow Quill Paperbacks, 1980).

57. Kate Millett, *Sexual Politics* (Garden City, NY: Doubleday, 1970).

58. Sidney Tarrow, *Power in Movement: Social Movements and Contentious Politics* (Cambridge: Cambridge University Press, 1998), 2.

59. Jessy Chahine and Linda Dahdah, "Demo Plans Go Ahead Despite Warnings: Sfeir and Lahoud Call for Limiting Shows of Force," *Daily Star,* March 14, 2005.

60. "More than Two Kilometers of Young Men and Women Connected Hands in a Human Chain from Hariri's Grave to Location of the Explosion," *Annahar,* February 27, 2005.

61. Charles Tilly, "Repertoires of Contention in America and Britain, 1750–1830," in

The Dynamics of Social Movements: Resource Mobilization, Social Control and Tactics, ed. Mayer N. Zald and John D. McCarthy (Cambridge, MA: Winthrop, 1979), 126–155.

62. Anne-Marie El-Hage, "Manifestation—Un Sit-in Pacifiste, avec la complicité de l'armée, pour suivre en direct la séance parlementaire: 'Démissionnez,' demande la foule au gouvernement," *L'Orient-Le Jour,* March 1, 2005.

63. Alberto Melucci, "The New Social Movements: A Theoretical Approach," *Social Science Information* 19 (1980): 199–226.

64. Merei, "A Shiite Progressive Woman."

65. "More than Two Kilometers of Young Men and Women Connected Hands."

66. Ibid.

67. Samir Kalaf, "Lebanon's Youths Are Now Writing Their Own Future," *Daily Star,* March 29, 2005.

68. Ibid.

69. Ibid.

70. Merei, "A Shiite Progressive Woman."

71. Jihad Al-Turk, "Women in Martyrs Square: Their Strategic Participation by Shaking of Political Inhibitions in Order to Resurrect Lebanon." *Al-Mustaqbal,* March 10, 2005.

72. Giovanni Sartori, *The Theory of Democracy Revisited* (Chatham, NJ: Chatham House, 1987).

73. Mona Modad, "Is It Time for Women's Participation in Social and National Politics?" *Annahar,* March 13, 2005.

11

IMAGES OF MANIPULATION

Subversion of Women's Rights in the Maghreb

NADIA MARZOUKI

Whereas the West often portrays Muslim women in Middle Eastern countries negatively and from a biased standpoint, its images of the North African woman are largely positive. When "women of the Maghreb" are discussed, the focus is most frequently Tunisian women. Indeed, generalizations about the experiences of Tunisian women tend to subvert deeper inquiry concerning the lives of countless other Maghrebi women. A combination of indifference to and idealization of Maghrebi women reflects the limited strategic interest that North Africa holds for U.S. foreign policy,[1] especially in comparison to the Middle East.

Without question the lives of North African women are exceedingly different from the lives of their Iraqi, Lebanese, or Palestinian counterparts. However, women from these diverse regions have one thing in common: the ineffable experience of war. Furthermore, they all reside in regions with a colonial history and violent struggles for independence. In Algeria, for example, the wounds of civil war are still deeply felt today, in spite of the National Reconciliation policy adopted by President Bouteflika. Although one could say that no North African nation is currently at war, it would be inaccurate to refer to this region as a secure and peaceful geopolitical environment.

Authoritarianism, unemployment, poverty, and radicalism are major social and political features of North Africa today. As such, they increasingly erode the fragile landscape of peace. In this chapter I would like to emphasize the paradoxical situation of North African women whose struggle takes place in a context that can be described neither as war nor peace.

Although Mauritania is sometimes included in the Maghreb, I focus only on Tunisia, Morocco, and Algeria. From my perspective, their commonality stems from a form of state monopoly on women's issues. Some scholars have chosen to emphasize the dissimilarity in women's conditions in these three countries. For example, Mounira M. Charrad has discussed why the three have developed family policies that are so divergent.[2] According to Charrad, differences in contemporary family laws are related to disparities in the process of state formation. In each country, the state has developed a specific strategy to include or take control of tribes and kinship groups. This strategy critically affects the type of family law that is adopted.

Morocco's government has been formed in close alliance with kinship groups, which explains why until recently family laws have remained very conservative. In Algeria, state formation relied on a partial alliance with kinship groups. This alliance resulted in the ultraconservative nature of Algerian family law. In Tunisia, on the other hand, the relatively autonomous construction of the state in relation to kinship groups and tribes—as well as the formation of a large urban elite and bureaucracy during the colonization era—accounts for the liberal family law adopted as early as 1956. Regardless of differences, an intriguing similarity exists among the three countries. In Tunisia, Morocco, and Algeria, women's rights are granted by the ruling elite or the ruler himself.[3] This chapter examines the causes and implications of this phenomenon. Its approach is a constructivist one, in that it questions the assertion that the main obstacles to women's rights are "male domination" and the presupposition that the main solution to women's problems must be either purely Islamic or purely secular.

I first argue that the main cause of Maghrebi women's difficulties lies in the authoritarianism of the state in each of the three countries, even when the state claims to implement a secular and (supposedly) feminist policy. Second, I question assumptions about the North African male, assumptions that form the basis of most of the scholarship regarding women in North Africa. Finally, I demonstrate that the only grassroots women's movements with any real influence or credibility are those presenting themselves as Islamic.

THE ROLE OF STATE AUTHORITARIANISM

Until the mid-1960s no legitimate field of study explored Arab and/or Muslim women's issues. The question of Muslim women was considered part of the broader analysis of modernization and development. Since the 1970s, however, gender studies research has been increasingly applied to the Arab world. Indeed, Muslim women's issues have now become universally accepted as a natural extension of gender studies. In the case of the Maghreb, however, I contend that it is inappropriate to examine women's conditions and status exclusively from the point of view of gender studies. Instead, these issues should be examined in relation to state authoritarianism.[4] In North Africa, state authoritarianism has played a critical role in slowing the progress of women's rights. Rather than look through the lens of a patriarchal[5] or Islamic tradition or at the impact of the colonial experience, I argue that one would do well to explore the direct link between the authoritarian state feminism of North African regimes and women's conditions.

Although the history of women's rights is very different in Algeria, Tunisia, and Morocco, one can nevertheless find significant similarities. First, the state has always used women's issues as a tool to compete against Islamic conservatives. Next, secular grassroots women's movements have never been able to succeed. Finally, any rights granted to women result from a state decision (a gratuity of sorts) rather than from women's activism.

Tunisia offers the best example of state feminism (Bessis 1999). Bourguiba, leader of the independence movement and the first Tunisian president, established the Personal Status Code (Code du Statut Personnel) in 1956; the code granted Tunisian women a number of fundamental rights.[6] At the time Bourguiba's decision was perceived as nothing less than revolutionary. Although one must acknowledge the positive impact of this reform on Tunisian women's lives, it should be noted that the reform had negative effects as well. Bourguiba's policy halted the formation of feminist grassroots activism, implying that because basic rights had already been granted by the "Father-President," all other claims were illegitimate and potentially harmful to national unity. Following the 1987 coup in which Ben Ali became president, women were briefly concerned that he would change or cancel the CSP. However, it soon became clear that women's rights were a crucial part of Ben Ali's strategy to crush Islamists and to consolidate the image of Tunisia as a modern, secular, and democratic country.

Symptomatic of this institutionalized state feminism was the creation of the National Union of the Tunisian Woman (Union Nationale de la Femme Tunisienne [UNFT]). A 1958 initiative by Bourguiba, this organization claimed to represent and defend the interests of all Tunisian women. Presenting itself as a nongovernmental organization (NGO), the UNFT has maintained extremely close ties to the government. The organization publishes a monthly review, *Femme,* which has a photograph of and a quote from President Ben Ali on the cover of each issue. The cover of the December 2006 issue reads: "The UNFT begs President Ben Ali to be a candidate for the presidential election in 2009."[7] Other covers show Leïla Ben Ali, the president's wife, being awarded a number of prizes for her feminist actions. While the UNFT tries to sell the image of a woman-friendly, secular, and modern country, an increasing number of Tunisian women are taking up the headscarf (Beaugé 2006). Although functionalist approaches—explaining the new headscarf popularity as a way to express a political view—do not exhaust the phenomenon, it is clear that the propagation of headscarves on Tunisian streets is related to women's discontent with the absence of real freedom. The Tunisian case exemplifies how an authoritarian state, pretending to support women's progress, has blocked the emergence of a credible grassroots women's movement and has delegitimized the very concept of feminism, a notion too often associated in the public's mind with authoritarian secularism.

In Morocco, where the king is also the "Descendant of the Prophet" and the "Commander of the Faithful," the relationship between women, the state, and Islamic conservatives is addressed in a different way. After independence, King Hassan II did not change the *Moudawana*, or traditional family code. Rather, the first efforts to defend women's rights initially came from the major Moroccan political parties, such as the Istiqlal Party.[8] In 1969 King Hassan II created the National Union of Moroccan Women (l'Union Nationale des Femmes Marocaines), chaired by his two daughters. The union mainly represented the urban elite's interests. It was often blamed for being too closely allied with the Makhzen and for monopolizing the "feminist discourse" by claiming to represent all Moroccan women's interests.[9] No matter how sincerely they tried to improve the living conditions of impoverished, rural Moroccan women, the first generation of Moroccan feminists (to a large extent) primarily represented the interests of the urban elite. This elite feminism coupled with the state's fear of pluralism blocked any real progress for women.

In the late 1980s the Moroccan regime became somewhat more liberal, allowing new women's organizations to develop. Within a few years, numerous organizations had been created, leading to significant fragmentation in the Moroccan women's movement.[10] While the Tunisian government restrained women's activism by monopolizing and unifying the feminist discourse, the Moroccan kingdom allowed the women's movement to weaken itself by encouraging its fragmentation. In 1992 Moroccan women's organizations launched a campaign calling for the reform of the ultraconservative *Moudawana*.[11] Islamic conservatives, including the Ulama and Islamist political parties, responded to this campaign by accusing female leaders of being manipulated by Westernized men seeking to undermine the Moroccan Islamic tradition. The king was much more concerned with the Islamic conservatives' reaction than with the women's claims. Interestingly, he asked women not to create a political party, arguing that the reform of the *Moudawana* was a family issue and not a political one.

This fear of women's politicization underscores the fact that feminism has always been a purely political currency for North African regimes. The question of women's emancipation has been instrumentalized by North African authoritarian states in their rivalry with Islamic conservatives and in their quest for international legitimacy. In 1998 yet another effort to reform women's status failed. The "National Plan of Action for the Integration of Women in Development" presented by Said Saadi, secretary of the family, was severely criticized by Islamists. They claimed the plan merely reflected demands of Western organizations such as the World Bank. When King Mohamed VI finally amended the *Moudawana* in 2004, it was not because of the 1992 campaign or because of feminist efforts. Although changing the *Moudawana* could be considered a victory *for* Moroccan women, it is not a victory *of* Moroccan women. Indeed, the reform of the *Moudawana* was not so much decided by King Mohamed VI regardless of Islamic conservatives' opposition but rather a calculated decision made against them. A few months after the Casablanca terrorist attacks of May 2003, the king could find no better way to reaffirm his power against Islamists and to correct the international perception of Morocco as controlled by extremists.

Morocco thus provides a credible example of how, just as in Tunisia, women's issues have been manipulated to consolidate the king's power against Islamists and to seek international legitimacy. If the Islamists finally accepted the reform, after having strongly opposed it a few years earlier, it was only because of the impressive ability of the king to centralize the state's decision-making process — the same process that had led to the *Moudawana* reform. The king thus succeeded in reconciling the feminists, the Ulama, the political parties, and international organizations (Roussillon 2004).[12]

Comparing and contrasting the three North African nations reveals that conditions for women are most deplorable in Algeria. Although Algerian women played a crucial part in the war for independence, afterward their political roles were markedly reduced. Whereas approximately 11,000 women fought in the civil resistance as *maquisardes*,[13] the first Constitutional Assembly (Assemblée Constituante) in 1962 included only 10 women (out of 194). A year later, the National Liberation Front (Front de Libération Nationale [FLN]) — the nationalist movement that had fought the war for independence — created the National Union of Algerian Women (Union Nationale des Femmes Algeriennes), the primary purpose of which was to echo the FLN point of view regarding women. After 1963 the FLN rejected the notion of "women's emancipation" on the grounds that it was a throwback to French colonial rule.

In 1984 a new family code was adopted defining Algerian women as minors.[14] This family code, generally interpreted as a concession by President Chadli Benjedid to the Islamic conservatives, was created in an effort to preserve social order. Here again the authoritarian regime sacrificed women's rights in order to restrain the Islamist opposition. The Algerian case provides an interesting counterargument to the idea that grassroots activist movements necessarily lead to political liberalization. Ironically, the more liberal family code was adopted in Tunisia without the influence of feminist grassroots organizations. In contrast, although Algeria's feminist organizations played a crucial role in the struggle for independence, women's conditions deteriorated significantly after independence.[15]

In Tunisia, Algeria, and Morocco, despite differences in the history of women's struggles, women's rights remain, for the most part, dependent on the authoritarian state agenda. Women's issues in North Africa are often linked to the region's "Islamic tradition" or to "the colonial past." It is time to question these culturalist and postcolonial approaches that tend to omit the political analysis of the state. Instead, the topic of North African women and the absence of basic rights should be integrated into a broader political framework that focuses on issues of the state and democratization. No longer can this area of research be relegated to the field of gender studies, pretending that no link exists between the lack of pluralism and women's sociopolitical conditions.

THE NORTH AFRICAN MALE: WHO IS HE?

In the literature on North African women, one finds very little of substance concerning North African men.[16] For example, what do Algerian men think of the 1984 family code? What is the opinion of Tunisian men regarding state monopoly of feminist discourse? Were *all* Moroccan men opposed to the reform of the *Moudawana?* Because no comprehensive research has been done addressing these questions, most studies about North African women continue to reinforce the assumption that most men are potentially dangerous and hostile to women's emancipation. Interestingly, authoritarian governments tend to put forward the same image when attempting to justify the need for feminist reforms (in Tunisia, for example) or the absence of those same reforms (in Algeria). The presupposition underlying authoritarian policy—similar to most Western feminist scholarship—is that the Arab man in the street, "l'homme de la rue arabe," is essentially hostile to women's emancipation and remains tenaciously attached to social order and traditions.

A closer analysis of the relationship between state authoritarianism and women's rights suggests that this view supposedly held by men is not rooted in a so-called Islamic tradition but rather is itself a construction of state authoritarianism. Male domination is simultaneously an instrument of and an effect of state authoritarianism. Oppressing women and exerting violence against them is not a "right" or a sign of power; on the contrary, it shows that men are themselves completely dominated by the authoritarian state (Addi 1999).

This ambivalence inherent in the phenomenon of oppressed-oppressing men appears very clearly in the families of the "disappeared"[17] and in recent cases of violence exerted against single women. Since 1993 between 3,000 and 4,000 individuals, mostly male, have "disappeared" after being arrested by security forces, allegedly because they were suspected of being involved with Islamic armed groups. Wives and children of the disappeared are now victims of multiple forms of violence: material violence, because they are often left without resources, and symbolic violence, because they are to some extent ostracized by the society at large.

On July 14, 2001, a mob of three hundred men, ages fifteen to thirty, attacked about twenty single women living and working in Hassi Messaoud, a city 1,000 kilometers south of Algiers, where many foreign oil companies employ single women who come from the north in search of work. Many of these women are wives of the disappeared. The assailants accused them of being prostitutes and of stealing work from local men. This crime is all the more appalling in that it was not committed by a group of radically insane men—as suggested by the media—but by "ordinary" young men with no prior criminal records. Many were neighbors or landlords of the victims.

This extraordinary case of violence can be viewed as an extension of the violence sparked by the Algerian government's 1992 decision to cancel elections. After the Algerian civil war, which raged for five years (1992–1997), the ideals of national reconciliation and cohesion remained abstract. The subsequent surges of violence reflect the depth of frustration, anger, and despair of the Algerian people, who have lived in a repressed society and polity since 1992. The timid response of the local officials to this attack is especially mystifying. Instead of condemning the attack, local officials locked all single women of Hassi Messaoud in a barrack to "protect" them. The case of the disappeared and examples of violence such as the Hassi Messaoud incident suggest that *both* men and women are victims of an authoritarian and failed state.

GRASSROOTS WOMEN'S MOVEMENTS AND ISLAM

A more comprehensive form of analysis regarding North African women is required, one that links the issues affecting women, men, and the state. However, I do not mean to deny the autonomous female space in which women can develop creative ways to escape or expand the limits imposed on them by the state. Because secular authoritarian regimes have delegitimized the idea of secularism—now always equated with Western imperialism or state repression—the only women's movements with some degree of power, autonomy, and legitimacy are those that present themselves as Islamic. To understand these movements, it is crucial to move beyond commonly drawn polarities, that is, the emancipating character of liberal secularism versus the oppressive character of Islamic tradition.

My objective is not to examine whether or not Islam runs fundamentally contrary to women's emancipation. Rather, I am simply recording the language that North African women use to express their needs for improved conditions and policies. No matter how one interprets this trend, it is a fact that Islam, not Western secularism, has become the language North African women increasingly rely on to communicate their disapprobation and to secure their rights.

This Islamicization of North African women is reflected in the women's section of Al Adl wal Ihsane (Justice and Spirituality), led by Nadia Yassine. Al Adl wal Ihsane is an Islamic movement established in 1973 by Abdessalem Yassine. It has continually criticized the authoritarianism of the "Makhzen" (the power base of Moroccan politics) and, in particular, refuses to acknowledge the article of the Moroccan constitution giving the king the title "Commander of the Faithful."[18] Nadia Yassine, Abdessalem Yassine's daughter, advocates women's emancipation and full participation in the public sphere. The program is not based on a Western, secular, and liberal paradigm; rather, it seeks to reconcile women's rights and the "true" spirit of Islam. Following her father's example, Nadia Yassine has always strenuously opposed the Makhzen and its policy toward women. In 2004 Nadia Yassine grudgingly accepted the reform of the *Moudawana* but at the same time voiced her disapproval. Although some individuals used her response as evidence of the supposedly antifeminist approach of Islamists, Yassine's argument was more complex. She criticized reform of the *Moudawana* on the grounds that the king adopted this initiative only to pander to international pressures following the tragic events of 9/11 and March 2003. Yes to woman's liberation, said Nadia Yassine, but no to the Moroccan people's alienation ("pour la libération de la femme, mais pas au prix de l'aliénation du peuple").[19]

Nadia Yassine's response reflects the attitudes of most North Africans. Almost without exception, secularism is now perceived as nothing more than a political strategy, a tool of the authoritarian state and/or of the imperialistic "North." Hence the need to disconnect secularization from the issue of women's empowerment, not only in North Africa, but throughout the entire Arab world as well.

According to a 2005 Gallup Poll,[20] most North African women want more freedom and more political participation. At the same time, they do not perceive "Westernization" as the right choice for their society. When asked what they most admired about their own society, most women answered the following: "people's adherence to Islamic values." Likewise, whereas 95 percent of Moroccan women believe that they should be able to exercise an autonomous vote, 98 percent think that Sharia (Islamic law) should be one source—or even the sole source—of legislation.

Although feminist Islamic movements such as Nadia Yassine's should be taken seriously, in that they represent an increasingly important trend in the Maghreb, they raise significant questions. Nadia Yassine's argument is based on the idea that the real cause of women's oppression is not Islam itself but the distorted manner in which authoritarian regimes have used religious texts. This view implies that there is actually something such as "pure" religious meaning that may be distorted or recovered. It also suggests that Islam offers the solution to most women's problems.

I earlier argued for a constructivist perspective by suggesting that the figure of the oppressive male is constructed by oppressive regimes. Likewise, from a constructivist perspective, one would do well to question claims of an authentic meaning of Islam or, for that matter, any phenomena that is put forth as "Islamically pure" (Roussillon 2004: 8). The distortion of Islam by authoritarian regimes and/or by radicals is as meaningful and as real as the supposedly true meaning of Islam that Islamic feminists want to recover. Interestingly, the feminists are using Islam as an instrument in much the same way as authoritarian regimes do. Only they are doing so for a significantly different—and more enlightened—purpose. I do not want to discredit the work of feminist movements trying to reconcile Islam and women's empowerment. But if one considers that there is no Islamic meaning independent from its context and that there is no "pure" religion independent from its use, then feminist strategies drawing on the return to an "authentic" meaning of Islam may ultimately be painting themselves into a corner.

Although movements such as Nadia Yassine's are important both politically and socially, their priorities are clearly embedded in spirituality and Islamic revival. These movements are less interested in political negotiations, in part because they consider the state excessively corrupt. While it is crucial to take these spiritual movements seriously, because they represent the most active basis of North African civil society today, democratization of political institutions—carrying the promise of social, political, legal, and institutional reforms—must be afforded as much importance as theoretical debates over religious meanings.

CONCLUSION

I have made the following three arguments: state authoritarianism significantly contributes to North African women's oppression; assumptions regarding the role of North African men in this oppressive dynamic should be reexamined; and, finally, the only influential grassroots North African women's movements are those inscribed in an Islamic tradition.

These three arguments imply that any attempt to help North African women is doomed to fail as long as Maghrebian authoritarian regimes remain unchallenged. I would even suggest that international aid is to a certain extent counterproductive. For example, one of the objectives of the Barcelona Process, established in 1995, was to support North African women's rights, notably by encouraging dialogue between representatives of the civil society on both sides of the Mediterranean. This offer of support to North African feminist NGOs has proven essentially ineffective, primarily because the authoritarian regimes of Tunisia, Algeria, and Morocco render any active NGO (such as the UNFT) powerless by placing them more or less under governmental control. Beatrice Hibou (2006) calls these organizations RGOs, really governmental organizations (*organisations vraiment gouvernementales* [OVG]). In short, supporting Maghrebian women's NGOs comes down to supporting the very authoritarian states responsible for the deplorable conditions against which women are struggling. As for other NGOs and international organizations, they are confronted with the same problem. Their support of "grassroots" women's organizations in the Maghreb is severely limited by strict control of the state (Brand 1998).

In Algeria, Tunisia, and Morocco, therefore, authoritarianism has become the only accepted tool for maintaining a very fragile social and political stability. Authoritarian rulers reject real political pluralism for fear that it might empower radical Islamists. However, the stability that authoritarianism is supposed to guarantee has become increasingly burdensome to the people. In many respects, the Mahgreb's peaceful social order seems as inauthentic as political democracy. Moreover, if anything disturbs this fragile peace, women—especially those in Tunisia—will probably be the first targets of violence, given that feminism has become so closely associated with authoritarianism. The terrible irony is that Maghrebi women are caught in a no-win situation: the limited rights they have been granted in "peacetime" may ultimately accelerate their social, cultural, and political downfall.

NOTES

1. The U.S. policy of supporting North African authoritarian regimes has been, in large part, coherent with the realist policy always favored by France, that is, one that mostly values the consolidation of stability on France's southern borders and fears the possibility of any Islamic regime coming to power. When some U.S. officials first attempted to have a dialogue with Algerian Islamists in the early 1990s and supported resumption of the democratic process, they were severely criticized by the French (see Fawaz Gerges, "The U.S.-French Clash over Algeria," in *America and Political Islam: Clash of Cultures or Clash of Interests* [Cambridge: Cambridge University Press, 1999], 155). It is true that since 9/11 U.S. officials have become more interested in North Africa and have been especially vigilant about radical groups such as Al Qaïda au Maghreb. However, if one looks at the general dynamics of international relations, North Africa very much remains the privileged field of action of Europe.

2. Mounira M. Charrad, *States and Women's Rights: The Making of Postcolonial Tunisia, Algeria and Morocco* (Berkeley: University of California Press, 2001).

3. Charrad acknowledges this at the end of her book. See *States and Women's Rights*, 23: "In all three Maghrebi countries, family law policy came 'from above' as a strategic choice by the elites in power."

4. Although I am here more interested in authoritarian state feminism than in authoritarianism, I am referring to Camau and Geisser's (2003) definition of authoritarianism. From their point of view, the current apparent *aggiorrnamento* of states such as Tunisia represents a consolidation of authoritarianism.

5. Much has been written about the supposedly patriarchal social structure of the Maghrebian family. See Germaine Tillion, *Le Harem et les cousins* (Paris: Editions du Seuil, 1966); Pierre Bourdieu, *Trois études d'ethnologie kabyle* (Paris: Droz, 1972); Camille Lacoste-Dujardin, *Des mères contre des femmes, maternité et patriarcat au Maghreb* (Paris: La Découverte, 1985).

6. The new code raises the minimum legal age at which women can marry to age seventeen, supports women's education and access to birth control, and replaces the traditional method of repudiation by a legal procedure of divorce.

7. "L'UNFT exhorte le président Ben Ali à se porter candidat aux elections de 2009." www.unft.org.tn/fr/publications/revue_femme.html.

8. The Istiqlal Party, the Socialist Union of Popular Forces, the Party of Progress and Socialism.

9. "The governing elite in Morocco centered around the king and consisting of royal notables, businessmen, wealthy landowners, tribal leaders, top-ranking military personnel,

security service bosses, and other well-connected members of the establishment." http://en.wikipedia.org/wiki/Makhzen.

10. Examples of women's organizations are the Democratic Association of Moroccan Women (1985), the Organization of the Istiqlalian Woman (1987), the Union of Feminine Action (1987), the Moroccan Association for Women's Rights (1992), the Democratic League of Women's Rights (1992), the Association of Progressive Women (1993), and the Organization for the Renewal of Women's Awareness (1994).

11. This campaign, during which women tried to gather one million signatures supporting a petition for the reform of the *Moudawana,* was called the One Million Signatures Campaign.

12. See the speech delivered on October 10, 2003, by King Mohamed VI: www.majliss-annouwaba.ma.

13. Algerian women, struggling against French colonial rule after 1945, were called *maquisardes* because they had to hide in the *maquis* (French for "thicket" or "undergrowth").

14. According to the 1984 code, women need a *wali,* or guardian. Repudiation and polygamy are allowed. Women cannot travel abroad without their husbands or without a male guardian's consent.

15. See Charrad, *States and Women's Rights,* 237.

16. In France, the sociologist Nacera Guenif-Souleïmas has challenged assumptions shared by many French feminists about the North African male immigrant in her book *Les Féministes et le garçon arabe* (Paris: Editions de l'Aube, 2006).

17. See Florence Beaugé, "En Algérie, aucun survivant Parmi les Disparus de la Sale Guerre," *Le Monde,* January 8, 2003.

18. For more information on Islamic movements in Morocco, see Malika Zeghal, *Les Islamistes marocains, le défi à la monarchie* (Paris: La Découverte, 2005).

19. http://nadiayassine.net.

20. Dalia Mogahed, "Perspectives of Women in the Muslim World," 2005. media.gallup.com/worldpoll/pdf/gallup+muslim+studies_perspectives+of+women_11.10.06_final.pdf.

PART THREE

EUROPE AND THE UNITED STATES

12

IMAGES OF WOMEN IN BOSNIA, HERZEGOVINA, AND NEIGHBORING COUNTRIES, 1992–1995

ZILKA SPAHIĆ-ŠILJAK

Images of women, especially as portrayed during the 1992–1995 war in Bosnia, Herzegovina, and neighboring countries, reflect ethnonational politics and ideologies prevalent at the time. This chapter begins by tracing the status and roles of Balkan women in public life, starting in 1946—the year in which they obtained suffrage. The first section provides a sociopolitical context, describing how women's rights in Bosnia and Herzegovina were framed by predominant images of "worker," "proletarian," and respectable "Communist." It should be noted that "motherhood" remained the predominant image by which the socialist egalitarian facade identified, repressed, and veiled the female population.

The second section covers the period of war (1992–1995) and the role of ethnonational ideologies in building new images of women, such as "Mother of the Nation," "[Mother of the] Homeland," "National Heroine," "Pride of the Nation," and "Ethic Paradigm" (i.e., woman as safeguard of ethnonational honor).

The third section deals with gender-based violence, in particular rape and other forms of sexual abuse, which proved highly successful in literally destroying women's bodies and figuratively destroying the "bodies" of nation-states. Gender-based violence effectively transformed the image of women from "the Nation's Pride" to "the Nation's Shame."

IMAGES OF WOMEN IN YUGOSLAVIA, 1945–1990

After World War II, the Socialist Federal Republic of Yugoslavia (SFRY) was established. This new republic, founded on socialist political concepts and ideology, became a center of mass industrialization and urbanization. In fact, Yugoslavia's economic development surpassed all other socialist countries in Eastern Europe. Its constitutional and legal framework offered equal opportunities to men and women in every sphere of life, including representation in politics.

From the beginning days of the Yugoslav republic, constitutional provisions were followed by intense activism on the part of women within the Communist Party (CP). The most prominent women's movement at the time was the Antifascist Front of Women (AFW). Its primary objectives were the eradication of illiteracy and the full participation of women in public life. A new image of women emerged: prominent proletarian figures marching shoulder to shoulder with men. Images of women building factories, roads, railways, and settlements for the working class became commonplace. The AFW successfully gathered women around this egalitarian vision. However, the AFW's close ties to the Communist Party resulted in limitations on its actual power. In fact, the Communist Party used the AFW as a successful tool to consolidate revolutionary power, mobilizing large numbers of women to rebuild the new republic and to solve accumulated social problems.[1] Consequently, the AFW lost all autonomy and ability to focus on women's issues; instead, it became the executor of previously prepared political goals of the CP.[2]

An expansive Communist bureaucracy emerged, with numerous branches and departments used for the purpose of exercising Party discipline. The real problems that women faced in daily life were largely ignored. Within ten years after the end of World War II, the AFW was abolished. The doyenne of the AFW movement, Neda Božinović, observed that patriarchy, more than any other obstacle, contributed to the dissolution of the AFW:

> I came to the conclusion that that event [the dismantling of the AFW], had at its base a patriarchal outline—it was difficult to accept women as equal people. Even then, socialism proclaimed equality for women, but under "our control"—control of the Socialist Party.[3]

Although gender equality had been formally guaranteed and advocated, in reality a patriarchal system prevailed, which managed to keep women out of politics and power and "outside the decision-making mainstream."[4] To confirm the validity of this statement, one need only examine statistical data regarding women's representation in economic and political life at that time. Despite equal access to all positions of employment, a hidden patriarchal agenda operated to systematically promote gender dichotomy. The result was a "feminization of occupations." In other words, female children were encouraged to attend schools that provided instruction in so-called women's occupations (i.e., education, health, and social care). These occupations provided ample time and opportunity for women to take care of their families. Child rearing and housekeeping remained indisputably natural female obligations. Woman and household symbolized nature, in the same way that man symbolized culture.[5]

In an attempt to reconcile their private and public lives, women accepted work in these less demanding occupations and also accepted lower incomes than their male counterparts. This resulted in the "feminization of poverty" and women's economic dependence on men. Between 1964 and 1969, women made up 51.7 percent of the education sector, 62 percent in health care, and 54 percent in social care;[6] by the 1980s the numbers had increased to 60 percent, 73 percent,, and 78 percent, respectively.[7] These statistics confirm that women were mostly oriented towards occupations considered natural extensions of housekeeping and nurturing. The remainder of employed women worked primarily in the so-called secondary sector of the textile industry "with old-fashioned technologies, lower educational structure, and lower wages and salaries."[8]

Women also participated in political life, holding 4 to 6 percent of elected political positions from 1953 to 1969[9] and 15 to 24 percent between 1974 and 1986, the era during which the delegate system was introduced in former Yugoslavia.[10] However, women remained on the margins of higher decision-making positions and power. Although women had formally obtained the right to education, to workforce participation, and even to full participation in politics, they had been unwittingly trapped. The patriarchal culture, with its traditional norms and values, still held sovereignty over family and social relations. Lidija Sklevicky concludes:

> Emancipatory values which were connected to existing traditional values on women's "natural" status in the culture, and "women's values" defined by tradition and social roles based on them, have been unequivocally incorporated into the process of socialist revolution and influenced women's political representation.[11]

Because of obstacles placed in their way, women tended to perceive their jobs as something that circumstance compelled them to do rather than as opportunities to fulfill their human potential and wishes. Since the majority of women were enmeshed in family obligations, they struggled between family and career and thus were saddled with a double burden. Women were raised and trained to be mothers and wives. Only if they fulfilled these duties properly would they earn the "moral right" to be engaged as workers in Yugoslavia's socialist system. Women were expected to run respectable households and dutifully raise their children. Concomitantly, they were required to achieve brilliant careers before they could hope to participate in politics.

Understandably, women were hesitant to step outside the assigned social and behavioral framework, fearing patriarchal judgment and social stigma. They shouldered the burden of responsibility for their children's success or failure, indeed for the welfare of the entire family. Even today when female children cause trouble, one may still hear the neighbors say, "If the mother were better, that would not have happened." However, if the children are successful, then the credit automatically goes to the father, and the mother's contribution is largely ignored.

In Muslim families, moral values were strongly emphasized, especially in regard to a woman's virginity and chastity. Not surprisingly, a man's virginity and chastity were never scrutinized or considered an appropriate topic for discussion. A popular saying illustrates this best: "Male shame can be washed away with a watering can, but female shame cannot be washed away by a whole river." Clearly patriarchy resulted in a win-win situation for men. Women were in charge of safeguarding moral values and family chastity and, above all, obliged to obey their husbands. Moral double standards remained deeply rooted in gender policies and culture, requiring that women subjugate themselves to male dominance. It is no wonder that mass rapes were chosen as the most powerful tool for destroying Muslim families and the population in Bosnia and Herzegovina.

IMAGES OF WOMEN AS THE "NATION'S PRIDE"

In the early 1990s the former Yugoslav republics, including Bosnia and Herzegovina, held multiparty elections for the first time. As a result, nationally based political parties came to power, signaling a new era of political and economic transition. In effect, the multiparty elections set the stage for a systematic disintegration of Yugoslavia—in the name of nationalistic concepts and territorial ambitions, primarily from Serbia and later from Croatia.[12]

The 1990s brought startling "democratic" changes. These changes, wrapped in national garments, affected women most profoundly—as women were the first to be fired and the last to be (re)hired.[13] Separating "political freedom" from the secure and stable system of social benefits that existed under socialism was meaningless to most of the population. However, women felt the new challenges most keenly, often in terms of daily survival.

During the Communist era in former Yugoslavia, the image of woman as "worker" and supporter of the socialist system had been emphasized. In the transitional period of the early 1990s, women's status was redefined according to policies of nation-state formation. New economic and political discourses mediated and reinforced strong gender identity. Generally, when societies undergo such transformations—attempting to connect present values with those of the traditional past and exploring new sources for the legitimization of power—women become a focal point for creating new identity. Unfortunately, in the former Yugoslavia, the transition was accompanied by terrible conflict and by horrific war crimes, so that womanhood was exploited and misused in creating new national images.

From a Croatian perspective, Vesna Kesić points out that women became the symbol of ethnic and ideological differentiation,[14] which can also be said for the other republics of former Yugoslavia. Instead of the Yugoslav models of workers and supporters of socialist order, women were redefined through new images in accordance with ethnonational goals. These goals placed women in the role of "reproducers," not only of the nation and its new members, but also of its very boundaries. Women were represented as the transmitters of culture and cultural values, key participants in the national struggle against the "other."[15] This process resulted in the misuse of women for the purpose of ethnonational ideological aims and ambitions.

Kesić, in analyzing the transformation that occurred in the new national order and political framework of Croatia, observed that women were glorified as the "Pride of the Nation." Once again, it should be noted that similar processes developed in Serbia and Bosnia-Herzegovina. In the first stage, nationalistic political discourses defined women as "Mothers of the Nation,"[16] "Mother–Nurturers,"[17] [Mothers of the] "Homeland," and "Ethic Paradigm" (woman as safeguard of ethnonational honor). This process was achieved in part by referencing prominent female saints and figures in national or religious history. Consequently, women's status was effectively reduced until only their reproductive function and role as child bearers held significance. Furthermore, women were expected to reciprocate the trust placed in them by solemnly fulfilling their obligation to produce sons/soldiers and daughters/ young mothers-of-the-nation. Accordingly, women were no longer perceived as individuals but as biological producers of new recruits to defend the nation. Their identity was completely reduced to motherhood, their only value tied to the family unit:

> The family is a metaphor for the nation and its life-giving work, but at the same time, also the only primary and ultimate social entity that was granted the right to separate existence and functioning within the totalizing comprehensiveness of the national collective.[18]

In short, women were subordinated to the higher goals of the nation; national interests took precedence over all individual wishes and rights. Curiously, this was the same logic through which Communist Party goals were achieved during the socialist period. One observes that nationalistic ideologues shrewdly manipulated the established gender dichotomies. The division of gender roles was completely transferred to the national discourse in former Yugoslavia, and individuals were expected to fulfill their assigned tasks and obligations. Women as "Mothers of the Nation" were destined to connect members of the nation through blood kinship. As Anđelka Milić explains, "Since 'blood kinship' establishes stronger connections between religious and spiritual relations among the same nations or members of the ethnic group, women are perceived as the 'cement' of cultural identity and continuity of the nation."[19]

Motherhood, perceived as essential to rebuilding the nation-state, was supported institutionally and politically through various pro-life campaigns. In Croatia, one such campaign declared, "Every Croatian woman should give birth to at least four new Croats."[20] A Catholic priest, Don Ante Baković, launched the Movement of the Croatian People (Pokret hrvatskog pučanstva), which advocated a pro-life policy and openly expressed criticism of and disregard for married couples without children.[21] Similar programs and ethnonational political discourses could also be found in the Serbian (Orthodox) and Bosnian (Muslim) populations. For instance, pro-life projects were launched in Serbia, with a clear nationalistic argument: "In order to survive, every woman must bear at least three children."[22]

The Islamic community of Bosnia and Herzegovina responded somewhat differently, and in a less aggressive manner where pro-life policies were concerned, than the two other religious communities. However, on occasion, the Islamic community also succumbed to nationalist pressures. The Reis ul-Ulema of Bosnia and Herzegovina, Mustafa Cerić, soon after being appointed to his position (1993), aggressively espoused the following policy: "I recommend to all Bosnian Muslims from East (Mashriq) to West (Magrib) wherever they are today, not to be reluctant in their love for Bosnia and their mothers and to come back. I promise, we are going to issue a fatwa for Muslim women to bear five children."[23] While the Islamic community never launched any institutionalized projects or issued fatwas regarding childbearing, certain imams did send Muslim women reminders of their obligation to help rebuild the Bosnian nation. These recommendations never carried serious consequence, however, or resulted in pro-life governmental or nongovernmental projects. Nevertheless, demographics invariably became a political issue, with discourse turning intensely emotional as war-torn nations faced mass destruction and exodus.

In such circumstances, as I have previously stated, women were asked to sacrifice themselves, and in return, the national body promised to protect and honor them as Mothers of the Nation. Men were also expected to obey higher national goals as Fathers of the Nation. Their duty was "to present a unified territory to others, to govern and manage it, and to keep and protect it from enemy assault."[24] They were forced to kill, destroy, and rape, all the while protecting national pride. Because women's bodies were considered territory, violating the integrity of that territory could be a crime or a victory—depending on the participant's point of view.

Because patriarchy was the underpinning of all societies in Eastern Europe, women's bodies traditionally fell under male supervision. In spite of the socialist ideal to promote gender equality, the majority of women never lived according to that model. As a result, a collective sense of remorse, ambivalence, and confusion followed the Communist years. In this unstable milieu, national elites emerged to "heal the moral crises" that the Communist system had produced, especially within the family. A revival of religious discourse strongly supported their efforts.

Conservative politicians warned that socialism had destroyed traditional family values. In order to establish a healthy democratic society (a prerequisite for nation building), women had to return to their traditional roles. Indeed, for the nation to survive, women had to reassume their "natural" position in life—at home and with the family. The consequences of nationalist efforts and programs soon became apparent. In the early 1990s one began to notice a significant reduction in the number of women in public life and politics—down to a negligible 2 to 4 percent.[25] Women lost the positions and benefits they had worked steadfastly to acquire and were ultimately pushed back into isolation, narrowly confined to the private sphere of life: "In the nationalistically imagined nation and state, women are segregated and excluded from full citizenship and from the distribution of power."[26] When the war ended in 1995, women had to struggle to regain rights they had obtained fifty years before and to remove the imposed national garments and assigned images of "Mothers of the Nation" and the "Nation's Pride."

TRANSFORMATION TO IMAGES OF NATIONAL SHAME

During the war, women in Bosnia, Herzegovina, and neighboring countries were subjected to mass rapes and various forms of sexual violence, largely because they were perceived as vulnerable targets, nothing more than objects to be humiliated and destroyed. Due to the extensive practice of mass rapes, other forms of sexual violence received less attention. However, testimonials ultimately surfaced from women who survived in war camps:

> Sexual violence also encompasses forced prostitution, sexual slavery, forced impregnation, forced maternity, forced termination of pregnancy, forced sterilization, indecent assault, trafficking, strip searches and inappropriate medical examinations.[27]

Inarguably, different forms of sexual violence against women, including mass rapes, have been implemented time and again during war to terrorize the population. However, during the 1992–1995 war in former Yugoslavia, these crimes against humanity reached new proportions. The gender dimension of the war—together with the mass killings and systematic destruction of cultural heritage in Bosnia, Herzegovina, and neighboring countries—translated into successful ethnic cleansing projects that devastated entire groups of people and obliterated all remnants of their existence from memory.

Women in Black, the prominent women's nongovernmental organization (NGO) based in Belgrade, has worked diligently to call public attention to these crimes. By campaigning in the streets and through other activities, they have become respected human rights activists and protectors of justice. One of their leaders, Staša Zajović, views ethnic cleansing not as "a consequence, but rather [as] one of the main aims of the war." Elaborating on the ethnic cleansing issue, Zajović contends that "cleansing in our language (Bosnian/Serbian/Croatian) is a local word for abortion."[28] Consequently, cleansing the national territory and violating women's bodies (viewed in terms of territory) became the single, prime objective of nationalist ideologues.

Although rape and sexual violence occurred in all former republics of Yugoslavia, these acts were committed "first and most notoriously by Serb forces and later by Croats and Muslims, against ethnic others."[29] Muslim women especially became paradigmatic symbols of suffering and mass rapes. Thousands of women were raped, tortured, and kept in war camps until they reached advanced states of pregnancy so that they would deliver "new soldiers."

While much has been made of the ethnic dimensions of rape, feminists insist on naming these atrocities "gender-based violence."[30] They view this gender-based violence as deeply rooted in the patriarchal value system, in which women are treated as the property or territory of men, nation, or people. This type of violence is closely related to power, and feminists argue that "rape serves to prove power and establish hierarchy."[31]

The point must be made that during the time period under discussion (the early 1990s), international law did not recognize rape as a criminal act against the integrity and dignity of human beings. It therefore took years to bring these cases before the courts. Sexual violence and rape were usually depicted as isolated individual cases and not as strategic tools for systematic destruction of certain ethnic groups and nations. Only after the experiences of Rwanda, Kosovo, and Bosnia-Herzegovina did the world community begin to acknowledge the proportion and consequences of these crimes. At the dawn of the twenty-first century, under strong pressure from human rights activists and feminist organizations, the civilized world decided to classify rape as a war crime. This huge moral and legal victory assuaged, if only in a small way, the suffering of thousands of women humiliated by the brutal acts.

One must duly acknowledge the efforts of international media and human rights organizations to raise awareness regarding collective rape and the torture of women in war camps. For example, Amnesty International conducted thorough investigations into these crimes and provided astonishing testimonial evidence—information that was used to successfully prosecute war criminals. Its reports demonstrated that mass rapes had been committed systematically:

> The available evidence indicates that in some cases the rape of women has been carried out in an organized or systematic way, with the deliberate detention of women for the purpose of rape and sexual abuse. Incidents involving the sexual abuse of women appear to fit into a wider pattern of warfare, characterized by intimidation and abuses against Muslims and Croats which have led thousands to flee or to be compliant when expelled from their home areas out of fear of further violations.[32]

As previously mentioned, rape and other brutal forms of sexual abuse were committed by all sides (Serbs, Croats, and Bosnians) in the war, but Amnesty International's report clearly indicates that Muslim women were the primary victims and Serbian armed forces the main perpetrators. Nevertheless, Serbian and Croatian authorities refused to accept responsibility for the crimes committed by their soldiers in Bosnia and Herzegovina. Not only did they deny the accusations, but they also tried to shift emphasis to those crimes committed by neighboring forces against their own women. In short, they would only admit that all sides in the conflict were equally guilty.[33]

Two international courts have been established to prosecute war crimes committed in former Yugoslavia. The International Criminal Tribunal for the former Yugoslavia (ICTY) and the International Criminal Court (ICC) have both investigated a number of cases, followed by convictions for genocide, war crimes, crimes against humanity, and rapes. The ICTY convicted three Bosnian Serbs (Zoran Vuković, Radomir Kovać, and Dragoljub Kunarac) for the rape of Bosnian Muslim women—some as young as twelve and fifteen. This conviction held particular symbolic value, given that "it was the first time an international court had judged a combination of sexual enslavement and rape to be a crime against humanity."[34]

The War Crimes Chamber of Bosnia and Herzegovina was also given a mandate to prosecute war criminal cases, and in 2006 it sentenced the Bosnian Serb N. Samardžić to twenty-four years in prison for war crimes, including rape and torture.[35] It should be noted, however, that conviction rates for gender-based violence remain discouragingly low. The Sarajevo-based women's organization Women Victims of War has consistently protested that only a small percentage of women are coming forward to prosecute their cases because witnesses are not adequately protected and because there exists a marked insensitivity on the part of the court itself.[36]

Perception differs among the victims, national groups (Bosnians, Croats, Serbs), and the international community as to the nature and consequences of sexual abuse and rape in Bosnia and Herzegovina. For the majority of victims, discussion of these crimes has never been an option, due to the social stigma, "shame," and "guilt" associated with such acts. In the cultures of Bosnia and Herzegovina especially, a woman's role is to guard moral values and her own chastity. Therefore, those who experience sexual violence, no matter the circumstance, are strongly discouraged from speaking openly about such experiences. Instead, they are taught to take personal responsibility for any such assaults and violence and to hide their suffering and feelings.[37] Only in this way can they hope to maintain their families' dignity.

Given the moral double standards of the patriarchal societies in which they live, few women would dare report sexual violence and rape perpetrated against them. Furthermore, public acknowledgment of such crimes could have deleterious results. Who would want to associate with the families of these women, to arrange marriages or do business with them, much less accept them as morally valuable members of society? It is no wonder, given the cultural "blame and shame" complex perpetrated by the patriarchy, that victims have been strongly discouraged from sharing their personal stories.

Fortunately, a certain number of women have been willing to report their tragic experiences to women's NGOs or to centers for the investigation of war crimes in the hope of alerting the world community to atrocities committed in Bosnia and Herzegovina. Only in this way have these women achieved a type of moral victory. Within their families and communities, however, they remain isolated and abandoned, victimized once again—this time by the phenomenon of shame.

Without a community's understanding, without proper psychological support, and without the acceptance of their husbands, these women often see themselves through the eyes of their society, as "ruined moral territory." Their image has been transformed from a glorified National Heroine and National Pride to that of National Shame. They have come to represent the Fallen Nation, a perception that results in divorce and separation for many families unprepared to cope with the consequences of sexual abuse, rape, and torture.[38] Although NGOs have attempted to work with these victims, countless numbers of them have automatically turned to the Islamic authorities for forgiveness and spiritual peace.

In a certain way, then, the Islamic community was called upon to respond to the accumulated frustration and suffering of these women. Since the community was not prepared to deal with such issues, they decided to send the message that raped women should be considered our heroines. Along with this message came the recommendation that family members and society accept these women and help them heal from their traumas. It was an encouraging and positive first response but one that fell entirely short, neither offering concrete assistance nor help in any tangible way.

Muslim intellectuals criticized the silence and indifference of the Islamic community leadership. The prominent Bosnian Islamic scholar Enes Karić, for example, in an interview titled "We Are Worse to Ourselves than the Chetniks [pejorative term for Serbian aggressors]," stated:

> We have today thousands of raped women and instead of attracting foreign reporters and media to pay attention to it, the Islamic Community does not even provide a meeting hall for reporters and people who could come there, talk and cry together.[39]

Although the Muslim media (e.g., *Ljiljan* and *Preporod*) reported specific stories about rape victims[40] and included positive coverage of imams publicly displaying empathy to these women, it was not enough. For the most part, women had to cope with their pain alone. Consequently, some of them described the indifference of local authorities and religious leaders as far more hurtful than the actual brutality they had experienced. Again, men demanded that these women—the same women pushed into the role of "safeguards" of family values and, by extension, protectors of the moral fabric of their societies—internalize their misery and maintain "dignified" silence:

Dear sister, why do you not try to keep quiet and think about your husband and children? If you continue to be persistent and speak publicly, you will not get anything but shame.[41]

It is difficult to imagine that women who have been raped and unspeakably brutalized should then be required to make themselves invisible. In this regard, Rada Iveković has written that "the subjectivity of woman is doubly denied: she is not only exposed to humiliation, her existence is also disputed." The entrenched patriarchal system has chosen to sink quietly into denial rather than work actively toward healing and recovery. In short, men have been unwilling to accept responsibility for national defeat and therefore have steadfastly avoided any reminders of their past shame and humiliation.

CONCLUSION

When Communist regimes controlled Bosnia, Herzegovina, and neighboring countries within former Yugoslavia, women's images as Worker, Proletarian, and Supporter of the Socialist System were purposefully emphasized. During the subsequent transitional period to nation-state societies, women's status was redefined—according to new economic policies and nationalistic political discourses that mediated and reinforced strong gender identities. Finally, during the war period, the new images of woman as Pride of the Nation and National Heroine were transformed into Shame of the Nation and Fallen Nation, as a result of the widespread use of torture, sexual abuse, and rape. Women's bodies took on a different meaning, as symbols of national territory to be conquered and defeated. Although gender-based violence has finally been recognized as a war crime by international law, the tremendous social stigma of shame and guilt remains part of the war's legacy, leaving the majority of female victims voiceless, powerless, and without necessary resources for healing and recovery.

NOTES

1. Marija Divićić, *Organizacija antifašističkog fronta žena u Sarajevo u Socijalističkoj Jugoslaviji* (Organization of AFW in Sarajevo in Socialist Yugoslavia) (Sarajevo: Historical Archive, 1988), 295–296.
2. Ibid.
3. Gordana Stojaković, *Neda: jedna biografija* (Neda: A Biography) (Novi Sad: Futura publikacija, 2002), 48.

4. Markov Slobodanka, *Položaj i uloga žena? u sistemu polititčkog odlučivanja* (Status and Role of Women in the Political Decision-Making System) *Šema,* no. 3 (1984): 54.

5. Sherry B. Ortner, "Is a Female to Male as Nature Is to Culture?" in *Women, Culture and Society,* ed. M. Z. Rosaldo and L. Lamphere (Palo Alto, CA: Stanford University Press, 1974), 87.

6. *Statistical Yearbook of SR Bosnia i Herzegovina,* 1970, 61.

7. *Statistical Yearbook of SR Bosnia i Herzegovina,* 1989, 83–84.

8. Stipe Šuvar, "Diskusija u raspravi: Društvena svest, marksistićka teorija i emancipacija žena-danas" (Discussion in Debate: Social Consciousness, Marxist Theory and Emanacipation of Women Today), *Žena* (Woman), no. 2–3 (Zagreb, 1972), 73.

9. *Statistical Yearbook of SR Bosnia i Herzegovina,* 1989, 23:32.

10. Ibid., 32–33.

11. Lidija Sklevicky, *Konji, žene, ratovi* (Horses, Women, and Wars) (Zagreb: Zenska Infoteka, 1996), 57.

12. Ivo Banac, *Cijena Bosne* (The Price of Bosnia) (Sarajevo: Vijeće kongresa bošnjaćkih intelektualaca [Council of the Congress of Bosniak Intellectuals], 1996).

13. See Martina Belić, *Žene i rad* (Women and Work), (Zagreb: B.a.b.e., 2000); Zilka Spahić-Šiljak, "Political Representation of Women in Croatia: Analysis of the Sociocultural, Socioeconomic, and Political Obstacles for Full Representation of Women in Politics," M.A. thesis, CIPS, University of Sarajevo (International Master's Program Sarajevo-Bologna), 2001–2002, 48.

14. Vesna Kesić, "Gender and Ethnic Identities in Transition: The Former Yugoslavia-Croatia," in *From Gender to Nation,* ed. Rada Ivekovic and Julie Mostov (Ravena: Longo Editore, 2001), 65.

15. Floya Anthias and Nira Yuval-Davis, Introduction to *Woman-Nation-State,* ed. Nira Yuval-Davis and Floya Anthais (London: Macmillan, 1989), 6–11.

16. Kesić, "Gender and Ethnic Identities in Transition," 65.

17. Anđelka Milić, *Žene, politika, porodica* (Women, Politics, Family) (Belgrade: Institute for Political Studies, 1994), 155.

18. Ibid., 149.

19. Ibid., 155.

20. Kesić, "Gender and Ethnic Identities in Transition," 65.

21. Sabina Ramet, *Religion and Politics in Times of Change: Catholic and Orthodox Churches in Central and Southeast Europe,* trans. Jasminka Bošnjak (Belgrade: Centre for Women's Studies, 2006), 106.

22. Wendy Bracewell, "Women in Transition to Democracy in South-Eastern Europe," in *The Balkans: A Religious Backyard of Europe,* ed. J. M. Faber (Ravena: Longo Editore, 1996), 215.

23. Mustafa Cerić, "Pobjeda ili ćasna smrt" (An Interview: Victory or Honour Death), *Ljiljan,* Sarajevo-Ljubljana, no. 37 (1993), 7.

24. Milić, *Žene, politika, porodica,* 154.

25. Spahić-Šiljak, "Political Representation of Women in Croatia," 49.

26. Kesić, "Gender and Ethnic Identities in Transition," 80.

27. Marie Vlachova and Lea Biason, *Women in an Insecure World: Violence against Women, Facts, Figures, and Analysis* (Geneva: Geneva Centre for the Democratic Control of Armed Forces [DCAF], 2005), 113.

28. Staša Zajović, "Abuse of Women on a National and Militarist Basis," in *Women for Peace* (Belgrade: Women in Black, 1995), 176–177.

29. Elissa Helms, "Gendered Visions of the Bosnian Future: Women's Activism and Representation in Post-War Bosnia-Herzegovina," Ph.D. dissertation, University of Pittsburgh, 2003, 6.

30. Mirko Petrović, "O povijesnom revizionizmu Vesne Kesić" (On the Historical Revisionism of Vesna Kesić), *Zarez,* no. 45–46, Zagreb (2000): 22–35.

31. Rebeka Anić, *Nasilje nad ženama u obitelji: teološko-pastoralni vid* (Domestic Violence: Theological-Pastoral Perspective) (Split: Franciscan Institute for Culture of Peace, 2006), 91.

32. Amnesty International, *Bosnia-Herzegovina: Rape and Sexual Abuse by Armed Forces.* Report, January 21, 1993.

33. Jasna Bakšić Muftić, "Zločin silovanja-lokalna i međunarodna dimenzija" (The Crime of Rape in Bosnia-Herzogovina: Local and International Dimensions), in *Izazovi Feminizma* (The Challenges of Feminism), ed. Jasminka Babic-Avdispahic et al. (Sarajevo: IF Bosnae, 2004), 52.

34. *International Justice Failing Rape Victims,* prepared by IWPR staff in The Hague, London, and Sarajevo, January 5, 2007. www.iwpr.net/?p=tri&s=f&o=328311&apc_state=henitri2007.

35. Merdijana Sadović, *Foca Rape Sentence,* IWPR, December 15, 2006. www.iwpr.net/?p=tri&s=f&o=326212&apc_state=henitri200612.

36. Ibid.

37. Dardić Dragana, "Domestic Violence," in *In-Depth Study on Domestic Violence in Bosnia and Herzegovina* (HCa, B Luka, Žene Ženama Sarajevo, and Lara Bijelina, 2006), 31.

38. Bakšić Muftić, "Zločin silovanja-lokalna i međunarodna dimenzija," 50.

39. Enes Karić, "Mi smo sebi gori od četnika" (An Interview: We Are Worse to Ourselves than Chetniks), *BH Dani,* no. 3, November 11, 1992, 8.

40. Ines Sabalić, "Pečat na tijelu" (Seal on the Body) *Ljiljan,* no. 20 (1993): 13.

41. Working on the *In-Depth Study on Domestic Violence in Bosnia-Herzogovina* from 2004 to 2006, I met women in Tuzla and Sarajevo who complained about the indifferent reaction of some imams to both domestic violence and rapes that the women had survived during the war. Instead of finding compassion and peace for their wounded souls, these women encountered barriers of silence and shame, still prevalent in the cultural context and minds of Bosnian people.

13

MUSLIM WOMEN IN THE SPANISH PRESS

The Persistence of Subaltern Images

ÁNGELES RAMÍREZ

This chapter explores how and in what ways the terrorist attacks in Madrid influenced the Spanish media's representation of Muslim women. As I began researching this topic, the assumption was that their image had been reframed as part of a larger threatening aggressor group: Muslims. If this were the case, it might coincide with the new forms of Islamophobia already identified in Europe. The metamorphosis from an old Islamophobia anchored in colonial relations to a new breed, tied to the attacks and to identifying Islam with terrorism, would be of primary interest.[1] Had March 11 eradicated the subordinate image of Muslim women, supplanting it with a new and more threatening image—that of a veiled aggressor?

ISLAMOPHOBIA: A NEW BRAND OF RACISM

To begin with, it seemed evident that the train bombings had to some degree transformed Maurophobia (a phenomenon closely tied to Spain's colonial and postcolonial relationships with Morocco)[2] into Islamophobia. Unlike Maurophobia, in which Islam was never a relevant factor, Islamophobia (as a new type of racism) used Islam alone as a primary basis for discrimination. According to Pnina Werbner:

> What we have, then, uniquely in the case of contemporary Islam, is an oppositional hegemonic bloc which includes intellectual elites and the consumerist masses, as well as "real" violent racists, like members of the British National Party, who exploit anti-Muslim discourses to target Muslims in particular (as statistics show) for racial attacks.[3]

What is the media's role in all of this? Discourse is the form of racism through which the elites explain themselves.[4] The press writes and gathers, in different genres, the constructions and images of Islam. In fact, they naturalize them and make them appear to be consensual questions, which ensures their legitimate reproduction. Moreover, a coterie of "specialists" has begun to proliferate, representing themselves as expert voices on Islam in various news publications. This is as common in other European nations as it is in Spain. For example, Geisser points to the French intellectual who has created discourse that "naturalizes" exclusion, contributing significantly to Islamophobia.[5] This type of specialization has also arisen in Germany.[6]

In Spain, journalists pontificate on Islam when, in fact, they may have no real personal experience or expertise in this area. As of this writing, each of Spain's major newspapers includes a staff of writers generally acknowledged as academically qualified and intellectually capable. With the exception of one author at ABC, however, these are persons whose academic and/or professional backgrounds stray far from Islamic studies; that is, they are not specialists in the field.

To make matters worse, the general tendency of the press is to lean right, especially in regard to immigration issues—an unfortunate phenomenon pointed out by Van Dijk in his assessment of the Dutch case.[7] As immigration concerns become politicized in Spain and as the presence of terrorist groups wreak havoc in the name of Islam, Spanish newspapers have promoted an ultraconservative level of discourse. A newspaper's tendency to voice concerns on behalf of the political right reinforces and legitimizes the sensation of a threat, one of the main thematic categories of racism.[8]

Furthermore, everything that refers to Moroccans—to *moros*—the secular object of phobia in Spain, leaves its stain on Islam and is perceived as Muslim. An increasingly collective sense of fear, coupled with vague implied threats, lends legitimacy to Islamophobia, a legitimacy that its ancestor Maurophobia never enjoyed.

MUSLIM WOMEN AND JOURNALISTIC DISCOURSE

From the beginning of Europe's relationship with the Middle East, it has used the theme of discrimination to further its own political agendas. European travelers, politicians, and writers have labeled Muslim women as oppressed. Their observations on this Arab-Muslim social construct have facilitated arguments regarding the overall inferiority of Arabs and Muslims and allowed colonial masters to condemn the conquered peoples.[9] Another overriding Western theme, which buttressed the belief in Arab inferiority, concerned the incompatibility of democratic values and Islam.[10]

Post-3/11, for the first time in Spain's history, the Spanish press equated a Muslim woman (the only one accused in the bombings) with aggression. Up to that point, the press had represented Muslim women as subordinate and powerless, stereotypes that suddenly conflicted with this newer, assertive image. The headscarf, in particular, received significant scrutiny. Muslim women wearing a headscarf had always been equated to that which was rural, ignorant, and rigid. The Spanish press viewed the headscarf as nothing less than a symbol of obscurantism and portrayed the women wearing headscarves as victims of behind-the-scenes manipulation. Through the lens of the Spanish press, one habitually viewed Muslim women in contexts of instability, passivity, and poverty, contexts that seemed incompatible with the newer, more assertive image. Could these women in headscarves, portrayed by the press as hopelessly victimized, be moving beyond the "oppressed" stereotype? To explore this question, I analyzed three Spanish newspapers: *El País, El Mundo,* and *ABC.*

Some 2,182,000 individuals read *El País* daily.[11] It is the second most widely read newspaper and the leading paper for daily news. The newspaper's politics align with the Spanish Socialist party, and as such, it has followed a trajectory towards social democracy, which is its current position. As for the issues of immigration and Islam, *El País* maintains a laical stance—without, however, proposing changes in the relationship between the Spanish government and the Church.

El Mundo is the second leading paper for general news and has a daily readership of approximately 1,443,000. In its initial years, *El Mundo* was considered a liberal publication, presenting a leftist critique of Socialist government, but it has slowly evolved towards supporting the conservative Popular Party. For some years now, the publication has fallen in line with the Spanish right, although its readers hail from backgrounds similar to those of *El País*—and to a large extent, are individuals disappointed by *El País'* accommodating position (i.e., towards the Socialist Party). The positions of *El Mundo* regarding the relationship between Church and State are similar to *El País,* even nearer to laicism "à la française."

The third newspaper, *ABC,* maintains a faithful following of readers, although the numbers are more modest: approximately 681,000 daily. *ABC* is monarchical and Catholic; its social model reflects the values of the Catholic Church, especially concerning the relationship between Church and State and the traditional family. *ABC* is composed of Spanish nationalists who stay very near to the Spanish right (specifically, the Popular Party), although the Church is its main referent point.

To analyze the impact of the March 11 attacks on media discourse around

Muslim women, I selected pertinent articles from March 11, 2004, to November 1, 2007, and contrasted their content with articles dating from September 1, 2000, to March 10, 2004. In researching the different newspaper genres, I looked at three sections of each publication: feature articles, readers' opinion pieces, and editorials.

The key words I used to scan the material were *velo*/veil and *pañuelo*/headscarf. These two words were frequently mixed in with articles mentioning *chador* and *hijab*. Concerning terminological use (and misuse), I discovered an article written by the ombudsman of *El País* in which she concluded there was no difference between calling the *hijab* a headscarf or veil.[12] *El País* even dedicated a double page to the different names for the *hijab*, depending on its form. The most careless reporting overall on this same topic was by *ABC*, which referred to the *hijab* as a "shador" in its editorial.[13]

As Rabah (1998) has noted, the use of one term or another is no accident. In Spanish, the Islamic veil (*velo*) has a stronger connotation than *pañuelo*—which can be translated as "scarf," "headscarf," or "handkerchief." The word *velo* is much more specific, referring to a scarf that women place on their heads to enter a church or to signify mourning, compulsory in Spain as recently as forty years ago. Interestingly, *velo* also connotes anything that hides the view of another thing, that is, that keeps something obscured. In *El País*, the word *pañuelo* took prominence. *El Mundo* and *ABC* preferred *velo*, *chador*, or *hijab*.

The journalistic discourse in these three dailies is usually quite moderate, including the articles and editorials. Even *ABC*, the newspaper closest to the Church, generally eschews aggressiveness towards Islam. However, post–March 11, the discourse in the opinion sections began to assume a distinctly vitriolic tone. Moreover, pejorative references were used to describe girls wearing the headscarf, such as "little girl" Shaima[14] and "little girl" Fatima. These are old expressions, connected to the folkloric speech of the Gypsies and the poor in Andalusia.

Unfortunately, no counterdiscourse was presented to balance the negative images put forth concerning Islam, Muslims in general, or Muslim women in particular. In short, with respect to the question of Islam and Muslim women, one might expect that the dailies, given their disparate political positions, would offer opposing arguments. However, this was not the case. The tone of and information contained in the articles, as well as the editorials, hardly differs among the three papers. What is most interesting here is that the columnists at the three dailies, all with different ideological positions, do not differ essentially in their approaches to Islam. This consensus on Islam lends legitimacy to stereotypes and fixed images, so that consensus becomes a criterion of truth.

THE HEADSCARF: PROTEST AND PUBLICATIONS

In Spain, women wearing the headscarf have become an obvious symbol for transplanted Islam. Protest over the presence of Muslim girls wearing headscarves in Spanish public schools first took place in February 2002; this protest occurred in a small town fifty kilometers from Madrid. A second similar protest arose during October 2007 in the Catalan town of Girona. Between these two events, in summer 2004, France passed a law regulating the use of religious symbols in its public schools. This law attempted to establish a universal norm regarding the Muslim headscarf. In general, it can be said that the Spanish papers were, for different reasons, extremely critical of the French headscarf law, especially from a civil liberties perspective.

News pertaining to the controversial French law first appeared in June 2003. *El País* treated the topic as cause for profound dissent in France, focusing primarily on the call from feminists and intellectuals to reinforce laicism.[15] In general, *El País* hinted that the problem was related not to Islam but to the fractured relationship between different religions and the French state.[16] In fact, almost a year later, *El País* followed the case of two French girls expelled from school under the headscarf law. They were introduced as daughters of a professor who had emigrated from Algeria to work at Peugeot—a fact that made the family more familiar and therefore more acceptable to the average Spanish reader. The newspaper also emphasized the solidarity of the girls' classmates.[17]

El Mundo followed France's "headscarf problem" as well, noting that many Muslim groups felt discriminated against and pointing out that other religious symbols were allowed in French public schools. *El Mundo* presented this headscarf affair as an imposition by the French government. The paper claimed that Chirac had banned headscarves, yarmulkes, and crucifixes in school, "despite protests from Muslims,"[18] and that the holidays of Yom Kippur and Eid ul-Adha could not be celebrated as such. It also pointed to the dissent of France's Green Party on this issue, emphasizing that no real political consensus had been achieved. Furthermore, the paper suggested that Chirac's concern about moving the headscarf law forward appeared to be based on election concerns.

ABC focused on the union of three religions against the headscarf law,[19] but only in response to the demands of the moment, and ended by calling attention to the electoral importance of Muslims and the fact that policies had to change to adapt to them.[20]

THE HEADSCARF AND MARCH 11

As for the March 11 train bombings, *El País* published an obituary of each of the 192 victims—including that of a thirteen-year-old Moroccan girl. The obituary portrayed her as an adolescent like any other, highlighted her friendship with Spanish girls, and tiptoed around the fact that she wore a headscarf. The text read, "She was proud of the headscarf that covered her hair," although in the newspaper's photograph she was not wearing one. The article also reported that she seldom spoke Arabic, thus positioning her as a Spanish girl and not as a foreigner. The features (dress and language) that distinctly identified her as a Moroccan seemed purposefully blurred.[21]

El País also ran an article about another Muslim woman, Naima Oulad Akcha, sister of two of the terrorists who blew themselves up in an apartment in Leganés;[22] Naima was accused of collaboration in the bombings. *El País* emphasized the fact that she was single and very religious.[23] Furthermore, it described her physically as "covered from top to bottom by a veil and the headscarf," a circumstance that "caused problems when taking her photograph for the police file without her headscarf."

In the case of the teenage victim, an attempt is made to conceal her Muslim identity, bringing her closer to "us"; in the second case, that of the accused, the opposite process occurs. Naima Oulad Akcha is presented as a person who puts her beliefs above societal norms, resisting removal of her headscarf for the police photo. The accused is clearly one of "them."[24] It must be noted Akcha was finally exonerated, but the tone and content of the *El País* article suggest that she had already been found guilty.[25]

In *El Mundo* an interview appears with the mother and two sisters of one of the terrorists involved in the March 11 attack. The sisters, twenty-five and twenty-seven years old, respectively, are described as living "a Western lifestyle." The article is titled "Muslim Women without a Headscarf."[26] The mother's choice to wear a headscarf is ascribed to her age and, in a lighter tone, to the fact that her hair is falling out. This implies that the only headscarf in the family is "deactivated" and therefore, not a potential threat. The three women are introduced as members of a working-class family. Reference is made to "their bosses," which automatically places them in a subservient position. The women are worthy of the appreciation of their neighbors and employers, who continue to treat them well despite the fact that they are related to terrorists. Although the paper mentions that these women pray five times a day (as devout Muslims), the point is made that they "do not go to Mosque every Friday." Again, by underscoring the fact that the sisters avoid wearing a headscarf, the paper is eager to show the "normalcy" of this family.

To understand the newspaper's motivation for doing so, one must remember that *El Mundo* upheld the thesis, along with the Spanish right, that March 11 was an attack by Basque pro-independent terrorists and not Islamists.[27] But what is most interesting is that both *El Mundo* and *El País* adopted the same strategy; that is, they decided the best way to exonerate Muslims in articles or print interviews was to minimize the impact of their "being Muslim." In this way, Islam—usually symbolized by the headscarf or by an incompatibility with democratic values—was made invisible in order to play on the readers' sentiments. The reverse strategy was used when the opposite goal was desired.

THE 2002 AND 2007 HEADSCARF AFFAIRS

As previously mentioned, the initial headscarf controversy took place in 2002. The case involved a teenage girl (Fatima) who had been asked to leave, first by a semiprivate Catholic school and then by a public school, for wearing a headscarf. At least this is how the press presented the issue. What really happened was revealed in later interviews with teachers employed at the public school. Apparently the young girl arrived in Madrid during the middle of the school year and was placed by the Municipal School Commission in a semiprivate religious school.[28] The nuns did not look kindly on the girl attending school wearing the *hijab,* and the student was informed she had to remove it. The girl then left the religious school. Later, the territorial head of education decided to enroll the girl in a public school,[29] undermining the Commission's decision. But the Parent-Teacher Association at the public school questioned this decision, complaining that when the semiprivate schools had problems, the public schools were invariably shouldered with responsibility for admitting "difficult students." At that same time, the director of the public school made distinctly provocative comments, referring to the headscarf as discriminatory.[30]

Overall, the newspapers placed special emphasis on the director's negative comments rather than on the issue of the schools' authority. As for the girl in the headscarf, *El Mundo* emphasized that she had arrived in Spain with her mother and sisters only four months earlier from a village deep inside Morocco. Moreover, she was portrayed as introverted; neither of her parents could speak Spanish. The journalists who tried to interview the girl had met with resistance. In this same *El Mundo* article, girls without headscarves were shown to be better adapted to Spain. The article reads, "The only feature that betrays their Moroccan origin is their eyes." According to the writer, these same girls without headscarves expressed themselves more articulately; and their families had resided in Spain significantly longer.

ABC's handling of the Moroccan teen's story was similar. The journalist attempting to speak with the girl's mother found "a frightened woman who did not dare respond under any circumstances."[31] In the same *ABC* article, one of the neighbors commented that "the girl's father always forced his wife and daughter to cover their heads and that it was a very, very conservative family."

El País, however, handled the story differently, reporting that the neighbors "assured [journalists] . . . the people were normal." Ali Elidrissi, the father, worked in construction. "I make a good living," he was reported as saying.[32] The intention at *El País* was to present the Moroccan family, their customs, and their coexistence with neighbors in the town as normal:

> Until last week, the Elidrissi family was unknown to their neighbors. And some [of their] neighbors seem very unenthusiastic about the arrival of foreigners. But other neighbors, like the owner of an electrical appliance repair store located across from Fatima's house, do not hesitate to defend their Moroccan neighbors. The owner doesn't know the Elidrissi family either, but affirms, "In the neighborhood we all get along well, because the Moroccans are not difficult people." As far as the Muslim community's way of dressing, they [the neighbors] note that only older women wear the headscarf and "not all of them."

In October 2007, the second headscarf affair unfolded in a public school in Girona (Cataluña). According to a news item in *El País*,[33] a seven-year-old girl (Shaima) was ordered to take off her headscarf. The phrases "little Muslim girl" and "Islamic headscarf" were used in the article. No reference was made to the parents' nationality. According to *El País*, the parents insisted that their daughter wore a headscarf because she wanted to, because it was her personal choice. In other words, she had not been coerced. The school principal affirmed that school rules and regulations forbade students from wearing the

headscarf. The head of education for the province, however, called for tolerance and respect for the use of the headscarf.

This led to a revival of the debate on the headscarf in Europe and a reminder of the rules.[34] The same day, *El País* presented a bit more of Shaima's
story. The family had emigrated first from Morocco to Switzerland—where
"things were very bad"—and then to Spain. The mother was shown wearing
a *chador;* the family's economic situation was unstable. The *El País* article
emphasized that the girl wore a headscarf to emulate her grandmother, with
whom she had lived in Rabat.

On October 4, 2007, all of the political parties expressed their opinions
on the headscarf. The PSOE (Socialist Party) was against regulation. The political left (United Left, IU) opted for a French-style law as long as it applied
to Catholics as well. The traditional right, in the name of maintaining individual culture, championed a general regulation. Spain's government dodged
the headscarf question altogether. At the same time, Spanish theologians
refrained from condemning the headscarf.

News coverage offered the impression that in Shaima's case, the "responsible party" was the girl who personally wanted to wear the headscarf, whereas
in Fatima's case, the father was clearly the force behind his daughter's behavior. In Shaima's case, *El País* represented the family's situation as precarious,
even nomadic. After all, the family had threatened to leave Spain if their
daughter's headscarf crisis were not resolved. This piece of information is
particularly revelatory: *El País* portrayed the family as willing and determined
to emigrate once again if the situation did not improve. This dramatic report,
carrying overt and subtle messages, implied that the family would readily
accept being uprooted once again rather than conform to minimal social
requirements. *ABC* mentioned the story but only superficially. *El Mundo*
refrained from reporting Shaima's story at all.

In short, El *Mundo* and *ABC* handled the first headscarf affair almost the
same way. Both suggested that the root causes lay in economic instability and
in the family's immigrant ("recent arrivals") status. In making the Muslim-
Gypsy comparison, the press related the use of the headscarf to educational
failure. *El País* took another position, however, normalizing the family situation and turning the father, mother, and siblings into familiar people, much
like its readers. The second headscarf affair was handled much more tan-
gentially by *El País* and in *El Mundo*'s case, not at all. *ABC* provided ample
space to the second event, connecting the story with a defense of its own
interests.

MUSLIM WOMEN IN THE PRESS: EDITORIALS

In general, editorials in Spanish newspapers before and after March 11 were quite moderate with respect to Muslim women and the *hijab*—especially in the case of *El País* and *El Mundo*. Solutions were proposed in the editorials that championed dialogue and integration. However, tolerance for the headscarf in school did not include the assumption that Muslims were free to dress as they wish.

El País championed permissiveness for the headscarf in school. In a February 2002 editorial regarding Fatima's case, the relationship between the *hijab* and discrimination against women was raised—and any comparison with female circumcision, as the Popular Party labor minister had attempted, was rejected.[35] In the last editorial (October 14, 2007) relating to Shaima's case, the position remained the same: girls should be allowed to go to school wearing a *hijab,* and under no circumstances should this right be legislated.

El Mundo took a similar position, starting from the premise that the headscarf (which it termed a "chador" until 2003), though discriminatory,[36] should in no case be prohibited or regulated. In another editorial, *El Mundo* proposed integrative solutions with respect to the use of the headscarf in those schools that require a uniform.[37]

Of the three newspapers, the *ABC* editorials most clearly opposed use of the headscarf. Stating that the headscarf law had upset certain Muslims in France, the paper commented on the issue as a "revealing symptom of how each person faces their role when it comes time to share the same social space in a country whose immense majority forms part of what is known as Christian culture."[38] ABC clearly states that the headscarf (which it indiscriminately refers to as "shador") represents discrimination against and subordination of Muslim women.[39] Their assertions leave no doubts:

> The use of the Islamic headscarf could be, of course, a discretional exercise of individual freedom, but in its natural context, which is not European, it symbolizes a way to order society in accordance with directives that, despite being internalized by women, are opposed to the equality of the sexes.[40]

In summary, the editorials appearing in *El Mundo* and *El País* argue proximity, in the sense of demonstrating a marked degree of tolerance for the headscarf, whereas ABC suggests that it should be prohibited altogether.

OPINION ARTICLES AS ELITE
ISLAMOPHOBIC DISCOURSES

After March 11, the lid was removed from Pandora's box and Islamophobes found it much easier to use aggressive vocabulary against Muslims. This section analyzes two types of opinion articles: those that address the question of the headscarf and those that focus on Islam and its relationship with the West. In this discourse, there is little difference among the three newspapers. The old stereotypes regarding Islamophobia are present in each, while almost no contrary discourses take on or question this stereotypical language.

In *El País,* other (dissenting) voices are heard on occasion, but they are an absolute minority in terms of number and proportion. While there is a paucity of specific discourses on Muslim women, they are presented in the general framework as representatives of obscurantism. For example, in an *El País* opinion piece titled "Women without Attributes," the author supports admitting girls (who wear a headscarf) to school, despite the fact that the *hijab* "is not a simple piece of cloth that the child wears to imitate her mother, but a symbol of the dogma, training and silence that awaits her."[41] The author implies that providing the Muslim girl access to education "may be the only way that within a few years we will see little Shaima with her face uncovered, having become an adolescent who can dress as she wishes, even showing her belly button if she wants, feeling proud of her body and her mind." The assumption here is that wearing the *hijab* is synonymous with being poorly educated. If the girl were educated, surely she would remove it. With a few exceptions, all of which attempt to contextualize the headscarf in quite specific political, legal, and social structures,[42] those few individuals who defend the right to wear a headscarf do so from a legalistic perspective or as a strategy to prevent exclusion and to minimize cultural differences.[43]

Feminist discourses appear in *El País* opinion pieces arguing that children wear the headscarf because of tradition, a phenomenon that can be explained away as "[an] obsession for loading women's heads (physically and symbolically) with cultural traditions."[44] One author poses the following response in questioning why girls wear the headscarf:

> Why? Maybe because immigrant families succumb to the pressures of the clergy, of gossipy neighbors, of all the miserable, repressive sort of people that Spanish society knew in the 1940s and 1950s. Why do we let them succumb now without finding the least support or the least condemnation in the society that surrounds them?

Finally, this same "feminist" author alludes to a letter sent to the newspaper by a nineteen-year-old Muslim girl who claims to wear the headscarf based on personal choice. The author then recalls that at age nineteen she, too, made many foolish decisions. In short, there can be no reasonable explanation for wearing the headscarf: either families are pressured to make their girls wear a headscarf or it is all youthful silliness. No one considers the possibility that Islam lived in this way corresponds to well-considered decisions. The question is reduced to either coercion on the part of the clergy or ignorance that will pass with education.

In another *El País* opinion piece, "The Eight-Year-Old Girl Who Wanted to Cover Her Hair," the choice to wear a headscarf is compared to what would happen (hypothetically) if a young girl said she wanted a female circumcision.[45]

The columnists in *El Mundo* also take a firm position against the headscarf, connecting the issue with broader discussions around the meaning of Islam and its relation to the world and Western values. Those opinion pieces that appear to hold alternative positions are not so much defending the headscarf as criticizing certain social sectors for their mismanagement and articulation of the problem.[46] In the article "Allowing the Islamic Headscarf Is Encouraging Communitarianism," the author, Ivan Tubau,[47] connects integrism with the Muslim headscarf in France.[48] "Should the French government give in to the threat of integrism by removing the prohibition against the Islamic headscarf, the Jewish yarmulke and the Christian cross?" In yet another *El Mundo* piece, the writer makes wild assertions between the choice to wear a headscarf and potential fanaticism:[49]

The spectacle[50] made me think, especially because I read a report about an alarming number of young French girls converting to an extremist form of Islam based more on fashion than on [religious] conviction.
. . . When a young girl decides to wear the headscarf as an anti-establishmentarian statement and not because of her authentic religious belief, this is serious because she can easily become a full-blown fanatic, as we have seen throughout history with other religions.

Like the other two papers, columnists at *ABC* also voice strong opposition to Muslim girls' right to wear the headscarf. In an *ABC* article from February 2002, Ignacio Sánchez Cámara offers his opinion on the headscarf, which he regards as neither aesthetic nor opportune.[51] He fears that at some point in time, some adolescent will appear in the costume of a shackled slave because, as he suggests, "the roads of submission are infinite."

Although opposed ideologically, two individuals—Mario Vargas Llosa (from the independent secular right) and Jiménez Losantos (a well-known Spanish neo-con)—published very similar opinions on topics related to Muslim women. In autumn 2007, Mario Vargas Llosa wrote an article for *El País* in which he described the headscarf as

> the symbol of a religion where discrimination against women is still, unfortunately, stronger than in any other, a traditional defect of humanity of which democratic culture has managed to free itself in part. . . . And if the issue is respect for all cultures and customs, why does democracy not also allow planned marriages and ultimately, female circumcision of girls, which millions of believers in Africa and other places in the world practice?[52]

The author deftly slips from a discussion of the headscarf to the issue of female circumcision, which he connects with Muslim believers. Five years earlier, Jiménez Losantos had made the following observation in *ABC:*

> Behind the headscarf is a jail. If we don't understand or don't want to understand that Islam is an implacable system of repression and submission of the woman to the man and of women to the men in their families, clans or Mosques, [then] all the controversy unleashed by the hijab, veil, headscarf or chador . . . is an absurd anecdote.[53]

While Losantos's language is slightly more radical, his message resonates with that of Vargas Llosa.

In early 2007 *ABC* printed an opinion article by Serafín Fanjul—a weekly contributor to the paper and one of the few writers with credentials in Arab studies—warning of the dangers of a proposal to concede moral recognition to the descendants of the Moors expelled from Spain in the seventeenth century. Why? Because this could mean "automatic entry into Spain through the front door, with flags unfurled and triumphant, of any Moroccan who can bribe someone in his extremely corrupt bureaucracy to falsify his roots."[54] Warning of the "hyper-birth rate of the Moroccans already here" and the potential for invasion, the author sensationalizes two particular fears associated with Muslim immigration.

At *El País,* the author who has written most prolifically on Muslim values and Islam's relationship with the West is the political scientist Antonio Elorza. While his articles cover Spain's contemporary political affairs, his primary focus has always been Basque nationalism, a focus veering sharply from

Islamic issues. From September 1, 2000, to March 11, 2004, only 12 percent of the articles by Elorza dealt with Islamic questions. After that date and up to November 1, 2007,[55] the number rose to 30 percent.

A central, consistent argument in Elorza's work is that Al Qaeda's terrorism is justified by Islamic orthodoxy.[56] Al Qaeda's terrorist strategy "is . . . adopted by integrist sectors that create it out of a partial but Orthodox strategy coming from the Koran and the Hadith" (October 22, 2001). In this way, Elorza establishes a genealogy of integrism from Islamic sources (April 16, 2004, and October 10, 2001), an integrism that comes to light when they (Muslims) are threatened.[57] After all, according to Islam, the believer is obligated to fight against the infidel (April 3, 2002). In this same article, Elorza hints that being overly tolerant (with regard to the headscarf) is tantamount to being an accomplice of Zawahiri.

CONCLUSION

The classic media conceptualization of Muslim women as secondary, subordinate, and powerless is still dominant in Spain. Wearing the headscarf—that most obvious of Muslim symbols—is explained away by immigrant status and inadequate education, as well as a failure to integrate. In this respect, the representation of Muslim women in the Spanish press neatly fits within preexisting images of former Maurophobic constructions.

Depending on the intended impact or desired journalistic effect, Muslim women have been presented by the Spanish press in one of two ways: either they wear the headscarf or they do not. The absence of a headscarf signals adaptation, modernity, and culture. Its presence is perceived as a threat to democratic values.

In general, the Spanish press has afforded no thoughtful analysis to the deeper significance of the headscarf, nor has it attempted to provide a forum for those women who wear it. The manner in which the Spanish press exploited the headscarf issue after March 11 reveals much about the *hijab*'s utility. When the intention of a particular newspaper was to bring readers closer to the Muslim woman (or women) featured in an article, the headscarf was made invisible—thereby creating a sense of sameness and solidarity. When the press wanted to accentuate feelings of opposition and alienation, the *hijab* became a central focus. In this way, the headscarf issue was manipulated to reinforce tension between "us" and "them" and to drive a wedge of incompatibility between Western values and the Muslim worldview.

Of the three newspapers analyzed, *ABC* (monarchist, religious, traditional, and right wing) portrayed Muslim women (especially Moroccan women) as prisoners of an unstable life and victims of ignorance. *El Mundo* (right wing, strongly opposed to the Socialist party) did the same. The focus of *El País* (Social Democratic) was more integrative in that the paper made some effort to present "normalized" Moroccan families. However, with the passage of time, even *El País* began handling Muslim-related issues much like the other papers.

From an editorial perspective, while *El País* and *El Mundo* argued for tolerance on the headscarf issue, *ABC* remained absolutely opposed to permitting the headscarf in school. The three papers appeared most similar in their opinion sections. The different columnists, although situated along lines that reflected their papers' political leanings, paradoxically maintained very similar positions when discussing the Muslim headscarf. They broadened the field only in the conception of Islam and its relationship to the West, which never veered very far from the views of Huntington and the clash of civilizations. By arriving at and maintaining the same hypotheses, all of the papers lent credibility to their positions and successfully constructed arguments reflecting elitist racism.

NOTES

1. Vincent Geisser, *La Nouvelle Islamophobie* (Paris: La Découverte, 2003).

2. This idea, supported by Martín Corrales, implies that being Moroccan connotes a series of characteristics that justify exclusion. This construct dates from Spain's first incursions into Morocco. Eloy Martín Corrales, "Maurofobia/islamofobia y maurofilia/islamofobia en la España del siglo XXI," *Revista CIDOB d'Afers Internacionals,* 66–67 (2004): 39–51.

3. Pnina Werbner, "Islamophobia: Incitement to Religious Hatred—Legislating for a New Fear?" *Anthropology Today* 21 (2005): 8.

4. Teun Van Dijk, "Discurso de las elites y racismo institucional," in *Medios de comunicación e inmigración,* ed. Manuel Lario Bastida (Murcia: CAM, 2006).

5. Geisser, *La Nouvelle Islamophobie.*

6. See Kai Hafez, Karin Hörner, and Verena Klemm, "The Rise and Decline of Opinion Leaders: The Changing Image of Middle East and Islam in German Mass Media," in *Islam and the West in the Mass Media: Fragmented Images in a Globalizing World,* ed. Kai Hafez, 273–289 (Creskill: Hampton Press, 2000).

7. Van Dijk, "Discurso de las elites y racismo institucional," notes that when Dutch newspapers began to disassociate themselves from (arguing against) racism, they simultaneously began to support anti-immigration policies.

8. Van Dijk, "Discurso de las elites y racismo institucional."

9. See Leila Ahmed, *Women and Gender in Islam: Historical Roots of a Modern Debate* (New Haven: Yale University Press, 1993); Lila Abu-Lughod, "Do Muslim Women Really Need Saving?" *American Anthropologist* 104 (2002): 783–790; Ángeles Ramírez, "Olvidadas," *El País,* March 1, 2002.

10. Edward Said, *Cubriendo el Islam: Como los medios de comunicación y los expertos determinan nuestra visión del resto del mundo* (Barcelona: Debate, 2005).

11. The data on the number of readers for each paper come from the General Media Survey from the Association for Media Research, General Summary for October 2007 to May 2007.

12. "¿Velo o pañuelo?" (Veil or Headscarf?), by Malén Aznárez, Ombudsman, *El País,* December 21, 2003.

13. *El Mundo* editorial, March 19, 2007.

14. Used in, among others, opinion articles by Susana Fortes in *El País* (October 21, 2007); or "little girl Fatima" (*la niña Fátima*) in the article by Manuel Delgado, "The Little Girl in the Headscarf," *El Mundo,* February 19, 2002; "little girl Elidrissi" in the article by Federico Jiménez Losantos, *El Mundo,* February 18, 2002; "little girl Fatima" in "The Blonde was a Brunette," by Ignacio Camacho, *ABC,* February 18, 2002.

15. *El País* article, December 8, 2003.

16. *El País* article, December 17, 2003.

17. *El País* article, October 21, 2004.

18. *El Mundo* article, February 19, 2003.

19. *ABC* article, December 17, 2003.

20. *ABC* article, January 16, 2004.

21. *El País* article, March 24, 2004.

22. Three weeks after the March 11 attack, on April 3, authorities surrounded an apartment in Leganés, near Madrid, where suspects in the train bombings were living. Apparently, police had studied the activity of the suspects' cell phone cards, which had been identified in the attack. Surrounded by the police with no chance of escape, seven of the alleged terrorists committed suicide amid hymns and declarations of martyrdom.

23. *El País* article, May 14, 2004.

24. Van Dijk, "Discurso de las elites y racismo institucional."

25. See Mariana Tello Weiss, "El otro entre Nosotros: Una approximación antropológica a las construcciones sobre el 'Terrorismo Islamista' en la prensa tras el 11M," Ph.D. dissertation, Universidad Autónoma de Madrid, 2007.

26. *El Mundo* article, March 3, 2004.

27. Between the March 11 attack and the elections on March 14, the right, which was in power at the time, held that the attack had been the work of ETA. If they had admitted from the beginning that Islamic terrorists were responsible, the Spanish people would have known that the bombings were an act of revenge by Al Qaeda for the Spanish government's support of the U.S. invasion of Iraq. In fact, protest against Spain's collusion with North American imperialism was clear in subsequent elections that turned against the Popular Party. Throughout the entire trial of those accused in the March 11 attacks,

the right, which ultimately lost the 2004 elections, continued to maintain that ETA was responsible.

28. This concerned the authority of the Board of Education, an organization dependent on the City Hall, which, among other tasks, places students in public and semiprivate schools in the municipality.

29. This body is dependent on the Madrid Autonomous Community. Its tasks include training teachers and overseeing school inspections.

30. Laura Mijares and Ángeles Ramírez, "Mujeres, pañuelo e islamofobia en España: Un estado de la cuestión," *Anales de Historia Contemporánea,* no. 24 (2008): 121–135.

31. *ABC* article, February 16, 2002.

32. *El País* article, February 16, 2002.

33. *El País* article, October 2, 2007.

34. *El País* article, October 3, 2007.

35. *El País* editorial, February 17, 2002.

36. *El Mundo* editorial, February 16, 2002.

37. *El Mundo* editorial, February 18, 2002.

38. *ABC* editorial, March 6, 2005.

39. *ABC* editorial, December 4, 2006. Also see *ABC* editorial, October 3, 2007.

40. *ABC* editorial, March 6, 2005.

41. "Mujeres sin atributos" (Women without Attributes), by Susana Fortes, *El País,* October 21, 2007.

42. For instance, "Multiculturalismo e islamofobia," (Muliculturalism and Islamophobia), by Gema Martín, *El País,* March 1, 2002; "Olvidadas" (Forgotten Women), by Ángeles Ramírez, *El País,* March 11, 2006; "Sexismo neolocolonial" (Neocolonial Sexism), by Ángeles Ramírez, *El País,* October 8, 2006.

43. "El desvelo del velo" (The Unveiling of the Veil), by Eugenia Relaño, *El País,* November 1, 2007; "El pañuelo de las musulmanas y la vorágine culturalista" (Muslim Women's Headscarf and the Culturalist Vortex), by Andrés Pajares, *El País,* February 20, 2002; "Cuando la amenaza es un pañuelo" (When the Threat Is a Headscarf), by Jordi Sánchez, *El País,* October 8, 2007.

44. "La tradición sienta mal a las mujeres" (Tradition Doesn't Suit Women Well), by Soledad Gallego-Díaz, *El País,* October 12, 2007. Gallego-Díaz is not just a columnist; she holds a position at the paper, making her opinions more like an editorial than those of other columnists.

45. Empar Moliner, *El País,* October 8, 2007.

46. "Occidente en un pañuelo" (The West in a Headscarf), by Antonio Galeote, *El Mundo,* February 24, 2002; "Niña y pañuelo" (The Little Girl and the Headscarf), by Antonio Gala, *El Mundo,* February 19, 2002.

47. *El Mundo,* September 4, 2004.

48. In Spanish, *integrism* refers to religious fanaticism and is especially linked to Islamic terrorism and the ideological basis for such terrorism.

49. "La teta y el velo" (The Breast and the Headscarf) by Zoe Valdés, *El Mundo,* March 1, 2004.

50. The writer is referring to the "spectacle" of veiled girls in French cities.

51. "Ni estético ni oportuno" (Neither Aesthetic nor Opportune) by Ignacio Sánchez Cámara, *ABC,* February 18, 2002.

52. "El velo no es el velo" (The Headscarf Is Not a Headscarf), *El País,* October 7, 2007.

53. "Detrás del velo" (Behind the Headscarf), by Federico Jiménez Losantos, *ABC,* February 18, 2002.

54. "Immigrantes y moriscos" (Immigrants and Moors), by Serafín Fanjul, *ABC,* January 4, 2007.

55. These are the dates that delimit the time frame for this chapter.

56. "La ignorancia del infiel" (Ignorance of the Infidel), by Antonio Elorza, *El País,* October 22, 2001; "Las dos caras del Corán" (The Two Faces of the Koran), by Antonio Elorza, *El País,* September 25, 2002; "Religión y violencia" (Religion and Violence), by Antonio Elorza, *El País,* April 16, 2004.

57. "Velos y quebrantos" (Headscarves and Suffering), by Antonio Elorza, *El País,* April 3, 2002.

14

THE 7/7 LONDON BOMBINGS
AND BRITISH MUSLIM WOMEN

Media Representations, Mediated Realities

FAUZIA AHMAD

This chapter explores media representations of Muslims, and British Muslim women in particular, following the London bombings of July 7, 2005, and attempted bombings in London and Glasgow during June 2007. As in the period following 9/11, Muslim women, their role in Islam, and the issue of dress, received special scrutiny in the British media. I question whether those projected images of Muslim women reflect lived realities, or merely reflect a victim-based pathology of Muslim women selectively maintained by the mainstream media.

Many of the issues discussed here in relation to media representations of Muslim women are not new. Just as the *burqa* attained a heightened symbolic and iconic quality following 9/11 and the war in Afghanistan, Muslim women, their bodies, and their dress, have become a renewed site or "abstracted category"[1] for both media and political debate over the past several decades. I refer to high-profile controversies before 7/7 such as the case of Shabina Begum and her two-year high court battle to wear the *jilbab* (2004–2006).[2] Then came the subsequent banning of the *niqab* on some university campuses when this article of clothing was deemed a "security risk" following 7/7. Finally, inflammatory comments were made by Jack Straw, then leader of the House of Commons, questioning the "integration" of young Muslim women wearing the *niqab*. These examples highlight how Muslim women's bodies, their apparent "victimhood," and, ironically, their perceived threat to "British values" continue to remain a source of fascination in the media and government-led agendas. In my opinion, this "victim-focused" and pathological discourse is one that repeats simplistic "modern/Western" versus "traditional/Muslim" dichotomous frameworks.

This chapter draws on the unique reflections of six British Muslim women responding to the issue of British media constructs of Muslim women, post-7/7.[3] The women also addressed the manner in which these representations influenced Muslim women's civil liberties. All these individuals, politically and socially active in Muslim organizations, have been at the front line responding to and advising the media, public sector workers, and government agencies on issues affecting Muslim women and have been providing grassroots services to various Muslim communities.

Representational issues include the use of derogatory language, misrepresentations of Islam, visibility/invisibility, and Muslim women's perceptions of their personal sense of security and safety; all are significant factors in discussing the ways Muslim women's civil liberties have been affected by the London bombings and the ensuing fallout. One study of British Muslim responses to media coverage of 9/11 revealed how Muslim women experienced a "loss of control" of the images used to represent and portray them.[4]

The antiwar movement that emerged after the U.S. decision to invade Afghanistan encouraged a number of British Muslim women to become more politically and visibly active in such movements.[5] Their political and social activism led some of them to become spokespersons and articulate advocates for Muslim women. Their activities challenge dominant stereotypes of Muslim women as passive, oppressed, and subjugated, but to what extent has this been recognized in the media?

THE LONDON BOMBINGS

After London was named host of the 2012 Olympics, a day of celebration and national pride ensued. However, the next morning, Thursday, July 7, 2005, Londoners on their daily to commute to work experienced one of the most traumatic events since the IRA bombings in Canary Wharf in 1996. Four suicide bombers struck in central London, killing 52 people and injuring more than 770. Three bombs went off at 08:50 BST inside underground trains just outside Edgware Road and Liverpool Street stations, with one other exploding on a train traveling between King's Cross and Russell Square. The final explosion happened about an hour later on a double-decker bus in Tavistock Square. Rolling coverage of news networks revealed the extent of the explosions and brought the realization that these were indeed the work of a coordinated terrorist attack. The walking wounded, dazed and frightened, mingled with confused crowds of commuters, as medical teams, fire crews, and police tried to contain the situation.

About a week later, police confirmed what Muslims in the United Kingdom were dreading—that the bombers were indeed young British-born Muslims. The prime minister, Tony Blair, who was hosting the G8 Summit in

Gleneagles, Scotland, appeared at midday flanked by G8 leaders. In a brief statement, Blair said that he believed the attacks were intended to coincide with the G8 summit and represented an attack on "our values and our way of life." A subsequent speech delivered later that day from Downing Street drew on the press statement of the Muslim Council of Britain (MCB) condemning the terrorist attacks but interestingly implied that the MCB "[knew] that those people acted in the name of Islam."[6] Many national newspapers were also quick to apportion blame, and several papers drew comparisons with the Madrid bombings and with 9/11. "Al-Qa'eda brings terror to the heart of London," was the *Daily Telegraph*'s headline on July 8, with a dramatic full-page picture of a bomb victim with bandages across her face. The tabloid *Daily Star* read:

> We will not be broken: This was our 9/11 and Tony Blair spoke for all of us when he told those responsible: "You will not destroy us." . . . Osama bin Laden and his wretched followers should know: we will not be broken and we WILL get justice for the dead of 7/7.

Britain's most popular tabloid newspaper, the *Sun,* similarly evoked comparisons with 9/11 and World War II:

> Our spirit will never be broken: Adolf Hitler's Blitz and his doodlebug rockets never once broke London's spirit. Years later, the capital was bloodied but unbowed by two decades of deadly attacks by the mad bombers of the IRA. So yesterday's outrage by fanatics of al-Qaeda — Britain's 9/11 — will achieve only one end. . . . To make this nation ever more determined that those who violate our way of life must never win. . . . In the words of Winston Churchill in 1941: "Never give in. Never. Never. Never."

AN ATTACK ON CIVIL LIBERTIES

Hostile repercussions for Britain's varying Muslim communities ensued, mirroring the anti-Muslim backlash following the U.S. 9/11 attacks. Within hours of the London bombs, Muslims or anyone looking like a Muslim (including Sikhs) began reporting incidents of reprisal attacks.[7] Reports of arson and graffiti attacks on mosques and Muslim or Asian organizations, family homes, Sikh temples, and individuals emerged alongside numerous reported incidents of verbal abuse, death threats and harassment, racist bullying and spitting. An arson attack by two white men on a mosque in Birkenhead, Wirral, within the first five days following 7/7 left the assistant imam trapped in his upstairs bedroom. He was pulled to safety by fire crews, while in Nottingham, a forty-eight-year-old Pakistani man was killed in what police described as a racially motivated attack.[8] The anti-Muslim backlash had public repercussions for Muslim academics in Britain as well.[9]

A second attempted series of bomb attacks on London's travel networks on July 21 proved unsuccessful. However, severe disruption to travel services followed, creating further tension not just among the public but also, more significantly, in police responses to potential terror suspects. Within the first two days of the July 7 attacks, police recorded seventy racist incidents against minorities. Within two weeks, the number of religious hate crimes recorded by the Metropolitan Police stood at eight hundred, five times the number recorded the previous year during the same period. The flawed and fatal shooting of the innocent Brazilian, Jean Charles de Menezes, in Stockwell tube station on July 22—the day after the failed bomb attacks—added to the death toll of innocent victims. There were also a number of high-profile police raids on Muslim properties, often based on faulty intelligence. One of the most notorious occurred in the east end of London (an area known for its concentration of Muslims) when 250 police in full protective gear raided two neighboring homes falsely reported as a chemical weapons factory. One of the accused inhabitants, Mohammed Abdul Kahar, was shot in the shoulder.[10]

Muslim women in Britain, especially those highly visible in their *hijab, jilbab,* or *niqab,* experienced particular vilification on the streets, in the media, and from some politicians. During this time, Muslim women were advised by their own Muslim communities not to venture outdoors unaccompanied. The late Shaikh Dr. Zaki Badawi even suggested that Muslim women should remove their *hijab* if they feared for their safety, though this advice was dismissed by some Muslim women's organizations (such as Pro-Hijab) as unnecessary. Fariha Thomas, of the Glasgow-based Muslim Women's Resource Centre Amina, noted an increase in Islamophobic incidents, such as "name-calling, being stared at, some hijab's being pulled off." She went on to say:

> While the number of reported incidents may not be high, immediately after the bombing (around the time of Jack Straw's comments on the niqab) there was an increase in incidents. This leads to women feeling unsafe in public spaces and in unfamiliar environments where they are likely to be in a minority and therefore curtails life options. Women "keeping their heads below the parapet"—not doing anything to draw attention . . . increases opportunities for increased segregation.

She also noted feeling compromised in her personal safety and experienced increased scrutiny when traveling, especially through Glasgow Airport. This compromising of Muslim women's safety clearly had an impact on their civil liberties. Other women related similar personal experiences. For instance, Sarah Sheriff, an adult education tutor who was also the former deputy editor of the *Muslim News* newspaper; cofounder and chair of a Muslim women's advocacy organization, the Muslim Women's Helpline; and an activist in several other Muslim and interfaith charities, reported:

> Members of my family are anxious and urge each other not to get involved in any activity that might bring unwarranted attention. I often have the thought crossing my mind that I or somebody in my family (especially the males) might be targeted by the police and we might be raided. My private "day-mare" or nightmare is of a raid happening whilst I'm having a shower! I worry when a male family member travels in the evening to his university. I've supported my sister-in-law in arguing that my nephew shouldn't go around with his Muslim Pakistani friends on a roam around the town centre as, apart from other scenarios, they could be targeted as suspicious.

Aaliyah Shaikh, a researcher at the Muslim Youth Helpline and a Muslim chaplain at one of the central London hospitals, related a distressing personal incident and the lack of understanding she received from the police. Although the event occurred about eighteen months after 7/7, it nonetheless reflects the general increase in tension and hostility to Muslims:

> I got spat at by a white guy and called a "fucking Muslim" at a train station, and I know other people who have suffered the same, or had their hijab torn off, and that's invading your personal space and degrading you and treating you like dirt. . . . When I contacted the police, they didn't really do anything. They asked *me* to actually take a DNA test. . . . It wasn't taken seriously. In fact the policeman didn't even understand what Islamophobia was.

Similarly, Kulsum Butt, a writer and antiwar activist, noted the strain in personal relationships with non-Muslim friends after 7/7 and recalled the following harrowing experience:

> I was going to get petrol and there was this Hindu man—I was wearing a scarf—and he started calling me "Bin Laden" and a terrorist! . . . He

was just so aggressive towards me, he wouldn't stop until I had to resort to calling him terrible things. Some people stood and watched, and some shook their heads.

Media hype and sensationalized reporting have contributed to many British Muslims experiencing a deep sense of alienation. Media representations that speak disparagingly of Muslims as "these people"[11] suggest that Muslims represent the "enemy within" and are not part of British society. Government responses have merited criticism among Muslim and non-Muslim groups alike for adopting an "us"/"them" approach—dismissing Muslim concerns with foreign policy in Iraq and Afghanistan, for example, as "false grievances" (Tony Blair's words). By placing responsibility for rooting out terrorism and "evil ideology"[12] at the doors of the Muslim community, the British government refuses to acknowledge any links between its foreign policy and the London bombings or to accept any responsibility for the subsequent loss of life caused by the bombs.[13]

Existing research shows the British Muslim response to media coverage of 9/11 as one of ongoing frustration. The U.K. Muslim community especially objects to the use of subjective terminology (such as "Islamic terrorist" and "Muslim fundamentalist") and the misappropriation of terms such as "jihad" to project negative images of Muslims.[14] My previous research on this same topic identified the ways in which respondents felt that language was employed as a tool to stigmatize Islam and believed that a lack of journalistic social responsibility further contributed to a sense of Western double standards.[15]

High-profile raids and arrests following the Glasgow attempted car bombings in June 2007 further demonized Muslims, especially those working in the medical profession. Muslim women were also implicated in these bomb plots and arrested alongside their partners, though later released without charge. Some sections of the media insisted that Muslim women now posed a real and dangerous threat to British values.

MEDIA DISCOURSES AND DISTORTIONS

It is important to recognize that the media is not a monolithic entity. The fact that concerted efforts have been made by large sectors of the British media, and some journalists in particular (such as Madeleine Bunting, Gary Younge, Seumus Milne, and Robert Fisk) to educate the public about Islam and Muslim cultures and to encourage further thought must be acknowledged. This applies not just to the broadsheets, TV news, and documentaries. After 9/11 the hugely popular tabloid the *Sun,* not normally known for its sensitive coverage of racialized minorities, issued front-page spreads urging people not to blame ordinary Muslims. Furthermore, in 2004 the *Sun* hired Anila Baig, who was launched in a front-page cover story wearing a *hijab* and introduced as "Our woman in a headscarf."[16]

However, in the post-9/11 and post-7/7 era, British political and media discourses about Islam, Muslims, and Muslim women appear to be framed, regulated, and "othered" through a number of overlapping themes. These themes include a tendency to inject negativity into Muslim-related stories, to refrain from making basic distinctions between Islam and Muslims, and to attach artificial and polarizing labels such as "moderate" and "extremist" to Muslim identities. Finally, Muslims are blamed for failing to "integrate" in critiques of multiculturalism; this inability is represented as a "failed project," invoking the "clash of civilizations" analogies. All these contribute to further "us"/"them" distinctions.[17]

A key crisis in the British media and its coverage of British Muslims post-7/7 was the controversy over the Danish cartoon affair, which culminated in protests orchestrated by the banned (but re-formed as the "al Ghurabaa") Muslim group, Al-Muhajiroon. A number of young men were arrested for incitement to murder and racial hatred following the protests at the Danish embassy in London in February 2006. The controversy sparked international debate about the limits and abuses of free speech in democratic societies. In Britain, as in other parts of Europe, media commentators who supported the "right to offend" rehearsed arguments around the failure of multiculturalism. This failure led to the prioritizing of cultural differences, lack of integration of Muslim minorities, and debates on the incompatibility of Muslim with non-Muslim values rooted in the "clash of civilizations" hypothesis. This discourse has replayed itself in media representations of Muslim women in the British press, especially since 9/11 and 7/7.

The perception of multiculturalism as a failed project has inevitably been strengthened by using issues such as forced marriages, female genital mutilation, and honor killings to sharpen the focus on Muslim communities and Muslim women as a case in point.[18] Furthermore, the privilege bestowed by the media on self-professed former Muslims, such as Ayaan Hirsi Ali, to be spokespersons on Islam and Muslim women continues to be a source of irritation for many Muslim women. This is especially true when the voices and opinions of these individuals appear to be legitimized as "authentic" merely because they are dissenting.

As many Muslims in Britain have frequently noted, fair and balanced reporting of Muslim-related stories is limited and not mainstreamed, or "normalized." The negative focus often associated with news stories on Muslims is still prevalent,[19] despite the presence of Muslims working within the mainstream media, some in senior or high-profile positions.[20] As Sarah Sheriff explained:

> The omission of Muslims in positive roles and making positive contributions makes it all the more stark that the majority of news items feature Muslims in negative lights: terrorists, honour killers, forced-marriage perpetrators, criminals, woman oppressors etc. Some practising Muslims do get an opportunity from time to time to write a column, but it's too few and far between. When non-Muslims engage in activities that Muslims are always portrayed as being guilty of, e.g., BNP bomb plots, Sikh forced marriages or honour killing incidents, etc., there isn't the same stigmatisation. Having Muslim faces in the media has not resulted in enough "normalising" news coverage. There are also too many films, dramas and documentaries that reinforce negative images of Muslims.

Aaliyah Shaikh also noted how opportunities for positive images of Muslims and Muslim women, if initially attempted, were often lost through the inclusion of one or two negative or stereotyped comments or actions: "Basically, *they* [the news media] *always manage to turn a positive into a negative*" (my emphasis). Narzanin Massoumi added:

> Since 7/7 there has been a notable increase in Islamophobia, particularly in the media and I think, as a result, Muslim women can be used in very cynical ways in the media. I think there are two ways in which they are presented, one whereby these women are presented as victims of their religion as a means to emphasise the illiberal nature of Islamic values. Discussions following Jack Straw's comments with regards to the niqab seemed to follow this discourse. On the other hand, particularly since 7/7, there has been increased attention given to Muslim women who are seen to be a pacifying force on Islamic radicalism.

John Richardson's detailed discourse analysis of media reporting of Muslims in the British broadsheets suggests that this theme of negativity is endemic.[21] Muslim sources, he says, are only attributed in critical, negative contexts.

HISTORICAL AND CONTEMPORARY
REPRESENTATIONS OF MUSLIM WOMEN

Historically, Muslim women have been framed within competing gendered and racialized discourses of victimhood and exotic objectification.[22] Often viewed as "defenders of Islamic heritage,"[23] Muslim women have been depicted interchangeably with Muslim culture itself—static and immobile, incapable of fluidity, and/or not open to change. Such pathologized accounts silence and obscure forms of agency and difference that restrict Muslim women's experiences and identities within artificial binaries such as "modern" (read Western, educated) and "traditional" (read Muslim, uneducated, backward).[24] Reductionist and victim-focused representations of Muslim women set within stories of forced marriage, honor killings, and *hijabs, jilbabs,* and *niqabs* have long been a source of irritation and frustration for many Muslim women. According to Fariha Thomas:

> The media still likes to portray the image of Muslim women as oppressed. They are still infatuated with issues such as forced marriage and female genital mutilation, and do not put into context the violence against women in all societies, reinforcing stereotypes that Muslim and Asian women are far more badly treated, and more oppressed.

Although some of the women cited in this chapter have acknowledged efforts by journalists and media outlets to include more positive Muslim women's voices in media stories, the majority say that these efforts are too limited. When asked if media representations reflected Muslim women's lived realities, all the respondents answered with a firm negative. Sarah Sheriff cited examples of Muslim women's positive achievements being ignored in the media. She suggested, perhaps cynically, that to highlight these would be to "undermine the stereotypes that the media have spent such a long time creating and perpetuating." She went on to say:

> The successful, well-socialised Muslim woman is completely invisible. When Muslim women achieve, for example, Iranian women scaling Mount Everest, this is not given any attention, especially by women's magazines/ programmes, for example *Women's Hour.*[25] Successful women's projects and mobilisations are still not given credit—it always appears that some white politician or activists or co-opted "liberated" Asian/Muslim woman is the champion of Muslim women, drawing attention to or trying to confront things that many of us have been addressing for a long time. It seems as if we

are only called upon when Muslims are being problematised and validation for the problem and "their" solution is required by an authentic voice.

Narzanin Massoumi, an activist in the antiwar movement and a doctoral student researching Muslim women political activists, pointed to the complexity of male/female relationships and the media's tendency to portray Muslim men and women as enemies:

> I don't think they emphasise the extent to which Muslim women are engaged with non-Muslims; they are assumed to be very segregated, passive and unengaged with society in general. The relationships they have with the men in their lives are also misrepresented. Current media representations seem to illustrate the men in these women's lives as enemies. Rarely are the relationships that Muslim women and men have with each other seen as supportive or mutually beneficial.

Inherent in the post-9/11 obsession with Muslim women has been the sheer volume of articles written *about* Muslim women rather than *by* them, despite the presence and availability of numerous articulate Muslim women writers. This has contributed to the sense of a "loss of control" in terms of their images and rights to self-definition.[26] The post-7/7 period in Britain has seen the same phenomenon. A trawl through the online photo libraries for stock images used for news items reveals vast collections of *niqab*-clad Muslim women.

POLARIZING MODERATE MUSLIMS

Media and political discourses on Islam and Muslims very often fail to recognize differences between basic terms such as "Islamic" and "Muslim." Douglass and Shaikh distinguish between the *signifier* "Islamic" and the *signified* "Muslim," highlighting ways in which the prefixing of "Islamic" on familiar routines, places, or events transforms the commonplace and everyday into an "alien" form that signals difference and marginality.[27] One of the most striking examples of a failure to appreciate and differentiate between the two terms has led to contested terms such as "Islamic terrorism." Criticism of such terms by Muslim organizations has led to some restraint by politicians and certain sectors of the media; however, what has ensued is the use of equally contentious and confusing terms, such as "Islamist" and "moderate Muslim." The latter term especially holds the connotations "stooge," "collaborator," and "sell-out."[28]

Muslim women, largely absent from most government consultations and many Muslim organizations, have chosen to organize their political efforts through alternative strategies. Interestingly, their positive interventions in very public arenas have remained invisible in much media commentary on or about Muslim women.[29] Narzanin Massoumi noted the ways government and media-led discourses presented internal debates in Muslim communities as one-sided and polarized, leaving little room for positive political dialogue:

> I think the key issue for Muslims in Britain is one of representation. Since the 7/7 bombings, the voices of British Muslims are presented as a polarisation between radical extremists versus those who are closely associated with the government. . . . There is a focus on those distancing themselves from the "bad" aspects of Islam and little focus on any forms of positive political dialogue. The British Muslim women that I have worked with, for example, have been involved in positive political dialogues with non-Muslims. They also offer a positive alternative of political resistance, giving a space to articulate critical views of the government's political agenda without resorting to Islamic political separatism. Such voices are rarely given a space to grow.

JACK STRAW AND THE *NIQAB* CONTROVERSY

If there has been a defining post-7/7 moment for Muslim women in Britain, it is the heightened media frenzy and photo-shooting spree (with cameras focused on *niqab*-wearing Muslim women) following comments from Jack Straw, the former foreign secretary. Media demonization of Muslim women who wear Muslim dress is not new. Prior to, during, and since September 11, 2001, well-known feminists and newspaper columnists such as Polly Toynbee (a self-confessed Islamophobe) have continued to insist that religion, and Islam in particular, oppresses Muslim women.

The *burqa* worn by Afghan women was widely viewed in the West as symbolic of Muslim women's subjugation and oppression and Islam's inability to coexist alongside Western concepts of modernity and democracy. Another columnist, Julie Birchill, in a pre-9/11 diatribe against Islam and Muslims, described Islam as "shit" and *burqas* as "mobile prisons" (the *Guardian*, August 2001), though she did later offer an apology. September 11 gave commentators the green light to equate Islam with fundamentalism, extremism, despotic and oppressive regimes (propped up, incidentally, by Western governments), and violence — thus at once representing and pathologizing Islam. Although some acknowledged efforts have been made in media representations of Islam and Muslims in Britain, the women I spoke to felt that little had changed overall.

The criminalization of Muslim women wearing the *niqab* and *burqa* was heightened when two separate criminal suspects attempted to escape police in 2005 using *burqas* as a disguise. The *Sun* reported the news of PC Sharon Beshenivsky's murder with a picture of a woman wearing a *niqab* and asked in the caption underneath: "*Veil . . . is this a Muslim woman or a ruthless gunman?*"[30] The fact that the 2005 male suspects were asylum seekers from Somalia, another group of stigmatized people in Britain, merely confirmed the *burqa*'s link with "undesirables." Face veils became a security risk and were banned from some university campuses.[31] Images that consolidated criminal linkages between Muslim women and the *niqab* became commonplace. These included photos of the wives of two of the 7/7 bombers in *niqab* and a *niqab*-wearing woman giving photographers a two-fingered "salute" (during the height of the Jack Straw affair). Then came the image of a *niqab*-wearing juror removed from court for hiding an iPod under her *hijab*. And, of course, there were the images of "a gaggle of women in burkas"[32] protesting outside the Old Bailey during the trials of four men accused of inciting murder and racial hatred following protests after the Danish cartoon affair.[33]

Jack Straw's infamous October 2006 comments (in an article for his local newspaper in Blackburn)[34] questioning the integration of Muslim women who wore the *niqab* encouraged the expression and normalization of Islamophobic sentiments in both broadsheets and tabloid press. Several senior politicians, including then–Prime Minister Tony Blair and members of the opposition, supported Jack Straw's views. The culture secretary, Tessa Jowell, insisted that "veils were a symbol of women's subjugation" and prevented women from taking a "full place in society."[35] Interestingly, Straw's comments coincided with news that the country's largest stockpile of chemical weapons had been found in the home of a supporter of the right-wing group the British National Party.[36] While this news did not make national headlines, the case of Aisha Azmi, a school teaching assistant suspended (and later sacked) from her job for refusing to remove her *niqab* in the presence of males, was front-page news.

Muslim women's organizations reported an increase in the number of *hijab*-wearing women experiencing some form of public abuse. Some of these women were spit at or verbally abused. Others were refused entry into public transport or had their *hijabs* pulled off and, in more serious cases, became targets of physical assault. *Niqab*-clad women were stigmatized and represented as a threat to British values and way of life for refusing to "integrate." Opinion polls showed support for a ban on face veils in public.[37] As Fariha Thomas noted, "The media had another field day in linking issues of women and backwardness with a 'failure to integrate' and 'lack of Britishness.'"

Narzanin Massoumi drew attention to the way media representations had led to an increase in the "visibility of Islamic dress as a marker of difference":

> I think it perpetuates an image of a division between "traditional" inassimilable Muslim women versus "modern" assimilated Muslim women. These "modern women" are seen to be those who have rejected these alien practices. In the media discussions and debates following Jack Straw's comments there were often Muslim women who neither wear the hijab nor the niqab articulating reasons as to why they didn't wear such garments. Such women are welcomed as recognising liberal values and held up in contrast to the supposedly backward fundamentalism of those women who do wear any form of Islamic dress. In doing so, it perpetuates the myth of self-segregating Muslims, who are choosing to separate themselves from British society.

However, Aaliyah Shaikh felt that Jack Straw's comments were "blown out of proportion" by some Muslims, suggesting that "the hijab has been made one of the five pillars of Islam, which it is not." The negativity of the images it provoked in the media—the serious, somber-looking women dressed head to toe in black—was not a reality she was familiar with, as the image masked the great diversity and achievements of Muslim women:

> The media continue to show typical images of women dressed in black and looking oppressed. I meet so many women who are funky, trendy and dressed in so many ways, but the images we see are old and are of women veiled in black from head to toe—but even many of these women are amazing in some of the things they do. But the images we always see look like women who are oppressed, suppressed and depressed, but they're not. Most women in this country have a choice to wear the hijab; some are forced, but they are a tiny minority. What about all these women . . . [in] great positions in public and private sectors? Most people don't want to look at them or hear about what they do. This is a great shame, especially for young people as these women are role models but young people don't get to see that. . . . There is not enough true representation of Muslim women in Britain.

As Aaliyah points out, in overprioritizing Muslim women's choice of attire, the media have failed to recognize Muslim women as achievers, contributors, or positive role models.[38]

The *niqab* also became a cheap and fast way to boost newspaper circulation. The *Sun* featured one of its topless glamour models wearing a *niqab* for a day. She was quoted as saying, "I feel more exposed wearing a niqab and am definitely attracting more attention than if I had stepped out naked. . . . But now I've had both experiences, I can honestly say my way of life feels more free and empowering."[39] Channel 4 used a *niqab*-wearing woman to present its "alternative" Christmas Day message—televised at an especially inopportune time—in the same time slot as the queen's traditional message to the nation. Serious news broadcasters also resorted to using images of *niqab*-clad women as shorthand for stories on Muslims. For example, in a "Survey of Muslim Voices"—part of the BBC Web site's coverage of the failed car bombing attempt in Glasgow and London in June 2007—the only photograph to appear was a closeup of a woman in *niqab*. The image was juxtaposed with a comment in which the woman refers to herself as "veiled." The reader was led to assume that the image and comment were connected to the same person. However, the actual photo (from Getty Images database) was that of a woman in Blackburn protesting against Straw's comments.[40]

Against a backdrop of angry tabloid headlines, such as "Tell extremists if they want to live under Sharia law, they can't live here" (*Sun*, October 18, 2006), the diversity of Muslim women's views were largely ignored. Instead, Muslim women were once again homogenized,[41] as staunch secular feminists such as Joan Smith argued that "the veil is a feminist issue" and a "dramatic visual symbol of oppression" that was "offensive."[42] Making tenuous links between Islam and male violence towards women, Smith insisted that most Muslim women, even those in Britain who exercised choice, were forced or at best influenced by male family members into wearing the veil. The practice of covering, she maintained, was a human rights issue. However, the obvious differentials in power between Jack Straw as a senior white male politician seeking to gain personal and political capital by commenting on Muslim women's dress and wider socioeconomic indicators that prevented integration were lost in all but a few broadsheet columns.[43]

CONCLUSION

Just as the plight of Muslim women in Afghanistan was used to justify military action following 9/11, media and political stereotyped discourses of Muslim women as victims of Islam have been used to further marginalize Muslim women's voices. The women cited in this chapter unanimously agreed that the British media significantly contributed to the vilification of Muslim women by representing them as a "threat" to liberal, secular "Western values." This outcome was achieved, at least in part, by deliberately and consistently linking the veiled Muslim woman's image to news stories about 9/11, the wars in Afghanistan and Iraq, and the tragic events of 7/7. The power relations embedded in discourses on representations of racialized and gendered groups and minorities have effectively ensured that Muslim women's rights to define their identities and experiences on their own terms, and in their own voices, have yet to be realized.

NOTES

1. Lazreg 1988.

2. There are several references in the British press to Shabina Begum, the fifteen-year-old Luton schoolgirl who embarked on a two-year court battle with her school, Denbeigh High, after she was suspended in 2004 for wearing the *jilbab*. Following an initial ruling in favor of the school, Shabina took her case to the Appeal Courts and won. However, the school then took the case to the House of Lords; the House ruled in the school's favor. See BBC News, "School Wins Muslim Dress Appeal," March 26, 2006, http://news.bbc .co.uk/1/hi/education/4832072.stm.

3. I would like to express a huge debt of thanks to the women who participated. They are, in alphabetical order, Kulsum Butt, Narzanin Massoumi, Salma Mirza, Aaliyah Shaikh, Sarah Sheriff, and Fariha Thomas. All usual disclaimers apply. I would also like to thank Faegheh Shirazi for her patience and support.

4. Ahmad 2006.

5. Ahmad 2002.

6. BBC News Online: "In Full: Blair on Bomb Blasts," Statement from Downing Street, Thursday, July 7, 2005, 17:30 BST. http://news.bbc.co.uk/1/hi/uk/4659953.stm.

7. For instance, the MCB received over 30,000 hate messages via e-mail within the first forty-eight hours of the bombings. See "Move to Limit Backlash against Muslims," Vikram Dodd and Alan Travis, Saturday, July 9, 2005. www.guardian.co.uk/attackon london/story/0,,1524576,00.html. Antiracist organizations such as the Institute of Race Relations compiled a full list of known and reported race and faith attacks from July 7, 2005, until September 15, 2007.

8. "Muslim leaders warn of mounting Islamophobia after attacks on mosques," Ian Herbert, Arifa Akbar, and Nigel Morris, *Independent*, July 12, 2005. http://news.independent .co.uk/uk/crime/article298513.ece.

9. A case in point was the tabloid vilification of Tariq Ramadan as a "preacher of hate" soon after 7/7.

10. "Forest Gate Terror Raid Cost £2M," BBC News, Tuesday, October 3, 2006. http://news.bbc.co.uk/1/hi/uk/5401386.stm

11. Ahmad 2002, 2006.

12. "Blair Speech on Terror," Saturday, July 16, 2005, BBC News. http://news.bbc.co.uk/1/hi/uk/4689363.stm.

13. The prime minister called an emergency meeting at No. 10 of Muslims regarded as representatives and leaders to discuss the London bombings. The "Preventing Extremism Together" working group or task force, as it was commonly known, was a product of that initial meeting but has been criticized for its approach, composition, and lack of any real political muscle. The main issue opined as the underlying reason for the bombings—anger at the Iraq war—was an issue *not* on the agenda for discussion. Frequent requests for a public inquiry into the bombings have been denied as irrelevant.

14. See Poole 2002; Richardson 2004; Ahmad 2006; IHRC, the EU Monitoring Centre, 2006.

15. Ahmad 2006.

16. There has been speculation among Muslim discussion groups that Baig wearing the *hijab* for the *Sun* was a publicity stunt, as she had not worn the *hijab* prior to joining the paper and early in 2007 stopped wearing the *hijab* altogether. In October 2006 she donned a *niqab* for a flight from Bradford to Paris and claimed that she was allowed through British airport security without her face being checked. In 2006 she signed a five-figure deal to write her memoirs.

17. Richardson 2006.

18. An illustrative example is the way the tragic death of Kurdish Banaz Mahmood, killed at twenty by her father and uncle in a so-called honor killing, was reported. Her sister Bekhal, who also feared for her life, had resorted to wearing the *niqab* for her safety. However, tabloid versions of her story about her sister were full of confusing inaccuracies stating that Banaz was "forced into an arranged marriage" and that their father was intent on "maintaining his strict Muslim traditions." These reinforced stereotypes of the oppressive Muslim father and family. See, for example, Oliver Harvey, "They Can't Have Same Life Here," *Sun,* June 13, 2007. www.thesun.co.uk/article/0,2-2007270252,00.html.

19. Richardson 2004.

20. Such as Aaqil Ahmed, commissioning editor of religion at Channel 4 and former deputy editor of documentaries at BBC Religion.

21. Richardson 2004, 2006.

22. See Lazreg 1988; Mohanty 1988; Khan 1998.

23. Rosario 1998.

24. Said's (1995) contention of the "deformed" nature of the Orientalist discourses that rely on the construction and legitimation of binary relationships that situate non-Western belief systems and cultures as "inferior" and "backward"—and the power relations inherent in these processes—is important to remember here. While Sayyid (1997) usefully highlights inconsistencies in some applications of "modern" and "Western," I have also described elsewhere (Ahmad 2001, 2003) the ways in which these terms are repeatedly applied to representations of Muslim women in Britain.

25. A popular and long-running daily morning radio show from the BBC, Radio 4.

26. Ahmad 2006.

27. Douglass and Shaikh.

28. Modood and Ahmad 2007.

29. Ahmad 2002.

30. Taylor 2006.

31. Curtis 2005.

32. C. Gill, "Veiled Protest as Race Hate Muslims Jailed,"*Daily Mail,* July 1, 2007. www.dailymail.co.uk/pages/live/articles/news/news.html?in_article_id=469285&in_page_id=1770.

33. The march and demonstration that attracted the most news coverage was relatively small but loud and organized on February 3, 2006, by fringe groups such as al Ghurabaa outside the Danish embassy. No more than 200 to 300 people attended. This can be compared to much larger, peaceful protests in London numbering some 3,500 the day after. There have since been suggestions that some sections of the media "encouraged" a group of men to "hijack" the peaceful protests. See "Press Pack 'Encouraged Activists,'" BBC News, Wednesday, March 15, 2006. http://news.bbc.co.uk/1/hi/uk/4809498.stm.

34. "I Felt Uneasy Talking to Someone I Couldn't See," Jack Straw's column in the Blackburn-based *Lancashire Telegraph* reproduced in the *Guardian,* Friday, October 6, 2006. http://politics.guardian.co.uk/homeaffairs/story/0,,1889231,00.html.

35. "Muslim Veil Is a Symbol of Women's Oppression," says Jowell, October 16, 2006. www.dailymail.co.uk/pages/live/articles/news/news.html?in_article_id=410622&in_page_id=1770.

36. "Ex-BNP Man Faces Explosives Charge," Andrew Hewitt, Wednesday, October 4, 2006. http://www.burnleycitizen.co.uk/display.var.951775.0.exbnp_man_faces_explosives_charge.php.

37. "Survey Finds Support for Veil Ban," Wednesday, November 29, 2006. http://news.bbc.co.uk/1/hi/uk/6194032.stm.

38. Recent research on Muslim women's academic achievements and career aspirations in Britain shows that Muslim women have high aspirations and are often supported by their families in the pursuit of these aspirations. However, stereotypes of Muslim women negatively influence the attitudes of education professionals and employers (Ahmad 2001; Tyrer and Ahmad 2006; Equal Opportunities Commission 2006).

39. "Keeley Has Less Stares Topless," Keeley Hazel, *Sun,* October 21, 2006. www .thesun.co.uk/article/0,,2-2006480904,00.html.

40. BBC News, "Muslim Voices on the Bomb Attacks," July 2, 2007. http://news.bbc .co.uk/1/hi/uk/6261988.stm.

41. Tarlo 2007.

42. Smith 2006.

43. For example, see Bunting 2006; Sardar 2006.

15

IMAGES OF MUSLIM WOMEN IN POST-9/11 AMERICA

OMAR SACIRBEY

Some seven years after the terrorist attacks of September 11, 2001, and the subsequent U.S. invasion of Afghanistan, stereotypical images of the Muslim woman abound in the U.S. media. Although media reporting of Muslim women has improved with time, primarily as a result of experience and constructive criticism from readers, large swaths of the American public still assume that Muslim women are weak and uneducated. This misperception is mainly due to the Muslim woman's adherence to Islam, a religion largely associated with the patriarchal enforcement of headscarves and burkas. Seen as instruments of oppression, these modest forms of clothing are used to link Islam with misogyny, violence, totalitarianism, and other negative aspects. Muslim women continue to be depicted as oppressed, ignorant victims.

During recent years, in an effort to provide a more objective and knowledgeable picture of Islam and its followers, American news organizations have begun to hire Muslim female journalists. One such journalist, who has provoked heated and sometimes acrimonious debates, is Pamela K. Taylor, a Muslim activist who converted to Islam in her twenties. She became the only Muslim female columnist for "On Faith," an online religious forum published by the *Washington Post* and *Newsweek*. In this position, Taylor presided over a podium in the American public sphere that few Muslim American women had ever enjoyed.

Taylor, a Harvard Divinity School graduate who co-chaired a group called Muslims for Progressive Values, submitted a column regarding media bias against Muslims ("Double Standards, Misinformation, and Vitriol") on March 30, 2007, criticizing, among other things, the common perception that the hijab is the mark of an authentic Muslim woman. Many readers applauded her. But others, despite her credentials and sound arguments, dismissed Taylor, who wears a hijab in the photo that accompanies her "On Faith" biography page.

In fact, the opening comment of what proved to be more than four hundred comments, read as follows: "If your Muslim values are so 'progressive,' then why do you still have to cover your head. Still a bit medieval, are we?" Similar comments, such as this one from "Joe," were overtly insulting: "I think I'll listen to the guys flying airplanes into buildings, rather than some white women looking for an apology."

Taylor's column and the readers' replies reflect a prevailing tension in the United States around the image of Muslim women. Cathy Young, an editor at *Reason* magazine, observed the following in her October 24, 2006, column, "For Westerners, the veil has long been a symbol of the oppression of women in the Islamic world. Some critics have used the plight of Muslim women to suggest that Islam is inherently evil and even to bash Muslims."

That many Americans still cling tenaciously to parochial perceptions about Muslim women, despite some U.S. news coverage that has attempted to counter prevailing stereotypes, raises two possibilities: either that Americans who hold those views are not reading or viewing informative news reports or that some people's prejudices are so deeply rooted that they find the hijab a convenient symbol to vilify a faith they do not understand and feel threatened by. In the worst-case scenarios, they associate the hijab with terrorism and respond with a level of hostility that has, on more than one occasion, provoked violence against hijab-clad women.[1]

According to Stephen Wessler, executive director of the Center for the Prevention of Hate Violence in Portland, Maine, "The hijab both reflects the stereotype that Muslim men oppress women, and it represents something that is viewed as different in a way that people feel is threatening."[2] Wessler, who has extensively studied relations between the mostly white community of Lewiston, Maine, and some thousand-plus Somali Muslim immigrants living there, claims that several Somali women have shared anecdotes with him about how they have endured verbal abuse and other forms of bias for wearing hijab. In Wessler's opinion, "The hijab is a symbol that allows Americans to feel self-righteous about freedom."

Apparently, the issue is not merely how to improve news coverage of Muslim women but rather how to counter pervasive anti-Muslim sentiment in the United States. One must question if impartial news coverage can undo bigotry or have any effect on the seemingly reflexive response of distrust and hostility engendered by the sight of a woman in hijab.

A 2004 survey from the Council on American-Islamic Relations (CAIR) reported that 51 percent of all Americans believe that the Islamic faith encourages oppression of women. And in its 2006 annual report, CAIR said the hijab was a "notable identification feature which triggered significant discrimination." The 2006 report also notes that 166, or 8.4 percent, of the 1,279 discrimination complaints that CAIR received that year were triggered by the hijab.

BLINDED BY BURKAS

Following 9/11, many Americans wanted to know more about the religion in whose name the terrorist attacks had been carried out. The American media shared this hunger and felt responsible to respond to the public's surging interest in Islam and Muslims.

Shaped by superficial and often fantastical accounts written by diplomats, travelers, and journalists over the centuries, prevailing images of the Muslim woman had ranged from the desert temptress to the oppressed and shackled Middle Eastern woman.[3] Americans in the seventeenth, eighteenth, and nineteenth centuries largely relied on European accounts of the Middle East and other parts of the Muslim world. These accounts were written by diplomats and travelers who, according to Moghissi, "accepted what they saw at face value, did little exploration, and sought to mark the insurmountable differences between European and Muslims, the exotic Muslim way of life and gender differences and relations between the sexes."

Several well-known American authors also traveled to the Middle East and wrote about Muslim populations, including Mark Twain and Herman Melville. While their accounts picked up on some of the subtleties of Muslim life, their works were exceptions in a sea of writings that demeaned Muslims, especially Muslim women. "Oversimplified western conceptions of women have been used throughout the long history of relations between the Christian West and the Islamic world, and are evident in representations from paintings and photographs of the eighteen century to contemporary film and TV images," wrote Georgetown University professor Elizabeth Haddad. "Their persistence is a result of a complex of factors, including both the credibility of the images themselves, based on the authority of the media in which they are found, and the ascendance of European and American global power."

These condescending writings on the Muslim world and Muslim women were not accidents resulting from simple prejudice and ignorance. "Europeans were curious to learn about 'other peoples,' but only at a level that would confirm their belief in the superiority of their own culture," wrote Judy Mabro in her book *Veiled Half-Truths: Western Travelers' Perceptions of Muslim*

Women. Indeed, European, and later American, leaders conveniently justified imperialistic policies with images of Muslim women as oppressed by Islam and needing to be liberated by Western, Christian values.

In her book *Veils and Daggars: A Century of National Geographic's Representation of the Arab World*, gender studies professor Linda Steet asserts that the iconic magazine has over the years perpetuated prevailing images of Muslim women as harlots, primitives, and other negative stereotypes. "Let there be no confusion," wrote Steet, who reviewed *National Geographic* issues from 1888 to 1988, "National Geographic is positively steeped in Orientalism and patriarchy."

While Orientalism infected U.S. media through much of the twentieth century, there were indications as the century came to a close that American journalists had begun to improve their reporting methods. Newspapers were increasingly conducting "question and answer" columns with Muslim women and allocating space to them in editorial pages, giving them the opportunity to voice their opinions unfiltered. Non-Muslim reporters were also finding language to describe Muslim women as strong and smart, alluding to their fidelity to religion as a means of empowerment.

But in the glut of television and film images that portrayed Muslim women in stereotypical ways, these reports continued to be the exception rather than the norm. Indeed, using imagery of oppressed Muslim women to justify imperialistic policies continued through the twentieth century, right up to the U.S. invasion of Afghanistan in 2001.

When journalists trailed U.S. and Allied troops into Afghanistan, they discovered the horrible conditions that women endured under the Taliban, reinforcing the ubiquitous perception of Muslim women as victims. Afghanistan became the first post-9/11 prism through which Americans viewed Muslim women in an "Islamic" society. The majority of Afghan women wore the burka, a sacklike garment covering the body from head to toe, with a mesh net obscuring the face. Thus, to most Americans, the burka came to symbolize Muslim women and their oppressive fate. Indeed, Laila Al-Marayati, director of the Los Angeles–based Muslim Women's League, noted in a 2002 *Los Angeles Times* editorial, "Headlines in the mainstream [U.S.] media have reduced Muslim female identity to an article of clothing—'the veil' . . . [or] burka." Her complaint was not that the media were covering the plight of women in Afghanistan but that the burka had come to overshadow far more pressing social and cultural issues these women faced. "The burka is not their major concern of focus," wrote Al-Marayati. "Their priorities are more basic, like feeding their children, becoming literate and living free from violence. Nevertheless, recent articles in the Western media suggest the burka means everything to Muslim women, because they routinely express bewilderment at the fact that all Afghan women didn't cast off their burkas when the Taliban was defeated." That Muslim women had been reduced to a single article of clothing was not some high-minded assertion debated by elitist Muslim feminists but rather a concern felt by rank-and-file Muslim women in America.

For example, Nada Selameh, an American-born Muslim I met at an American-Arab Anti-Discrimination Committee convention in 2005, related that she never wore hijab until she was twenty-six. Her decision to wear the hijab was intentional; she wanted to make the point that not every Muslim woman resembles those depicted on television. "I felt that I wasn't the female that they were showing as representative of Muslims," she explained. Although Selameh continues to defy the stereotypes associated with Muslim women, she readily admits to consciously choosing to wear the hijab. "When I'm not covered, you don't really know that I'm Muslim. I just blend in. But being covered, I kind of stand out and people know, "OK, she's Muslim." But I don't have ten kids. I'm not married. I'm educated. I work. I have a master's degree. So I'm not that person that they're showing."

Before Selameh agreed to an interview with me, she posed the following question: "Are you talking to other women, too, that don't wear . . . ?" she asked, finishing her sentence by pointing to the scarf wrapped around her head. Most women at the conference were not wearing hijab, and Selameh wanted reassurance that I would refrain from stereotyping all Muslim women. Indeed, only a handful of Muslim women at the conference were wearing hijab, and Selahmeh requested that the many different types and multifaceted aspects of Muslim women be represented.

"People in the U.S. have a hard time separating the hijab from the Muslim woman," noted Asma Barlas, an Islamic scholar at Ithaca College who writes about feminist interpretations of the Qur'an. "To most Westerners," she said, "an authentic Muslim woman is always wearing a hijab." It's not hard to understand how Americans have come to think of Muslim women as a veiled monolith, given the images usually presented to them, first and foremost from the war zones of the Islamic world.

Asra Nomani, a *Wall Street Journal* reporter turned Muslim feminist activist, made an interesting point in her November 7, 2006, article in the online magazine *Slate*. She called attention to the fact that publishing houses, art directors, and photo agencies were increasingly using stock photos of (supposedly) Muslim women in veils or hijabs to sell books about the Islamic world. For example, when plugging the term "Muslim woman" into the search engine of the electronic database of photo giant Corbis, 3,302 images of mostly veiled and covered women pop up.

At the same time, news reporters, photographers, and filmmakers in the United States, when working on stories involving Muslims, face the temptation to select images with an exotic or unusual appeal to the average news consumer. The *Detroit Free Press,* which covers the largest Arab-American community in North America, warned that this phenomenon could lead to excessive reliance on images of Muslim women who wear hijab. In "100 Questions and Answers about Arab-Americans: A Journalist's Guide," which the *Detroit Free Press* published online, question 98 asks, "Are there issues about the way Arab Americans are portrayed in the media?" The answer is revelatory: "In some cases, journalists seem to prefer to publish or air images of people who look different, or exotic. In trying for a more interesting image, they may emphasize the difference between Arab Americans and non-Arab Americans. Most Arab Americans do not wear traditional clothing. News organizations whose collective reports give the impression that Arab Americans generally dress differently than non-Arab Americans are being inaccurate."[4]

Not surprisingly, readers mistakenly get the impression that all Muslim women wear the hijab. Many non-hijabi Muslim women whom I interviewed remarked that people were often surprised to learn about their Muslim identity, given the absence of veils and/or headscarves. While many Muslim women struggle to demonstrate that the hijab is not necessarily a symbol of oppression, some also worry that the media has equated the hijab with piety and spirituality. One example is "Preserving Modesty, in the Pool," a *Seattle Times* piece from July 19, 2005, about a group of Muslim women who — thanks to the cultural sensitivity of a local indoor community pool — gather once a month, tape brown paper over the windows, and swim unseen by the eyes of men.

Contributing to the notion that the hijab goes part and parcel with Muslim women are female journalists such as Samieh Shalash, who wrote a piece in the July 25, 2005, *Lexington* [KY] *Herald-Leader* titled "What It's Like When I Wear the Hijab." Insisting that the hijab does not signify oppression, Ms. Shalash suggests that it's a universally accepted custom for Muslim women to express modesty. However, the notion that clothing defines modesty and is the mark of a good Muslim woman upset many of the Muslim women I interviewed, especially those who don't wear the hijab (except for prayer), expressing their faith instead through charity, good deeds, and/or spiritual devotion.

IMPROVED REPORTING

Under fire of criticism, journalists often respond that their job is to provide important news stories to their readers and not to serve in a public relations capacity for communities or organizations. Although far from perfect, the U.S. media have done a considerably better job reporting about Muslim women since the first few years after 9/11. As reporters became increasingly experienced covering Muslims both in the United States and abroad, their stories invariably strove for diversity of opinion and reflected a heightened understanding of the ethnicity and culture shared by Muslim women. Improved coverage also resulted from the fact that increasing numbers of Muslim women—or women with some family or cultural connection to the Islamic world—began entering the media in a professional capacity. To their credit, a plethora of news organizations continue to hire them.

For example, in 2000, *Newsweek* (circulation 3.14 million) hired Lorraine Ali as a general editor and music critic. Given that Ali is half Iraqi, *Newsweek* also had the vision to use her expertise when addressing questions pertaining to the Middle East and Islam.[5] After a spate of suicide bombings carried out by Muslim women, the magazine ran a December 2005 cover story called "Women and Terror." While the main feature delved into how Muslim women become extremists, *Newsweek* also included a piece by Ali headlined "Not Ignorant, Not Helpless." Ali wrote, "In America we've come to see (Muslim) women as timid creatures, covered from head to toe, who scurry rather than walk. . . . The West's exposure to Muslim women is largely based on Islam's most extreme cases of oppression: Taliban-dominated Afghanistan, Wahhabi-ruled Saudi Arabia and post-revolutionary Iran." Ali continued, "In reality, Muslim women are cops in Egypt, lawyers in Syria and make up the majority of medical students in Jordan."

On February 27, 2007, when *Newsweek* ran an interview with Hirsi Ali, the Somali-born Islam basher and critic who had just published her biography containing anti-Islamic diatribes, it also ran a parallel piece by Ali titled "Only One Side of the Story."

Other examples abound of U.S. media departing from the practice of stereotyping Muslim women as weak and dependent. Perhaps one of the most noteworthy is a December 15, 2006, piece by Andrea Elliot of the *New York Times*. Over a period of several months, Elliot reported on the remarkable life journey of Fadwa Hamdan, a devout Palestinian Muslim woman who divorced a neglectful husband, immigrated to the United States, and struggled to make a new life, eventually proving herself in another male-dominated world, the U.S. military. "Ms. Hamdan's passage through the military is a remarkable act of reinvention. It required courage and sacrifice," Elliot wrote, portraying Hamdan as a strong-willed fighter, who at the same time is a woman with strong feelings and deep-seated compassion.

Parade, the weekly Sunday magazine newspaper insert that reaches millions of American homes, has also profiled strong Muslim women—from cover stories about Jordan's Queen Rania to eye-opening pieces about Narmin Othman, Iraq's environment minister, to commentary concerning Dr. Massouda Jalal, Afghanistan's minister for women's affairs. Interestingly, the *Parade* July 2005 story on Dr. Jalal includes the fact that her husband "became her appointments secretary."

Small and medium newspapers have also contributed to the effort towards impartial news coverage of Muslim women. For example, on October 5, 2005, the *Richmond Times Dispatch* profiled Amina Wadud, the Qur'an scholar from Virginia Commonwealth University who a few months earlier had led a controversial mixed-gender prayer session. On June 10, 2006, the *Clarion Ledger* in Jackson, Mississippi, carried a sympathetic story about Okolo Rashid, the individual who opened the Museum of Muslim Cultures in Jackson. According to the story, Rashid's daughter Marya "said her mother breaks the stereotype that Muslim women are meek and live in the background."

Up until recent years, any news references to Islamic theology usually included misogynistic pronouncements, whether underscoring the importance of women covering their bodies or permitting men to take up to four wives. However, this too is changing. For example, the *Washington Post* ran a thoughtful piece on July 14, 2006, about measures taken by the Turkish clerical establishment to strike misogynistic sayings from the ahadith.[6] Carla Power of the *New York Times* followed with a February 25, 2007, piece titled "A Secret History." The article highlighted one modern-day scholar, Mohammad Akram Nadwi, who acknowledged the names of some eight thousand female Islamic scholars.

The media has also done well to cover important events concerning Muslim women. When Ingrid Mattson was elected the first female president of the Islamic Society of North America, numerous U.S. newswires and major newspapers covered the event. Mattson was also interviewed on *Fresh Air,* the popular National Public Radio program.

VEILED VILIFICATION

Despite these significant efforts to debunk pejorative stereotypes about Muslim women, many Americans unfortunately continue to view the veil or hijab with suspicion and associate it with terror. "The media, as it is now, is not strong enough to undercut the stereotypes and the bias that people have," claimed Wessler, the hate crimes expert from Portland, Oregon. Sandhya Somashekhar, a *Washington Post* reporter, noted in an August 29, 2005, story, "These days the hijab has become a flash point of controversy over women's rights, religious extremism and terrorism—a symbol in some eyes of a more radical Islam."

Paula Holmes-Eber, a Middle Eastern studies professor at the University of Washington, discussed this hijab-terror connection in her 2005 paper, "Conceptions and Misconceptions of Women in the Middle East." In her opinion, "Americans were making a very interesting connection between women, Islam, the Middle East and the terrorist attacks on New York and Washington." Holmes-Eber's remarks regarding the Western perspective of Muslim women and the veil are especially insightful. According to Holmes-Eber:

> Women in the Middle East—and likewise the wearing of the veil—have become a symbol to Americans of everything we dislike about this inexplicable part of the world, a representation of everything we fear about Islam, and yet also a romantic and exotic image of our fantasies about the Middle East. In our search to make sense of September 11, we have naturally focused on women in the Middle East as the key to our understanding. For perhaps, the thinking goes, if we can just understand "why they treat their woman that way," we will then be able to explain (the terrorist attacks of 9/11).[7]

Clearly the hijab and associated stereotypes have become convenient images with which to vilify Islam—convenient for everyday bigots as well as for politicians and other public figures who exploit these images to seek political gain. Mitt Romney, former governor of Massachusetts, is a stellar example. When campaigning for the Republican Party's presidential nomination, Romney made unabashed efforts to use "the veil" to score political points against Democratic congresswoman and House Speaker Nancy Pelosi. His efforts to smear Pelosi were based on the fact that she donned a headscarf while visiting a Syrian mosque in April 2007. "I just don't know what got into her head, to be completely honest with you," Romney was quoted as saying in the April 5, 2007, edition of the *New York Post*, a conservative tabloid.

Romney continued, "Having her picture taken with [Syrian president Bashir] Assad and being seen in a headscarf and so forth is sending the wrong signal to the people of Syria and to the people of the Middle East."

The Family Research Council, a conservative Christian group headquartered in Washington, D.C., also criticized Pelosi for wearing the scarf because doing so "is usually seen as a sign of submission in the Muslim world. If that's the case, American feminists should be outraged." (In fact, U.S. Secretary of State Condoleezza Rice and First Lady Laura Bush are among many high-profile women who have donned the scarf when in the Middle East.)[8] The vilification of the hijab should not be dismissed as a growing pain that all new religious and racial groups in the United States have had to endure. Rather, this behavior should be acknowledged as a phenomenon engendering hostility against Muslim women and potentially leading to violent acts against them.

Katrin Bennhold, a German journalist, wore the hijab for a flight from Washington, D.C., to Paris and described her travel experience in an October 19, 2006, piece for the *International Herald Tribune*. As might be expected, Ms. Bennhold received a wide spectrum of responses from fellow travelers, ranging from derogatory remarks and suspicious stares to friendly glances.

In the *Hartford Courant* (Hartford, Conn.), staff writer Tracy Gordon Fox wrote a March 12, 2007, story, "Behind Burka, Student Gets an Education in Bigotry,"[9] about a high school student who decides to wear a burka for a day and record her experience. "I hope all of your people die," was one of the fifty hostile comments the freshman received. "The remarks underscored a persistent animosity toward American Muslims that is driven largely by the terrorist attacks of 9/11 and the wars in Afghanistan and Iraq," Gordon observed in her piece.

CONCLUSION

Caught in a quandary, Muslim American women face hostility and violence from non-Muslim Americans for wearing the hijab and spiteful disapproval from fellow Muslims for *not* wearing the hijab. Against this no-win background, Muslim American women are taking proactive steps to shape their image in the U.S. media and to support those news associations genuinely striving to improve media coverage of Muslim women.

At its annual 2006 conference, the Religion Newswriters Association devoted an entire panel to "Covering Muslims in America," which included

Laila Al-Marayati and Asra Nomani. Various media organizations have compiled "how to cover Muslims" guides similar to the one published by the *Detroit Free Press,* and the Council on American-Islamic Relations, the Muslim Public Affairs Council, and the Islamic Society of North America have all held training workshops for journalists in North America. These organizations are addressing the same objective: to support impartial news coverage of Muslims and to ensure that journalists report what is factual, both in word and in image.

Also of great importance, according to Asma Barlas, is that news organizations acknowledge how far the Muslim world extends, miles beyond South Asia and the Middle East. Barlas would like to see increased news coverage of other Muslim regions and especially Indonesia—the most populous Muslim country in the world—as a way to break down the monolithic stereotypes many Americans hold of Muslim women.

Besides those Muslim women joining mainstream American news organizations, countless other Muslim American women are beginning to shape their own image as entrepreneurs. For example, in 2000 Tayyibah Taylor of Atlanta launched *Azizah* magazine, becoming the voice of the "contemporary Muslim woman." Ausma Khan gave up her professorship at Northwestern University in Chicago to become editor of *Muslim Girl* magazine, which premiered in January 2007. Khan explains, "Like a lot of people who are active in the Muslim community, we've been thinking about these issues for a long time and very concerned about the under-representation and lack of positive images of Muslims that are out there in the mainstream media." Khan asserts that the response from readers has been "overwhelmingly positive."

For other Muslim American women, carving a positive image in the United States means making efforts to contact news organizations when they find a story misleading, or for that matter, when they find a story positive. "When they hear from us," said Nahla Saleh of Columbus, "things will change. If we don't make our voices heard, it will never change."

NOTES

1. The Council on American-Islamic Relations, "The Status of Muslim Civil Rights in the United States," Washington, DC, 2005, 51.

2. Telephone interview with Stephen Wessler, March 29, 2007.

3. Jack G. Shaheen, *Reel Bad Arabs: How Hollywood Vilifies a People* (New York: Olive Branch Press, 2001), 2.

4. *Detroit Free Press,* "100 Questions and Answers about Arab-Americans: A Journalist's Guide," www.freep.com/legacy/jobspage/arabs/index.htm.

5. *Newsweek,* "Lorraine Ali, senior writer," www.msnbc.msn.com/id/4900569/site/newsweek/.

6. *Ahadith* is the plural form of the Arabic word *hadith,* which literally means "story."

7. Paula Holmes-Eber, University of Washington, "Conceptions and Misconceptions of Women in the Middle East," 3.

8. Family Research Council, "Americans Question the Pelosi Cover-up in Syria," April 6, 2007. www.frc.org/get.cfm?i=CM07D05.

9. www.campus-watch.org/article/id/3118.

BIBLIOGRAPHY

PUBLISHED SOURCES

Abdallah, Roula. "Fifteen Thousand White Roses Offered by the Beirut Social Development Organization." *Al-Mustaqbal,* March 1, 2005.

Abirafeh, Lina. "The Role of Religion in the Lives of Women in the New Afghanistan." *Critical Half* 1:1 (2003).

———. "Bourka Politics: The Plight of Women in Afghanistan." *Chronogram* 10 (2004).

———. "From Afghanistan to Sudan: How Peace Risks Marginalizing Women." *Forced Migration Review* 24 (2005).

———. "Lessons from Gender-Focused International Aid in Post-Conflict Afghanistan . . . Learned?" Bonn: Friedrich Ebert Stiftung, 2005.

———. "Freedom is Only Won from the Inside: Domestic Violence in Post-Conflict Afghanistan." In *Change from Within: Diverse Perspectives on Domestic Violence in Muslim Communities,* edited by Maha Alkhateeb and Salma Elkadi Abugideiri. Washington, DC, Peaceful Families Project, 2007.

Abu-Lughod, Lila. "Do Muslim Women Really Need Saving?" *American Anthropologist* 104:3 (2002): 783–790.

———. "Feminist Longings and Post-Colonial Conditions." In *Remaking Women: Feminism and Modernity in the Middle East.* Princeton: Princeton University Press, 1998.

Abu Saba, Mary Bentley. "Profiles of Foreign Women in Lebanon." In *Women and War in Lebanon,* edited by Lamia Rustum Shehadeh. Gainesville: University Press of Florida, 1999.

Addi, Lahouari. *Les Mutations de la Société Algérienne: Famille et lien social dans l'Algérie contemporaine.* Paris: La Découverte, 1999.

Aghaie, Kamran Scot. *The Martyrs of Karbala: Shi'i Symbols and Rituals in Modern Iran.* Seattle: University of Washington Press, 2004.

Ahmad, Fauzia. "British Muslim Perceptions and Opinions on News Coverage of September 11." *Journal of Ethnic and Migration Studies* 32, no. 6 (2006). Special issue.

———. "Modern Traditions? British Muslim Women and Academic Achievement." *Gender and Education* 13, no. 2 (2001): 137–152.

————. "Representing Muslim Women after September 11." Paper presented at the Centre of Islamic Studies Lunchtime Seminars, January 2002.

Ahmed, Leila. *Women and Gender in Islam: Historical Roots of a Modern Debate.* New Haven: Yale University Press, 1993.

Al-Ali, Nadje. *Iraqi Women: Untold Stories from 1948 to the Present.* London: Zed Books, 2007.

Aliy, Abolfazl, comp. *A Decade with the Graphists of the Islamic Revolution, 1979–1989.* Tehran: Art Centre of the Islamic Propagation Organization, 1989.

Alloula, Malek. *The Colonial Harem.* Minneapolis: University of Minnesota Press, 1986.

Ameli, Saied R., Syed Mohammed Marandi, Sameera Ahmed, Seyfeddin Kara, and Arzu Merali. *The British Media and Muslim Representation: The Ideology of Demonisation.* London: Islamic Human Rights Commission, 2007.

Al-Amin Merei, Anisa. "A Shiite Progressive Woman." *Annahar,* March 30, 2005.

Amin, Sonia Nishat. *The World of Muslim Women in Colonial Bengal.* Leiden: Brill, 1996.

Amnesty International Report 1993. "Bosnia-Herzegovina: Rape and Sexual Abuse by Armed Forces." Report released January 21.

Anić, Rebeka. *Domestic Violence: Theological-Pastoral Perspective.* Split: Franciscan Institute for Culture of Peace, 2006.

Anthias, Floya, and Nira Yuval-Davis. Introduction to *Woman-Nation-State,* edited by Nira Yuval-Davis and Floya Anthais, 6–11. London: Macmillan, 1989.

Ashford, Mary-Wynne, and Yolanda Huet-Vaughn. "The Impact of War on Women." In *War and Public Health,* edited by Barry S. Levy and Victor W. Sidel. London: Oxford University Press, 1997.

Aznárez, Malen. "¿Velo o pañuelo?" *El País,* December 21, 2003.

Bahramitash, Roksana. "Islamic Fundamentalism and Women's Economic Role: The Case of Iran." *International Journal of Politics, Culture, and Society* 16 (2003).

Bailey, David, and Gilane Tawadros, eds. *Veiling, Representation, and Contemporary Art.* Cambridge, MA: MIT Press, 2003.

Bakšić-Muftić, Jasna. "The Crime of Rape in BiH: Local and International Dimensions." In *The Challenges of Feminism,* edited by Jasminka Babić-Avdispahić et al. Sarajevo: IF Bosnae, 2004.

Banac, Ivo. *The Price of Bosnia* (Cijena Bosne). Sarajevo: Council of the Congress of Bosniak Intellectuals (Vijeće kongresa bošnjačkih intelektualaca), 1996.

Barnes, K., R. Chiarelli, C. Cohn, R. Johal, M. Kihunah, and M. Olsen. "UN Security Council 1325 on Women, Peace, and Security—Six Years On Report." 2006.

Bartels, Dieter Bartels. "Guarding the Invisible Mountain: Intervillage Alliances, Religious Syncretism and Ethnic Identity among Ambonese Christians and Moslems in the Moluccas." Ph.D. dissertation, Cornell University, 1977.

Bartlett, Linda A. "Maternal Mortality among Afghan Refugees in Pakistan, 1999–2000." *Lancet* 359 (2002).

Beaugé, Florence. "En Algérie, aucun survivant parmi les disparus de la sale guerre." *Le Monde,* January 8, 2003.

————. "Tunisiennes, retour de voiles." *Le Monde,* December 3, 2006.

Belić, Martina. "Women and Work" (Žene i rad). B.a.b.e. Zagreb, 2000.

Benjamin, Judy. "Afghanistan: Women Survivors Under the Taliban." In *War's Offensive on Women: The Humanitarian Challenge in Bosnia, Kosovo, and Afghanistan,* edited by Julie Mertus. West Hartford: Kumarian, 2000.

Berkowitz, Dan. "Suicide Bombers as Women Warriors: Making News Stories through Mythical Archetypes." *Journalism and Mass Communication Quarterly* 82, no. 3 (2005): 607–622.

Berkowitz, Dan, and S. Burke-Odland. "'My Mum's a Suicide Bomber': Motherhood, Terrorism, News, and Ideological Repair." Paper presented at the meeting of the Association for Education in Journalism & Mass Communication, Toronto, Canada, 2004.

Bertrand, Jacquest. "Legacies of the Authoritarian Past: Religious Violence in Indonesia's Moluccan Islands." *Pacific Affairs* 75 (2002): 57–85.

Bessis, Sophie. "Le Féminisme institutionnel en Tunisie." *Clio, Femmes du Maghreb* 9 (1999).

Blackburn, Susan. "Gender Violence and the Indonesian Political Transition." *Asian Studies Review* 23 (1999).

Borthwick, Meredith. *The Changing Role of Women in Bengal, 1849–1905.* Princeton: Princeton University Press, 1984.

Bourdieu, Pierre. *Trois études d'ethnologie kabyle.* Paris: Droz, 1972.

Bouta, Tsjeard, Georg Ferks, and Ian Bannon. *Gender, Conflict, and Development.* Washington, DC: International Bank for Reconstruction and Development, 2005.

Bracewell, Wendy. "Women in Transition to Democracy in South-Eastern Europe." In *The Balkans: A Religious Backyard of Europe,* edited by J. M. Faber. Ravena: Longo Editore, 1996.

Brand, Laurie. *Women, the State and Political Liberalization: Middle Eastern and North African Experiences.* New York: Columbia University Press, 1998.

Butler, Judith. *Bodies That Matter: On the Discursive Limits of Sex.* New York: Routledge, 1993.

Cainkar, Louise. "The Impact of the September 11 Attacks and their Aftermath on Arab and Muslim Communities in the United States." *GSC Quarterly* 13 (2004).

Camau, Michel, and Vincent Geisser. *Le Syndrome autoritaire: Politique en Tunisie de Bourguiba à Ben Ali.* Paris: Presses de la Fondation Nationale de Science Politique, 2003.

Candido. "Dichoso pañuelo de Fátima." *ABC,* March 4, 2002.

Cerić, Mustafa. "An Interview: Victory or Honour Death." *Ljiljan,* Sarajevo-Ljubljana, 37 (1993).

Chahine, Jessy. "We Are Coming to Free Our Country and Demand the Truth." *Daily Star,* March 14, 2005.

Chahine, Jessy, and Linda Dahdah. "Demo Plans Go Ahead Despite Warnings: Sfeir and Lahoud Call for Limiting Shows of Force." *Daily Star,* March 14, 2005.

Chahine, Jessy, and Rym Ghazal. "'People Power' Keeps up the Pressure: Protesters Determined to Stay Put." *Daily Star,* March 2, 2005.

Charlesworth, Hilary, and Christine Chinkin. "Sex, Gender, and September 11." *American Journal of International Law* 96:3 (2002): 600–605.

Charrad, Mounira M. *States and Women's Rights: The Making of Postcolonial Tunisia, Algeria, and Morocco.* Berkeley: University of California Press, 2001.

Chelkowski, Peter, and Hamid Dabashi, eds. *Staging a Revolution: The Art of Persuasion in the Islamic Republic of Iran.* New York: New York University Press, 1999.

Chivers, C. J. "Russian Security Forces Kill Last Rebels to End Standoff." *New York Times,* October 15, 2005, A3.

———. "Baghdad Burning: Women Write War in Iraq." *World Literature Today* 81 (2007): 23–26.

Clark, Kate. "The Struggle for Hearts and Minds: The Military, Aid, and the Media." In Nation-Building Unraveled? Aid, Peace, and Justice in Afghanistan, edited by Antonio Donini, Norah Niland, and Karin Wermester. Bloomfield: Kumarian, 2004.

Cooke, Ariel Zeitlin, and Marsha MacDowell, eds. *Weavings of War: Fabrics of Memory (an exhibition catalogue).* East Lansing: Michigan State University Museum, 2005.

Cooke, Miriam. *War's Other Voices: Women Writers on the Lebanese Civil War.* Syracuse, NY: Syracuse University Press, 1996.

———. *Women and the War Story.* Berkeley: University of California Press, 1997.

Counsell, Colin, and Laurie Wolf, eds. *Performative Analysis: An Introductory Coursebook.* London: Routledge, 2001.

Dadi, Iftikhar. "Shirin Nashat's Photographs as Postcolonial Allegory." *Signs: Journal of Women in Culture and Society* 34 (2008).

Dahdah, Linda, and Habib Battah. "People Power Forces Cabinet of Karami Government: 'No One Can Intimidate Us Anymore.'" *Daily Star,* March 1, 2005.

Dardić, Dragana. "Domestic Violence." In *In-Depth Study on Domestic Violence in Bosnia and Herzegovina,* edited by HCa, B Luka, Žene Ženama Sarajevo, and Lara Bijeljina, 2006.

Deeb, Lara. *An Enchanted Modern: Gender and Public Piety in Shi'i Lebanon.* Princeton Studies in Muslim Politics. Princeton: Princeton University Press, 2006.

Dempsey, Michael, and Hania Taan. "Lebanon Kicks off National Unity Festival: Thousands Take to Streets to Participate in Celebrations." *Daily Star,* April 11, 2005.

Divičić, Marija. *Organization of AFW in Sarajevo in Socialist Yugoslavia.* Sarajevo: Historical Archive, 1988.

Douglass, Susan L., and Munir A. Shaikh. "Defining Islamic Education: Differentiation and Applications." *Current Issues in Comparative Education* 7 (2004): 5–18.

Dris-Aït-Hamadouche, Louis. "Women in the Maghreb: Civil Society's Actors or Political Instruments?" *Middle East Policy* 14 (2007).

Dupree, N. H. "A Socio-Cultural Dimension: Afghan Women Refugees in Pakistan." In *The Cultural Basis of Afghan Nationalism,* edited by E. W. Anderson and N. H. Dupree. London: Pinter Publishers, 1990.

Eaton, Richard M. *Essays on Islam and Indian History.* New Delhi: Oxford University Press, 2000.

Elorza, Antonio. "La ignorancia del infiel." *El País,* October 22, 2001.

———. "Velos y quebrantos." *El País,* April 3, 2002.

———. "Las dos caras del Corán." *El País,* September 25, 2002.

———. "Religión y violencia." *El País,* April 16, 2004.

———. "Cerca del 11M." *El País,* February 22, 2005.

Equal Opportunities Commission. *Moving on Up? Bangladeshi, Pakistani and Black Caribbean Women and Work.* Manchester: EOC, 2006.

Erlanger, S. "Rebels Vow to Fight as Russians Shell Capital." *New York Times,* January 10, 1995, A1.

European Union Monitoring Centre on Racism and Xenophobia. *Muslims in the European Union, Discrimination and Islamophobia.* 2006.

Falah, Ghazi-Walid. "The Visual Representation of Muslim/Arab Women in Daily Newspapers in the United States." In *Geographies of Muslim Women, Gender, Religion, and Space,* edited by Ghazi-Walid Falah and Caroline Nagel. New York: Guilford Press, 2005.

Fanjul, Serafin. "Inmigrantes y Moriscos." *ABC,* January 4, 2007.

Fekete, Liz. "Anti-Muslim Racism and the European Security State." *Race and Class* 46 (2004).

Firestone, Shulamith. *The Dialectic of Sex: The Case for Feminist Revolution.* New York: Morrow Quill Paperbacks, 1980.

Fisk, Robert. *Pity the Nation: The Abduction of Lebanon.* New York: Thunder's Mouth Press / Nation Books, 2002.

Fleischmann, Ellen. *The Nation and Its "New" Women: the Palestinian Women's Movement, 1920–1948.* Berkeley: University of California Press, 2003.

Fortes, Susana. "Mujeres sin atributos." *El País,* October 21, 2007.

Foucault, Michel. *Surveiller et Punir.* Paris: Gallimard, 1975.

Freeman, Jo. *A Room at a Time: How Women Entered Party Politics.* Lanham, MD: Rowman & Littlefield, 2000.

Gala, Antonio. "Niña y pañuelo." *El Mundo,* February 19, 2002.

Galeote, Antonio. "Occidente en un pañuelo." *El Mundo,* February 24, 2002.

Gallego-Díaz, Soledad. "La tradición sienta mal a las mujeres." *El País,* October 12, 2007.

Geisser, Vincent. *La Nouvelle Islamophobie.* Paris: La Découverte, 2003.

Gerges, Fawaz. *America and Political Islam: Clash of Cultures or Clash of Interests.* Cambridge: Cambridge University Press, 1999.

Ghazal, Rym. "Anti-Syrian Protests Continue Despite Announced Redeployment: Campers Determined to Stay Until the Complete Withdrawal of Troops." *Daily Star,* March 8, 2005.

———. "Asma Andraos Honored as 'Hero of Change'" *Daily Star,* October 14, 2005.

El-Ghoul, Adnan. "Lebanese Bread through Army Cordon with Roses." *Daily Star,* March 1, 2005.

Gibson, K., and J. Graham. "Beyond Global vs. Local: Economic Politics outside the Binary Frame." In *Geographies of Power,* edited by Andrew Herod and Melissa W. Wright. Oxford: Blackwell, 2004.

Glatzer, Bernt. "Sword and Reason among Pashtuns, Notions of Individual Honour and Social Responsibility in Afghanistan." Paper presented at the 14th European Conference on Modern South Asian Studies, Copenhagen, August 1996.

Goodarzi, Mustafa, comp. *A Decade with Painters of the Islamic Revolution, 1979–1989.* Tehran: Art Centre of the Islamic Propagation Organization, 1989.

Graham-Brown, Sarah. *Images of Women: The Portrayal of Women in Photography of the Middle East, 1860–1950.* New York: Columbia University Press, 1988.

Guenif-Souleïmas, Nacera. *Les Féministes et le garçon arabe.* Paris: Editions de l'Aube, 2006.

Haddad, Scarlett. "Place des Martyrs, l'espoir retrouvé des jeunes: Nous ne quitterons qu'après le départ des Syriens." *L'Orient-Le Jour,* March 2, 2005.

———. "Les Femmes dans la Rue pour défier les poseurs de bombes." *L'Orient-Le Jour,* March 22, 2005.

Hafez, Kai, Karin Hörner, and Verena Klemm. "The Rise and Decline of Opinion Leaders: The Changing Image of the Middle East and Islam in German Mass Media." In *Islam and the West in the Mass Media: Fragmented Images in a Globalizing World,* edited by Kai Hafez, 273–289. Creskill: Hampton Press, 2000.

El-Hage, Anne-Marie. "Manifestation—Un Sit-in pacifiste, avec la complicité de l'armée, pour suivre en direct la séance parlementaire: 'Démissionnez,' demande la foule au gouvernement." *L'Orient-Le Jour,* March 1, 2005.

Hall, Stuart. *Representation: Cultural Representations and Signifying Practices.* London: Sage, 1997.

Hans, Asha. "Escaping Conflict: Afghan Women in Transit." In *Sites of Violence: Gender and Conflict Zones,* edited by Wenona Giles and Jennifer Hyndman. Berkeley: University of California Press, 2004.

Hansen, Lene. "Gender, Nation, Rape: Bosnia and the Construction of Security." *International Feminist Journal of Politics* 3 (2001): 55–75.

Hasso, Frances S. "Discursive and Political Deployments by/of the 2002 Palestinian Women Suicide Bombers/Martyrs." *Feminist Review* 81, no. 1 (2005): 23–51.

Hatoum, Leila. "Tens of Thousands Mark Civil War's Beginning with 'Unity Run': Young, Old, Christian and Muslim Run for Lebanon." *Daily Star,* April 11, 2005.

Hefner, Robert W., ed. *The Politics of Multiculturalism and Citizenship in Malaysia, Singapore, and Indonesia.* Manoa: University of Hawai'i Press, 2001.

Helms, Elissa. "Gendered Visions of the Bosnian Future: Women's Activism and Representation in Post-war Bosnia-Herzegovina." Ph.D. dissertation, University of Pittsburgh, 2003.

Hibou, Béatrice. *La force de l'obéissance: Économie politique de la répression en Tunisie.* Paris: La Découverte, 2006.

Hidalgo, Manuel. "La niña del pañuelo" (The Little Girl in the Headscarf). *El Mundo,* February 19, 2002.

Hiro, Dilip. *Holy Wars: The Rise of Islamic Fundamentalism.* New York: Routledge, 1989.

Hirschkind, Charles, and Saba Mahmood. "Feminism, the Taliban, and Politics of Counter-Insurgency." *Anthropological Quarterly* 75 (2002).

Holmes-Eber, Paula. "Conceptions and Misconceptions of Women in the Middle East." Lecture presented at the University of Washington, 2001.

Holt, Maria. "Lebanese Shi'a Women and Islamism." In *Women and War in Lebanon,* edited by Lamia Rustum Shehadeh. Gainesville: University Press of Florida, 1999.

Hosseini, Khaled. *The Kite Runner.* New York: Riverhead Books, 2003.

Howard III, John, and Laura Prividera. "Rescuing Patriarchy or Saving 'Jessica Lynch': The Rhetorical Construction of the American Woman Soldier." *Women and Language* 27, no. 2 (2004): 89–97.

Hughes, J. "Chechnya: The Causes of a Protracted Post-Soviet Conflict." *Civil Wars* 4 (2001): 11–48.

Hunt, Swanee, and Cristina Posa. "Women Waging Peace." *Foreign Policy* 124 (2001): 38–47.

Hunter Education Commission Report 1882. Superintendent of Government Printing, Calcutta, 1883.

Hussein, Saddam. *The Revolution and Women in Iraq.* Edited by Naji Al-hadithi. Translated by Khalid Kishtany. Baghdad: Translation and Foreign Languages Publishing House, 1981.

Inness, Sherrie A. *Tough Girls: Women Warriors and Wonder Women in Popular Culture.* Philadelphia: University of Pennsylvania Press, 1991.

———. "'Boxing Gloves and Bustiers': New Images of Tough Women." In *Action Chicks: New Images of Tough Women in Popular Culture,* edited by Sherrie Inness. New York: Palgrave Macmillan, 2004.

Isaenko, Anatoly, and Peter W. Petschauer. "A Failure that Transformed Russia: The 1991–1994 Democratic State-Building Experiment in Chechnya." *International Social Science Review* 75, no. 1–2 (2000): 3–15.

Ismael, Jacqueline, and Shereen T. Ismael. "Gender and State in Iraq." In *Gender and Citizenship in the Middle East,* edited by Suad Joseph. Syracuse: Syracuse University Press, 2000.

Iwasaki, Fernando. "El chador en el ojo ajeno." *ABC,* February 17, 2002.

Johnson, Chris, and Joylon Leslie. *Afghanistan: The Mirage of Peace.* London: Zed Books, 2004.

Johnston, Hank, and Bert Klandermans. *Social Movements and Culture.* Minneapolis: University of Minnesota Press, 1995.

Kalaf, Samir Kalaf. "Lebanon's Youths Are Now Writing Their Own Future." *Daily Star,* March 29, 2005.

Kamal, Sufia. *Ekale Amader Kaal.* Dacca, 1988.

Kandiyoti, Deniz. *The Politics of Gender and Reconstruction in Afghanistan.* Occasional Paper 4. New York: United Nations Institute for Social Development, 2005.

Karić, Enes. "An Interview: We are Worse to Ourselves than Chetniks." *BH Dani* 3 (1992).

Kawar, A. *Daughters of Palestine: Leading Women of the Palestinian National Movement.* Albany: State University of New York Press, 1996.

Kesić, Vesna. "Gender and Ethnic Identities in Transition: The Former Yugoslavia-Croatia."

In *From Gender to Nation,* edited by Rada Ivekovic and Julie Mostov. Ravenna: Longo Editore, 2001.

Khan, Shahnaz. "Muslim Women: Negotiations in the Third Space." *Signs: Journal of Women and Culture in Society* 23, no. 2 (1998): 463–494.

Khatun, Sayeeda Manowara. *Smriteer Paata.* Dacca: Jnan Prakashani, 1962.

Kitch, Carolyn. "Changing Theoretical Perspectives on Women's Media Images: The Emergence of Patterns in a New Area of Historical Scholarship." *Journalism and Mass Communication Quarterly* 74, no. 3 (1997): 477–489.

Kuzmaovic, Jasmina. "Legacies of Invisibility: Past Silence, Present Violence Against Women in the Former Yugoslavia." In *Women's Rights, Human Rights, International Feminist Perspectives,* edited by Julie Peters and Andrea Wolper. New York: Routledge. 1995.

Lacoste-Dujardin, Camille. *Des Mères contre des femmes: Maternité et patriarcat au Maghreb.* Paris: La Découverte, 1985.

Lazreg, Marnia. "Feminism and Difference: The Perils of Writing as a Woman on Women in Algeria." *Feminist Studies* 14 (Spring 1988): 81–107.

Lessing, Doris. *The Wind Blows Away Our Words.* London: Picador, 1987.

Lindholm, Charles. *Generosity and Jealousy: The Swat Pukhtun of Northern Pakistan.* New York: Columbia University Press, 1982.

Losantos, Federico Jiménez. "Detrás del velo." *ABC,* February 18, 2002.

Mabro, Judy. *Veiled Half-Truths: Western Travelers' Perceptions of Middle Eastern Women.* London: I. B. Taurus, 1991.

Maddy-Weitzman, Bruce. "Women, Islam, and the Moroccan State: The Struggle over the Personal Status Law." *Middle East Journal* 59 (2005).

Makdisi, Jean. *Beirut Fragments.* New York: Persea Books, 1990.

Makdisi, Ussama. "Reconstructing the Nation-State: The Modernity of Secularism in Lebanon." *Middle East Report* (Summer 1996).

Malallah, Hanaa'. "Consciousness of Isolation." In *Strokes of Genius: Contemporary Iraqi Art,* edited by Maysaloun Faraj, translated by Alia al-Dalli and Lily al-Tai. London: Saqi Books, 2001.

Malkki, Liisa. *Purity and Exile: Violence, Memory and National Cosmology among Hutu Refugees in Tanzania.* Chicago: University of Chicago Press, 1995.

Mamdani, Mahmood. *Good Muslim, Bad Muslim: America, the Cold War and the Roots of Terror.* New York: Doubleday, 2005.

Markov, Slobodanka. "Status and Role of Women in the Political Decision-making System." *Šema,* no. 3 (1984).

Martín Corrales, Eloy. "Maurofobia/islamofobia y maurofilia/islamofibia en la España del siglo XXI." *Revista CIDOB d'Afers Internacionals* 66–67 (2004): 39–51.

Martín, Gema. "Multiculturalismo e islamofobia" (Muliculturalism and Islamophobia). *El País,* March 1, 2002.

Melucci, Alberto. "The New Social Movements: A Theoretical Approach." *Social Science Information* 19 (1980): 199–226.

Mernissi, Fatima. *Beyond the Veil: Male-Female Dynamics in Modern Muslim Society.* Bloomington: Indiana University Press, 1987.

———. *The Forgotten Queens of Islam.* Translated by Mary Jo Lakeland. Minneapolis: University of Minnesota Press, 1993.

Mertus, Julie. *War's Offensive on Women: The Humanitarian Challenge in Bosnia, Kosovo, and Afghanistan.* West Hartford: Kumarian, 2000.

Mijares, Laura, and Ángeles Ramírez, "Mujeres, pañuelo e islamofobia en España: Un estado de la cuestión." *Anales de Historia Contemporánea,* no. 24 (2008): 121–135.

Milić, Anđelka. *Women, Politics, Family.* Belgrade: Institute for Political Studies, 1994.

Millett, Kate. *Sexual Politics.* Garden City, NY: Doubleday, 1970.

Mitchell, Tim. "Revolutionary Posters and Cultural Signs." *Middle East Report* 159 (1989).

Mitchell, W. J. T. *What Do Pictures Want? The Lives and Loves of Images.* Chicago: University of Chicago Press, 2006.

Moallem, Minoo. *Between Warrior Brother and Veiled Sister: Islamic Fundamentalism and the Politics of Patriarchy in Iran.* Berkeley: University of California Press, 2005.

Modad, Mona. "Is It Time for Women's Participation in Social and National Politics?" *Annahar,* March 13, 2005.

Modood, Tariq, and Fauzia Ahmad. "British Muslim Perspectives on Multiculturalism." *Theory, Culture and Society* 24, no. 2 (2007): 187–213.

Moghadam, Valentine M. "Peace-Building and Reconstruction with Women: Reflections on Afghanistan, Iraq, and Palestine." In *Empowerment: From Patriarchy to Women's Participation, Movements, and Rights in the Middle East, North Africa, and South Asia,* edited by Valentine M. Moghadam. Syracuse, NY: Syracuse University Press, 2007.

Mohanty, Chandra Talpade. "Under Western Eyes: Feminist Scholarship and Colonial Discourse." *Feminist Review* 30 (Autumn 1988): 65–88.

Murphy, Paul. *The Wolves of Islam: Russia and the Faces of Chechen Terror.* Washington, DC: Brassey's, 2004.

Myers, Stephen Lee. "Female Suicide Bombers Unnerve Russians." *New York Times,* August 7, 2003, A1.

———. "Insurgents Seize School in Russia and Hold Scores." *New York Times,* September 10, 2004, A1.

———. "Russia Finds No Corner Safe from Chechnya's War." *New York Times,* July 20, 2003, A3.

———. "Second Bombing This Week in Chechnya Kills 15 at Festival." *New York Times,* May 15, 2003.

———. "Suicide Bomber Kills 5 in Moscow near Red Square." *New York Times,* December 10, 2003, A1.

———. "Suicide Bomber Kills 9 at Moscow Subway Station." *New York Times,* September 9, 2004, A3.

———. "Suicide Bombings on Russian Train near Chechnya Kills 42." *New York Times,* December 6, 2003, A3.

NA. "Des Mamans du Liban se recueillent sur la sépulture, place des Martyrs." *L'Orient-Le Jour,* March 22, 2005.

NA. "Durrani Welcomes Victory of MMA Candidate F. P. Report." *Frontier Post,* Peshawar and Quetta, March 30, 2007.

NA. "The Government Falls under Popular Pressure and the Hammer of the Resistance." *Al-Mustaqbal,* March 1, 2005.

NA. "Hassan Al-Nassar: From Black Poems to a Disreputable Award." *Al-Rafidayn Weekly,* November 28, 2000.

NA. "Kandahar's Lightly Veiled Homosexual Habits." *Los Angeles Times,* April 3, 2002.

NA. "More than Two Kilometers of Young Men and Women Connected Hands in a Human Chain from Hariri's Grave to Location of the Explosion." *Annahar,* February 27, 2005.

NA. "La 'Révolution du Cèdre': Un avant-goût de liberté." *L'Orient-Le Jour,* March 3, 2005.

NA. "Seuls, en famille ou entre amis pour passer la nuit." *L'Orient-Le Jour,* March 1, 2005.

NA. "Tell Extremists If They Want to Live under Sharia Law, They Can't Live Here." Editorial. *The Sun,* October 18, 2006.

NA. "El velo no es el velo." *El País,* October 7, 2007.

NA. "Wary Chechens Scorn Plan by Yeltsin." *New York Times,* April 1, 1996, A8.

Nadhem, Hassan. "Abd al-Wahhab al-Bayyati." In *Biographical Encyclopedia of the Modern Middle East and North Africa,* edited by Michael R. Fischbach. Farmington Hills: Gale Cengage, 2007.

———. "Phantom Texts and the Violence of Reality." In *Al-Nass wa al Hayat* (The Text and the Life), ed. Hassan Nadhem (Damascus: Dar al mada Press, 2008), 3.

Naficy, Hamid. "Mediating the Other: American Pop Culture Representation of Post Revolutionary Iran." In *The U.S. Media and the Middle East: Image and Perception,* edited by Yahya R. Kamalipour. Westport, CT: Greenwood Press, 1995.

Nantais, C., and M. F. Lee. "Women in the United States Military: Protectors or Protected? The Case of Prisoner of War Melissa Rathbun-Nealy." *Journal of Gender Studies* 8 (1999): 181–191.

Al-Nassar, Hassan. *And Said Some Women.* Traun, Austria: Dhifaf, 2001.

———. *Stand Up! Sit Down!!* Beirut: Al-Muassa al Arabiyya li 'Dirasat wa 'l-Nashr.

———. *Widows' Doomsday.* Beirut: Dar al-Kunuzal-Adabiyya, 1999.

Nivat, Anne. *Chienne de Guerre: A Woman Reporter behind the Lines of War in Chechnya.* New York: Public Affairs, 2001.

———. "A War Russia Loses by Winning." *New York Times,* August 5, 2003, A15.

Ortner, Sherry B. "Is a Female to Male as Nature Is to Culture?" In *Women, Culture and Society,* edited by M. Z. Rosaldo and L. Lamphere. Stanford, CA: Stanford University Press, 1974.

Pajares, Andres. "El pañuelo de las musulmanas y la vorágine culturalista." *El País,* February 20, 2002.

Patkin, Terry Toles. "Explosive Baggage: Female Palestinian Suicide Bombers and the Rhetoric of Emotion." *Women and Language* 27, no. 2 (2004): 79–99.

Peteet, J. M. *Gender in Crisis: Women and the Palestinian Resistance Movement*. New York: Columbia University Press, 1991.

Petrović, Mirko. "On the Historical Revisionism of Vesna Kesić." *Zarez* 45–46 (2002).

Pickering, S., and A. Third. "Castrating Conflict: Gender(ed) Terrorists and Terrorism Domesticated." *Social Alternatives* 22 (2003): 8–15.

Pinontoan, Oktavianus. "Christian, Muslim Women Promote Peace in Maluku." *Jakarta Post,* December 31, 2002.

Poole, Elizabeth. *Reporting Islam: Media Representations of British Muslims*. London: I. B. Tauris, 2002.

Poole, Elizabeth, and John Richardson, eds. *Muslims and the News Media*. London: I. B. Tauris, 2006.

Rabah, Saddek. *L'Islam dans le discours mediatique: Comment les médias se réprésentent l'Islam en France?* Beirut: Al-Bouraq, 1998.

Ramet, Sabina. *Religion and Politics in Times of Change: Catholic and Orthodox Churches in Central and Southeast Europe*. Translated by Jasminka Bošnjak. Belgrade: Centre for Women's Studies, 2006.

Ramírez, Ángeles. "Olvidadas." *El País,* March 1, 2002.

———. "Women's Movements in Morocco: Gender Discourses and Political Strategies." *Etnográfica: Revista do Centro de Estudos de Antropologia* (2006): 107–120.

———. "Sexismo neocolonial." *El País,* October 8, 2006.

Rawi, Mariam. "Rule of the Rapists." *The Guardian,* February 12, 2004.

Relano, Eugenia. "El desvelo del velo." *El País,* November 1, 2007.

Richardson, John. *(Mis)Representing Islam: The Racism and Rhetoric of British Broadsheet Newspapers*. Amsterdam: John Benjamins, 2004.

———. "Who Gets to Speak? A Study of Sources in the Broadsheet Press." In *Muslims and the News Media,* edited by Elizabeth Poole and John Richardson. London: I. B. Tauris, 2006.

Rieff, David. "Did Live Aid Do More Harm than Good?" *Guardian,* June 24, 2005.

Roussillon, Alain. "Réformer la Moudawana, Statut et Conditions des Marocaines." *Maghreb-Machrek,* 2004.

Rucht, Dieter. "Campaigns, Skirmishes, and Battles: Anti-Nuclear Movements in the USA, France, and Western Germany." *Industrial Crisis Quarterly* 4 (1996): 193–222.

Rupp, Leila J., and Verta A. Taylor. *Survival in the Doldrums: The American Women's Rights Movement, 1945 to the 1960s*. New York: Oxford University Press, 1987.

Sabalić, Ines. "Seal on the Body." *Ljiljan* 20 (1993).

Sadler, Brent. "Hariri Sister Calls for Justice." CNN, March 14, 2005.

Said, Edward W. "The Clash of Definitions." In *Reflections on Exile and Other Essays*. Cambridge, MA: Harvard University Press, 2000.

———. *Covering Islam: How the Media and the Experts Determine How We See the Rest of the World*. New York: Pantheon Books, 1981.

————. *Cubrendo el Islam: Como los medios de comunicación y los expertos determinan nuestra visión del resto del mundo.* Barcelona: Debate, 2005.

————. *Orientalism.* New York: Vintage Books, 1994.

————. *Orientalism: Western Conceptions of the Orient.* Reprinted with a New Foreword. London: Penguin, 1995.

Salman, Wafaa. "The Life and Art of Madiha Omar." *Al-Wafaa News* 20 (1994): 3–7.

Samaddar, Ranabir. "The Historiographical Operation: Memory and History." *Economic and Political Weekly,* June 3, 2006.

Samra, Maher Abi. *The Women of Hezbollah.* Icarus Films, 2000.

Sanchez, Jordi. "Cuando la amenaza es un pañuelo." *El País,* October 8, 2007.

Sánchez Cámara, Ignacio. "Multiculturalismo contra integración." *ABC,* March 5, 2002.

————. "Ni estético ni oportuno." *ABC,* February 18, 2002.

Sarkar, Tanika. "Politics and Women in Bengal: The Conditions and Meaning of Participation." *Indian Economic and Social History Review* 21 (1984).

Sarkis, Hashim. "Territorial Claims: Architecture and Post-War Attitudes Toward the Built Environment." In *Recovering Beirut: Urban Design and Post-War Reconstruction,* edited by Samir Khalaf and Philip S. Khoury. Leiden: Brill, 1993.

Sartori, Giovanni. *The Theory of Democracy Revisited.* Chatham, NJ: Chatham House, 1987.

Sayigh, Rosemary. "Remembering Mothers, Forming Daughters: Palestinian Women's Narratives in Refugee Camps in Lebanon." In *Women and the Politics of Military Confrontation: Palestinian and Israeli Gendered Narratives of Location,* edited by N. Abdo and R. Lentin. Oxford: Berghahn, 2002.

Sayyid, Bobby S. *A Fundamental Fear.* London: Zed Books, 1997.

Schmemann, Serge. "The Chechens' Holy War: How Global Is It?" *New York Times,* October 27, 2003.

Schulze, Kirsten E. "Laskar Jihad and Conflict in Ambon." *Brown Journal of World Affairs* 9 (2002).

Shabout, Nada. "Preservation of Iraqi Modern Heritage in the Aftermath of the U.S. Invasion of 2003." In *Ethics and the Visual Arts,* edited by Gail Levin and Elaine A. King. New York: Allworth Press.

————. "The Iraqi Museum of Modern Art: Ethical Implications." In *Collections: A Journal for Museum and Archives Professionals from the Practical to the Philosophical* 2 (2006).

————. *Modern Arab Art: Formation of Arab Aesthetics.* Gainesville: University Press of Florida, 2007.

S.H. "Manifestation—Lorsque les femmes veulent faire entendre leur voix, place des Martyrs: Par milliers, elles ont réclamé la vérité de défié la peur et l'angoisse." *L'Orient-Le Jour,* March 29, 2005.

Sheea, Manal. "Thousands of Women Delivered One Message: Our Unity is Greater than All Their Explosions." *Annahar,* March 29. 2005.

Shaheen, Jack G. *Reel Bad Arabs.* New York: Olive Branch Press, 2001.

Shariati, Ali. *Shariati on Shariati and the Muslim Woman.* Translation by Laleh Bakhtiar. Chicago: ABC Group International, 1996.

Sheea, Manal. "The Sky Is Their Cover and the Flag Is Their Weapon, along with the White Flowers Which They Offered to the Soldiers, Demonstrators in the Freedom Square Awaited a New Dawn: We Will Not Leave Unless the Syrians Apologize and the State Shows Remorse for Their Crime." *Annahar,* March 1, 2005.

Shirazi, Faegheh. "The Daughters of Karbala: Images of Women in Popular Shi'i Culture in Iran." In *The Women of Karbala, Ritual Performance, and Symbolic Discourses in Modern Shi'i Islam,* edited by Kamran S. Aghaie. Austin: University of Texas Press, 2005.

———. *The Veil Unveiled: The Hejab in Modern Culture.* Gainesville: University Press of Florida, 2003.

Siapno, Jacqueline Aquino. "Gender, Nationalism and the Ambiguity of Female Agency." In *Frontline Feminism: Women, War, and Resistance,* edited by Marguerite R. Waller and Jennifer Rycenga. New York: Garland, 2000.

———. *Gender, Islam, Nationalism and the State of Aceh: The Paradox of Power, Co-optation and Resistance.* New York: Routledge Curzon, 2002.

Skaine, Rosemary. *The Women of Afghanistan Under the Taliban.* Jefferson: McFarland and Co., 2002.

Sklevicky, Lidija. *Horses, Women and Wars.* Zagreb: Zenska Infoteka, 1996.

Spahić-Šiljak, Zilka. "Political Representation of Women in Croatia: Analysis of the Sociocultural, Socioeconomic, and Political Obstacles for Full Representation of Women in Politics." M.A. thesis, University of Sarajevo, 2002.

Specter, M. "For Chechens in Mountains, Fighting Is Winning." *New York Times,* May 13, 1995.

Stanley, Alessandra. "As Chechens Take to Hills, Clans Gird for a Long Fight." *New York Times,* January 22, 1995, 6.

Steel, Jayne. "Vampira: Representations of the Irish Female Terrorist." *Irish Studies Review* 6, no. 3 (1998): 273–191.

Stojaković, Gordana. *Neda: A Biography.* Novi Sad: Futura publikacija, 2002.

Šuvar, Stipe. "Discussion in Debate: Social Consciousness, Marxist Theory and Emancipation of Women Today." *Žena* 2–3 (1972).

Talbot, Rhiannon. "Myths in the Representation of Women Terrorists." *Eire-Ireland* 35, no. 3–4 (2000): 165–186.

Tarrow, Sidney. *Power in Movement: Social Movements and Contentious Politics.* Cambridge: Cambridge University Press, 1998.

Tavernise, Sabrina. "Bomb Kills Russian Security Agent in Moscow." *New York Times,* July 11, 2003, A4.

———. "Terrifying Nights in a Theater Where Lights Never Dimmed." *New York Times,* October 26, 2002, A6.

Tello Weiss, Mariana. "El otro entre nosotros: Una approximación antropológica a las construcciones sobre el 'Terrorismo islamista' en la prensa tras el 11M." Ph.D. dissertation, Universidad Autónoma de Madrid, 2007.

Tetreault, Mary Ann. "The Sexual Politics of Abu Ghraib: Hegemony, Spectacle, and the Global War on Terror." *NWSA Journal* 18, no. 3 (Fall 2006): 33–50.

Thompson, John B. *Ideology and Modern Culture: Critical Social Theory in the Era of Mass Communication.* Stanford, CA: Stanford University Press, 1990.

Tillion, Germaine. *Le Harem et les cousins.* Paris: Editions du Seuil, 1966.

Tilly, Charles. "Repertoires of Contention in America and Britain, 1750–1830." In *The Dynamics of Social Movements: Resource Mobilization, Social Control and Tactics,* edited by Mayer N. Zald and John D. McCarthy, 126–155. Cambridge: Winthrop, 1979.

Treacher, Amal. "Reading the Other: Women, Feminism, and Islam." *Studies in Gender and Sexuality* 4 (2003): 59–71.

Tuchman, Gaye. "Introduction: The Symbolic Annihilation of Women by the Mass Media." In *Hearth and Home: Images of Women in the Mass Media,* edited by Gaye Tuchman, Arlene Kaplan Daniels, and James Benèt. New York: Oxford University Press, 1978.

Al-Turk, Jihad. "Women in Martyrs Square: Their Strategic Participation by Shaking of Political Inhibitions in Order to Resurrect Lebanon." *Al-Mustaqbal,* March 10, 2005.

Turpin, J. "Many Faces: Women Confronting War." In *The Women and War Reader,* edited by L. A. Lorentzen and J. Turpin. New York: New York University Press, 1998.

Tyrer, David, and Fauzia Ahmad. *Muslim Women and Higher Education: Identities, Experiences and Prospects.* ESF/Liverpool: John Moores University, 2006.

Valdes, Zoe. "La teta y el velo." *El Mundo,* March 1, 2004.

Van Dijk, Teun. "Discurso de las elites y racismo institucional." In *Medios de comunicación e inmigración,* edited by Manuel Lario Bastida. Murcia: CAM, 2006.

———. "Prólogo: Discurso racista." In *Medios de comunicación, inmigración y sociedad,* edited by Juan José Igartuna and Carlos Muñiz, 9–17. Salamanca: Ediciones de la Universidad de Salamanca, 2002.

Van Zoonen, Liesbet. *Feminist Media Studies.* Thousand Oaks, CA: Sage, 1999.

Varzi, Roxanne. *Warring Souls: Youth, Media, and Martyrdom in Post-Revolution Iran.* Durham, NC: Duke University Press, 2006.

Vesna, Kesić. "Gender and Ethnic Identities in Transition: The Former Yugoslavia-Croatia." In *From Gender to Nation,* edited by Rada Ivekovic and Julie Mostov. Ravenna: Longo Editore, 2001.

Vlachova, Marie, and Lea Biason. *Women in an Insecure World: Violence against Women, Facts, Figures, and Analysis.* Geneva: Geneva Centre for the Democratic Control of Armed Forces, 2005.

Wakefield, Shawna, and Brandy Bauer. "A Place at the Table: Afghan Women, Men, and Decision-Making Authority." Kabul: Afghanistan Research and Evaluation Unit, 2005.

Wali, Sima. "Afghanistan: Truth and Mythology." In *Women for Afghan Women: Shattering Myths and Claiming the Future,* edited by Sunita Mehta. New York: Palgrave Macmillan, 2002.

Werbner, Pnina. "Islamophobia. Incitement to Religious Hatred—Legislating for a New Fear?" *Anthropology Today* 21 (2005): 5–11.

Williams, Brian Glyn. "Commemorating 'The Deportation' in Post-Soviet Chechnya: The Role of Memorialization and Collective Memory in the 1994–1996 and 1999–2000 Russo-Chechen Wars." *History and Memory* 12, no. 1 (2000): 101–134.

Wilson, Scott. "Rallies Highlight Rifts in Lebanon: Lebanese Opposition Answers Hezbollah with a Huge Anti-Syrian Demonstration." *Washington Post Foreign Service,* March 15, 2005, A16.

Wines, Michael. "War on Terror Casts Chechen Conflict in a New Light." *New York Times,* December 9, 2001, A6.

Yegenoglu, Meyda. *Colonial Fantasies: Towards a Feminist Reading of Orientalism.* Cambridge: Cambridge University Press, 1998.

Zajović, Staša. "Abuse of Women on National and Militarist Basis." In *Women for Peace.* Belgrade: Women in Black, 1995.

Zeghal, Malika. *Les Islamistes narocains, le défi à la monarchie.* Paris: La Découverte, 2005.

ELECTRONIC SOURCES

Akbar, Arifa, Ian Herbert, and Nigel Morris. "Muslim Leaders Warn of Mounting Islamophobia after Attacks on Mosques." *Independent,* July 12, 2005. http://news.independent.co.uk/uk/crime/article298513.ece (accessed September 21, 2008).

Ali, Lorraine. *Newsweek.* www.msnbc.msn.com/id/4900569/site/newsweek/ (accessed September 21, 2008).

Al-Jazeera Net. "Taliban to Open Schools." January 21, 2007. http://english.aljazeera.net/NR/exeres/64E67830-5B5B-4303-8B31-0877CF632311.htm (accessed September 21, 2008).

Amnesty International. "Children in South Asia: Securing Their Rights." April 22, 1998. http://web.amnesty.org/library/index/engASA040011998 (accessed September 21, 2008).

BBC News Online. "Blair Speech on Terror." July 16, 2005. http://news.bbc.co.uk/1/hi/uk/4689363.stm (accessed September 21, 2008).

———. "Forest Gate Terror Raid Cost £2m." October 3, 2006. http://news.bbc.co.uk/1/hi/uk/5401386.stm (accessed September 21, 2008).

———. "In Full: Blair on Bomb Blasts." Statement from Downing Street, July 7, 2005. http://news.bbc.co.uk/1/hi/uk/4659953.stm (accessed September 21, 2008).

———. "Muslim Voices on the Bomb Attacks." July 2, 2007. http://news.bbc.co.uk/1/hi/uk/6261988.stm (accessed September 21, 2008).

———. "Lawyers 'Can Wear Veils in Court.'" November 10, 2006. http://news.bbc.co.uk/1/hi/uk/6134804.stm.

———. "Press Pack 'Encouraged Activists.'" March 15, 2006. http://news.bbc.co.uk/1/hi/uk/4809498.stm (accessed September 21, 2008).

———. "School Wins Muslim Dress Appeal." March 26, 2006. http://news.bbc.co.uk/1/hi/education/4832072.stm (accessed September 21, 2008).

————. "Survey Finds Support for Veil Ban." November 29, 2006. http://news.bbc
.co.uk/1/hi/uk/6194032.stm (accessed September 21, 2008).

Birchill, Julie. "Some People Will Believe Anything." *The Guardian,* August 18, 2001. www
.guardian.co.uk/lifeandstyle/2001/aug/18/weekend.julieburchill.

Bunting, Madeleine. "Jack Straw Has Unleashed a Storm of Prejudice and Intensified
Division." *The Guardian,* October 9, 2006. www.guardian.co.uk/commentisfree/story/
0,,1890821,00.html.

Bush, President George. "Bush Gives Update on War against Terrorism." CNN.com/
USA, October 11, 2001. http://archives.cnn.com/2001/US/10/11/gen.bush.transcript/
(accessed September 21, 2008).

Chapman, Hamed. "Targeting Extremists in Universities." *Muslim News,* no. 197, September 30, 2005. www.muslimnews.co.uk/paper/index.php?article=2131.

Curtis, Polly. "College Security Ban on Hijabs and Hoodies." *The Guardian,* November 24, 2005. http://education.guardian.co.uk/higher/news/story/0,,1649386,00.html.

Daily Mail. "Muslim Veil Is a Symbol of Women's Oppression, Says Jowell." October 16, 2006. www.dailymail.co.uk/papers/live/articles/news/news.html?in_article_id=
410622&in_page_id-1770.

Detroit Free Press. "100 Questions and Answers about Arab-Americans: A Journalist's
Guide." www.freep.com/legacy/jobspage/arabs/index.htm (accessed September 21,
2008).

Dobriansky, Paula J., Under Secretary of State for Global Affairs. "Remarks on Release of
Country Reports on Human Rights Practices for 2004." February 28, 2005. www.state
.gov/g/rls/rm/2005/42793.htm (accessed September 21, 2008).

Dodd, Vikram, and Alan Travis. "Move to Limit Backlash against Muslims." *The Guardian,* Saturday, July 9, 2005. www.guardian.co.uk/attackonlondon/story/0,,1524576,00
.html (accessed September 21, 2008).

Family Research Council. "Americans Question the Pelosi Cover-up in Syria." April 6,
2007. www.frc.org/get.cfm?i=CM07D05 (attempted September 21, 2008; no longer
accessible).

Fattah, Hassan M. "Violence Opens Old Wounds from Lebanon's Past." *New York Times,*
July 14, 2006. www.nytimes.com/2006/07/14/world/middleeast/14lebanon.html (accessed September 21, 2008).

Gill, C. "Veiled Protest as Race Hate Muslims Jailed." *Daily Mail,* July 1, 2007. www
.dailymail.co.uk/pages/live/articles/news/news.html?in_article_id=469285&in_page_
id=1770 (accessed September 21, 2008).

Global Media Journal. http://lass.calumet.purdue.edu/cca/gmj/fa07/gmj-fa07-mishra
.htm (accessed September 21, 2008).

Harvey, Oliver. "They Can't Have Same Life Here." *The Sun,* June 13, 2007. www.thesun
.co.uk/article/0,,2-2007270252,00.html (accessed September 21, 2008).

Hazell, Keeley. "Keeley has Less Stares Topless." *The Sun,* October 21, 2006. www.thesun
.co.uk/article/0,,2-2006480904,00.html (accessed September 21, 2008).

Herbert, Ian, Arifa Akbar, and Nigel Morris. "Muslim leaders warn of mounting Islamopho-

bia after attacks on mosques." *The Independent,* July 12, 2005. http://news.independent
.co.uk/uk/crime/article298513.ece.

Hewitt, Andrew. "Ex-BNP Man Faces Explosives Charge." October 4, 2006. www.burnley
citizen.co.uk/display.var.951775.0.exbnp_man_faces_explosives_charge.php (accessed
September 21, 2008).

Iraq Working Group. "Iraq Constitution-Making: What Happens Now?" www.usip.org/
events/2005/0823_constitution.html (accessed September 21, 2008).

IRR News Team. "The Anti-Muslim Backlash Begins." July 14, 2005. www.irr.org.uk/2005/
july/ak000008.html.

IWPR Staff. "International Justice Failing Rape Victims." The Hague, London, and Sarajevo, January 5, 2007. www.iwpr.net/?p=tri&s=f&o=328311&apc_state=henitri2007
(accessed September 21, 2008).

Lovell, Jeremy. "Amnesty: Iraqi Women No Better Off Post-Saddam." February 22, 2005.
www.commondreams.org/headlines05/0222-08.htm (accessed September 21, 2008).

Macleod, Scott. "Days of Cedar." *Time,* November 2, 2005. www.time.com/time/
magazine/article/0,9171,1112768,00.html (accessed September 21, 2008).

Mahmoud, Mona. "Postwar Artists, Art World Will Illustrate New Time and Place."
USA Today, July 7, 2005. www.usatoday.com/news/world/iraq/2005-07-21-artists-
iraq_x.htm (accessed September 21, 2008).

Mamdani, Mahmood. "Whither Political Islam?" *Foreign Affairs* (2005). www.foreign
affairs.org/20050101fareviewessay84113b/mahmood-mamdani/whither-political-islam
.html/ (attempted September 21, 2008; no longer accessible).

Mann, C. "Les Shahidé du monde traditionnel: Le suicide des jeunes filles afghanes."
TERRA Travaux, Etudes, Recherches sur les Réfugiés et l'Asile, February 2006. http://
terra.rezo.net/article.php3?id_article=404 (accessed September 21, 2008).

Medica Mondiale. "Study of Suicides among Afghan Women." December 2006. www
.medicamondiale.org/_en/presse/pm/aktuelles/mm-pm06-11-17.html (accessed September 21, 2008).

Mills, Margaret. "One Size Doesn't Fit All: Addressing Diversity in the Needs and Development Capacities of Afghan Women, Short and Long-Term." Social Science Research
Council, New York, 2002. www.ssrc.org/sept11/essays/mills.htm (accessed September 21, 2008).

Mishra, Smeeta. "'Saving' Muslim Women and Fighting Muslim Men: Analysis of Representations in the *New York Times.*" *Global Media Journal* 6 (2007). http://lass.calumet
.purdue.edu/cca/gmj/fa07/gmj-fa07-mishra.htm (accessed September 21, 2008).

Mogahed, Dalia. "Perspectives of Women in the Muslim World." 2005. media.gallup
.com/worldpoll/pdf/gallup+muslim+studies_perspectives+of+women_11.10.06_final
.pdf (accessed September 21, 2008).

Mohamed VI. Speech delivered on October 10, 2003. www.majliss-annouwaba.ma (attempted access September 21, 2008; link no longer accessible).

Muslim Council of Britain Press Release. "British Muslims Utterly Condemn Acts of
Terror." July 7, 2005. www.mcg.org.uk/media/presstext.php?ann_id=150.

The Nation, Peshawar, October 2003. www.specialoperations.com/Foreign/Pakistan/SSG .htm (accessed September 21, 2008).

Noorani, Dan. "Amnesty Law Condones Warlords' Past Abuse." Inter Press Service News Agency, March 23, 2007. http://ipsnews.net/news.asp?idnews=37056 (accessed September 21, 2008).

Peace Women. "Women's International League for Peace and Freedom, Suffering for Their Art." April 1, 2005. www.peacewomen.org/news/Iraq/April05/suffering.html (accessed September 21, 2008).

Radsch, Courtney C. "Artist Looks at Her Native Iraq behind Women's Veils." *New York Times,* March 21, 2005. http://proquest.uni.com/pqdweb?did=810622051&sid=1&Fmt =3&clientld=87&RQT=39&VName=PDQ (accessed April 20, 2007; attempted September 21, 2008; no longer accessible).

Rajiva, Lila. "Iraqi Women and Torture, Part IV: Gendered Propaganda, the Propaganda of Gender." August 9, 2004. www.dissidentvoice.org (accessed September 21, 2008).

Sadovic, Merdijana. "Foca Rape Sentence." IWPR, December 15, 2006. www.iwpr.net/ ?p=tri&s=f&o=326212&apc_state=henitri200612 (accessed September 21, 2008).

Sardar, Zia. "Jack Straw's Thinly Veiled Abuse of Power." *New Statesman,* October 16, 2006. www.newstatesman.com/200610160030.

Shaikh, Nermeen. "Interview with Mahmood Mamdani." *Asia Source,* May 5, 2004. www .asiasource.org/news/special_reports/mamdani.cfm (accessed September 21, 2008).

"Slogans Daubed on City Mosque." http://news.scotsman.com/edinburgh.cfm?id= 955692005. July 13, 2005.

Smith, Joan. "The Veil Is a Feminist Issue." *The Independent,* October 8, 2006. www .independent.co.uk/opinion/commentators/joan-smith/joan-smith-the-veil-is-a-feminist-issue-419119.html.

Straw, Jack. "I Felt Uneasy Talking to Someone I Couldn't See." *The Guardian,* October 6, 2006. http://politics.guardian.co.uk/homeaffairs/story/01889231,00.html (accessed September 21, 2008).

Stree. www.stree.biz/about_stree.html (attempted September 21, 2008; no longer accessible).

Tarlo, Emma. "Hidden Features of the Face Veil Controversy." International Institute for the Study of Islam in the Modern World, 2007. www.isim.nl/files/Review_19/ Review_19-24.pdf.

Taylor, A. "WPC Killer Fled UK in a Veil." *The Sun,* December 20, 2006. www.thesun .co.uk/article/0,,2-2006580832,00.html.

Taylor, Mathew, and Rebecca Smithers. "Extremist Groups Active Inside UK Universities." *The Guardian,* September 16, 2005. www.guardian.co.uk/terrorism/story/ 0,12780,1571636,00.html.

Tetreault, Mary Ann. "The Sexual Politics of Abu Ghraib: Hegemony, Spectacle, and the Global War on Terror." *NWSA Journal* 18 (2004): 33–50. www.dissidentvoice.org (accessed September 21, 2008).

"l'UNFT exhorte le président Ben Ali à se porter candidat aux élections de 2009." www .unft.org.tn/fr/publications/revue_femme.html (accessed September 21, 2008).

UNHCR. "Afghanistan, Operational Update." September 2006. http://www.unhcr.org/cgibin/texis/vtx/home/opendoc.pdf?tbl=SUBSITES&id=451a47ec2 (attempted September 21, 2008; no longer accessible).

Wheeler, Gary. "Visual Expressions of Violence and Symbolic Speech: Gendered Arts of War." www.heathertroy.net/GaryWheeler.pdf (accessed September 21, 2008).

Willisms. "More On the Babe Theory of Political Movements." www.willisms.com/archives/2005/03/more_on_the_bab_1.html (accessed September 21, 2008).

CONTRIBUTORS

Lina Abirafeh received a Ph.D. in development studies from the London School of Economics. She worked in Afghanistan from 2002 to 2006 as director of an international NGO and senior gender officer for a UN agency. Abirafeh currently serves as senior gender adviser for an international agency in Papua New Guinea.

Fauzia Ahmad is an honorary research fellow and consultant based in the Centre for the Study of Ethnicity and Citizenship, Department of Sociology, University of Bristol, U.K.

Sya'afatun Almirzanah has been chief associate professor of comparative religions at the Islamic University Sunan Kalijaga in Yogyakarta, Indonesia, since 1990.

Shamita Basu received a Ph.D. from the School of International Development Studies, Roskilde University, in Roskilde, Denmark. Her thesis deals with the relationship between religion and nationalism in the advent of modernity in colonial India.

Nada S. Fuleihan holds a master's degree in history from the American University of Beirut in Beirut, Lebanon. She teaches French and writes children's literature.

Abbas Kadhim holds a Ph.D. in Islamic studies from the University of California, Berkeley, with a specialization in Islamic theology and ethics. He is currently a visiting lecturer of Islam at Stanford University.

Carol Mann holds a doctorate in sociology from the École des Hautes Études en Sciences Sociales. In 2001 she created FemAid, a Paris-based nonprofit organization working with Afghan women and children in Pakistani refugee camps and serving children in Pakistan as well.

Nadia Marzouki is a visiting fellow at Princeton University and a doctoral candidate in political science, Institut d'Études Politiques de Paris. Her scholarly focus includes policies and discourses about Islam—in France and in the United States. She has also served as lecturer in political science at the École Polytechnique, Paris.

Ángeles Ramírez holds a Ph.D. from the Department of Social Anthropology at Universidad Autónoma de Madrid, where she teaches today. She is associate researcher at the

Center for Mediterranean Studies at Universidad Autónoma and at the Center for International Migration and Integration.

Omar Sacirbey received an M.S. degree in journalism from Columbia University, New York. He is a correspondent for the *Christian Science Monitor* and has written articles for the *Washington Post, Chicago Tribune, Los Angeles Times, Boston Globe,* and other major publications.

Nada Shabout is an associate professor of art history at the University of North Texas at Denton. Her primary area of research is contemporary Arabic art and, specifically, the metamorphosis of the Arabic letter.

Faegheh Shirazi is an associate professor in the Department of Middle Eastern Studies, Islamic Studies Program, at the University of Texas–Austin.

Zilka Spahić-Šiljak received a Ph.D. from the University of Novi Sad, Serbia. She is a human rights and Islamic feminist scholar, researcher, and activist. She also holds a law degree from the University of Sarajevo.

Rita Stephan is a Ph.D. candidate in sociology at the University of Texas–Austin. She serves as a lecturer at the University of Texas–Austin and at St. Edward's University, Austin. Stephan's special field of interest is political sociology with a focus on women and gender studies.

Sara Struckman is a Ph.D. candidate in journalism at the University of Texas–Austin. Her primary research interests include the media's role in social change and gender representations.

INDEX

www.ingramcontent.com/pod-product-compliance
Lightning Source LLC
Chambersburg PA
CBHW020337270326
41926CB00007B/216